# BIBLICAL MORALITY

Biblical Morality explores a selection of Old Testament narratives, drawing out their views on morality to offer a unique perspective on the meaning of the term 'biblical morality'. Mary Mills argues that Old Testament stories build upon a moral vision across the levels of cosmos, community and person; the author then uses these concepts as interpretative tools for reading texts, as well as literary-critical tools of characterisation, plot and time-space setting. When Old Testament stories are read by a number of different readers, diverse cultural meanings emerge; this book argues that any exploration of biblical morality must take into account plurality of meaning and not expect to settle for a single unified reading which produces a one-dimensional personal behavioural ethic.

Presenting a study of biblical morality which allows Old Testament stories to stand in their own right as relevant sources, this book allows for the relevance of 'moral boundaries' without drawing these simplistically or narrowly, and offers an accessible examination of biblical morality to all those exploring biblical texts, narrative criticism and morality and ethics more widely.

Mary E. Mills is a Lecturer in Theology at Heythrop College, University of London, UK, and is the author of many books including *The Puzzle of the Gospels* (HarperCollins); *Images of God in the Old Testament* (Cassell); *Historical Israel, Biblical Israel* (Cassell).

# HEYTHROP STUDIES
# IN CONTEMPORARY PHILOSOPHY, RELIGION & THEOLOGY


*Series Editor*
Laurence Paul Hemming, Heythrop College, University of London, UK

*Series Editorial Advisory Board*
John McDade SJ; Peter Vardy; Michael Barnes SJ; James Hanvey SJ;
Philip Endean SJ; Anne Murphy SHCJ


Drawing on renewed willingness amongst theologians and philosophers to enter into critical dialogues with contemporary issues, this series is characterised by Heythrop's reputation for openness and accessibility in academic engagement. Presenting volumes from a wide international, ecumenical, and disciplinary range of authors, the series explores areas of current theological, philosophical, historical, and political interest. The series incorporates a range of titles: accessible texts, cutting-edge research monographs, and edited collections of essays. Appealing to a wide academic and intellectual community interested in philosophical, religious and theological issues, research and debate, the books in this series will also appeal to a theological readership which includes enquiring lay-people, Clergy, members of religious communities, training priests, and anyone engaging broadly in the Catholic tradition and with its many dialogue partners.

*Published titles*
Radical Orthodoxy? – A Catholic Enquiry – Edited by Laurence Paul
Hemming
Challenging Women's Orthodoxies in the Context of Faith – Edited by
Susan Frank Parsons

*Forthcoming titles include:*
Postmodernity's God – Laurence Paul Hemming
God as Trinity – James Hanvey
Religion Within the Limits of Language Alone – Felicity McCutcheon
Reading Ecclesiastes –Mary Mills

# Biblical Morality

## Moral perspectives in Old Testament narratives

MARY E. MILLS

# Ashgate

Aldershot • Burlington USA • Singapore • Sydney

© Mary E. Mills 2001

Published by
Ashgate Publishing Limited
Gower House
Croft Road
Aldershot
Hampshire GU11 3HR
England

Ashgate Publishing Company
131 Main Street
Burlington, VT 05401-5600 USA

Ashgate website: http://www.ashgate.com

**British Library Cataloguing in Publication Data**
Mills, Mary E.
  Biblical morality : moral perspectives in Old Testament
  narratives. - (Heythrop studies in contemporary philosophy,
  religion and theology)
  1.Bible. O.T. 2.Ethics in the Bible 3.Christian ethics
  I.Title II.Heythrop College
  241

**Library of Congress Cataloging-in-Publication Data**
Mills, Mary E.
  Biblical morality : moral perspectives in Old Testament narratives / by Mary E. Mills.
    p. cm.-- (Heythrop studies in contemporary philosophy, religion, and theology)
  Includes bibliographical references (p. ) and indexes.
  ISBN 0-7546-1579-0 -- ISBN 0-7546-1580-4 (pbk.)
    1. Ethics in the Bible. 2. Bible. O.T.--Criticism, interpretation, etc. I. Title. II. Series.
BS1199.E8 M49 2001
241.5--dc21

2001034107

ISBN 0 7546 1579 0
Printed and bound in Great Britain by MPG Books Ltd, Bodmin, Cornwall

# Contents

# Preface

This study of Old Testament narratives and their moral perspectives is intended to be set in the context of more traditional approaches to ethical regulations in the Christian Bible. Whereas such studies take their origins from modern ethical categories such as war, marriage, and sexuality, and only then turn to possible biblical connections with these topics, the present volume starts explicitly from the Old Testament story and focuses on the moral vision which is part of that narrative. The intention is to expand the reader's horizons concerning biblical morality and to provoke consideration of its many facets. The study finds its place alongside Professor John Barton's volume *Ethics in the Old Testament* and I would like to pay tribute to his work as a source of inspiration for this project. As with previous books, much gratitude is offered to Anne Laing-Brooks SHCJ for her patient work as a reader of first drafts and as a commentator on style and expression of ideas. Gratitude is also due to St Mary's College, Strawberry Hill whose Research Committee provided a grant for the completion of this book.

Mary E. Mills

# Chapter One

# A Framework for Studying
# Biblical Morality

The possession of a moral perspective offers a person a means of establishing order in his or her own life. Since such a perspective involves the acceptance of behavioural boundaries set within a particular understanding of the universal order, it leads to the formation of a code of guidelines for appropriate and inappropriate actions. It can be argued that the Christian Bible offers its reader suitable material for the construction of such moral attitudes. However, arriving at the content of biblical or, in the case of this book, Old Testament morality is not a simple matter. It could be suggested that, since the Old Testament contains a number of collections of legal codes, what is required is to focus on these: more especially on the Decalogue, which offers the reader some general religious and social principles for action. As a further strand in this argument it could be stated that the Decalogue has a special command on the reader's attention. For these ten commandments, found in Exodus chapter twenty, are the very words of the deity, handed out at Mount Sinai and so having a dogmatic significance for biblical moral teaching. This approach of focussing on law would, however, exclude most of the law books of the Old Testament Torah from the area of morality, since it is story which is the dominant feature of these works as a whole. If the reader widens his or her consideration of morality, as informed by the Old Testament, to include narrative as a source of moral guidance, new emphases emerge. As John Barton writes: "In the Old Testament we are presented not with a carefully worked out code allegedly valid for all time, but with a way of handling life as it presented itself in all its brokenness and particularity in the societies which formed these texts as we now have them."[1]

In this wider perspective of Old Testament morality God no longer appears mainly as a rule-setter and a rule-monitor. Nor are the biblical texts viewed simply as a rule book, a set of legal codifications from which derives the measurement of persons and structures on a sliding scale of good (abides by the rules in the book) or bad (contravenes these rules). Although there are positive and negative evaluations of persons and actions to be found, these have to be reflected upon within the context of the entire story in which they are embedded. At the same time the manner in which appeal can be made to

---

1   Barton, J., *Ethics in the Old Testament*, London, SCM Press, 1998, p. 17.

the Old Testament as the authority for contemporary verdicts on life's events has to be re-thought. "As the Bible says . . . " or "The Bible tells us to . . . " are phrases often used to require of the hearer agreement with the speaker's view without further debate. This use of biblical text is often paradoxical since it claims that the speaker has an authoritative voice drawn from biblical teaching while reading biblical text in a manner already determined by pre-existing values. But in the broader approach to Old Testament morality it is less easy for any reader to claim that a single authoritative judgement on behaviour is demonstrated by the relevant literature. Nor can the reader so easily extract short passages and claim that isolated verses contain moral frameworks for ethical behaviour with regard to topics such as marriage, sexual behaviour, war and peace.

Barton's comment points to a further important issue for a modern reader – the connection between texts and the societies which form them. When the Hebrew Scriptures are read through, it is clear that they are addressed to a community, which can name itself as Israel. Although the exact content of that name varies from a single man, Jacob/Israel, in Genesis, to a tribal grouping, to a nation in its land, to the name of one half of a divided kingdom. The focus of these texts is the interaction of God, a society belonging to that deity and individual human beings within this society. In one of the major themes of the Old Testament – the Exodus, for example – the story moves between the God of Israel, Moses the chosen leader, other Israelites and their opponents, the Egyptians. This perspective is rather different from that of modern readers who consider the Bible an appropriate guide to interpreting their lives, for they are primarily concerned with the issue of personal behaviour, rather than social behaviour. In their view of biblical texts the emphasis falls on salvation through the subjective adaptation of life to a given and fixed set of pre-existing norms. Whereas the Exodus story, mentioned above, tells of a salvation offered to a people and to all who are joined with this people, as members of Israelite households in the Passover regulations, for instance.

The present study of Old Testament perspectives on morality aims to work from the approach to Old Testament morality represented by Barton's comment. It takes seriously the overall presentation of biblical characters as good and bad, the whole structure of stories, which contain an understanding of the working out of justice and righteousness in human affairs, and the complexity of biblical approaches to such topics as the origins of sin and evil in the universe. Consequently it will not focus on law and legality as such, but will explore Old Testament stories for the contribution these make to a broader picture of moral vision, which can accommodate even conflicting verdicts on the significance of human activity.

## The Forensic Face of Biblical Literature

It is certainly the case that sections of biblical text exist, which fuels the view that the Bible is full of rules. There are clear examples of texts which, in themselves, contain legal codes or offer exhortatory material relating to the proper pursuit of human life. In the Old Testament the term Torah has legal connotations; its English equivalent, Law, leads the reader immediately to precise matters of legal observance, of keeping the rules. It is significant to remember that Torah contains a richer range of meaning than just laws, being also a term to cover five books some of which are largely narrative in style and, ultimately, is a term carrying the value ' instruction' or 'teaching'. Here the purpose both of story and of legal statements is not ethical behaviour *per se*, but the place of such elements in a society's self-identity.

Nonetheless Torah books contain a large quantity of legal teaching. Readers of the Bible may well point to the Decalogue as the backbone of scriptural moral sense. Surely the basic elements of the relationship between God and humanity are set out therein. Biblical religion thus turns on 'what is required' of human beings. The case law of the book of the Covenant in Exodus and the cultic law which follows are obviously passages utilising a legal genre of writing.

The book of Deuteronomy offers a second account of the biblical Israel's law codes set in the context of Moses' instruction to the people. The law codes take their meaning from the overall shape of the book and carry through its ideology as established in chapters one to eleven.[2] Once again it would be possible to focus on the legal material as such and ignore the context. A reader could argue for the importance of worshipping a single deity and for avoiding superstitious religious practices from the laws in Deuteronomy chapter twelve, and for a 'spiritual' religion of personal ethical values from Deuteronomy chapter ten.

When the reader moves from Torah to Prophecy she or he encounters more passages which appear to have ethical significance. The judgement oracles contain a language of sin/punishment, offering a guide to interpreting the value of human society. The prophetic voice accuses a people of offending against the deity. Some part of that accusation has to do with social injustice. The 'haves' of society oppress the 'have-nots' and the prophet Amos, for example, calls for an end to this social oppression (Amos chapter five).

---

2   See eg. McConville, J., *Law and Theology in Deuteronomy*, Sheffield, Sheffield Academic Press, 1984 and *Grace in the End*, Carlisle, Paternoster, 1993, for a theological account of how commentary and law-codes are woven together in Deuteronomy through the writer's use of a common set of themes.

In the treatment of texts set out above, it is clear that there is biblical material relating to moral/ethical identity. But these passages, which are often of a legal type, do not appear in a vacuum but within works to which they contribute and from which they themselves acquire further levels of meaning. To examine that meaning more deeply must involve situating material, which is obviously forensic, in that broader textual context.


## The Bible and Ethics

To suggest that there are forensic elements in Old Testament books is not the same, of course, as stating that there is a close link between the two subjects, Bible and ethics. For professional readers of the Bible the actual texts come first; each book and each section of a book must be taken on its own terms and in its own language code. Moral philosophers, on the other hand, have their own methods of study, often seeking for systematic treatments of the term ethics itself. Different models have been addressed by moral philosophy – Aristotelian ethics, for instance, or the Utilitarian theories of the nineteenth century British thinkers. It has thus to be established whether Bible and ethics have common ground.[3] One recent work which reflects the range of debate on this matter, itself drawn from conference papers, and which puts forward a variety of opinions is *The Bible in Ethics*.[4] It will be helpful to consider some of the viewpoints expressed in this collected volume of papers.

There is the basic matter of what sort of dialogue, if any, can occur between practitioners in Bible and ethics. John Rogerson, for example, discusses the link between reading biblical text ethically and modern ethical discourse, in connection with Jurgen Habermas's 'Discourse Ethics'. Habermas's viewpoint is that "from the point of view of discourse ethics, obligations cannot be imposed; they must be seen to be justified and must be capable of being willingly accepted".[5] This approach might, at first sight, appear to be at odds with the idea that biblical ethics express laws handed down from an absolute divine source – in the Decalogue, for instance. But, since modern readers live at some distance in time and culture from the

---

3   For more information on the basic history of moral philosophy as an intellectual tradition see eg. Copleston, F., *A History of Philosophy* (nine volumes), Tunbridge Wells, Burns and Oates, 1966.

4   Rogerson, J., Davies, M. and M. Daniel Carroll R. (eds), *The Bible in Ethics*, Sheffield, Sheffield Academic Press, 1995.

5   Rogerson, J., *Discourse Ethics and Biblical Ethics* in Rogerson, J., Davies, M. and M. Daniel Carroll R. (eds), *The Bible in Ethics*, 1995, p. 20.

creation of the biblical text, it is inevitable that there will have to be some process of discussion, seeking a consensus, of what the decalogue and other law-codes mean in the modern world. Habermas's concept that the terms of ethical procedure stem from communication between individuals, and so are a collective rather than a personal matter, has a useful role to play in the interpretive task of reading the Bible ethically. Thus some continuity of thought may be established between the manner of reading biblical moral texts and the methods of ethical discourse.

John Barton's paper offers a further instance of such a possible link, and one that will be useful for following through the arguments of this present book. He suggests a way in which the need to read biblical material in detail, tackling each text on its own ground, can be matched with methods for reaching moral perspectives taken from a more philosophical background: that of the writings of Martha Nussbaum.[6] Barton argues that a foundational attitude of ethical enquiry is one which places emphasis on particulars and is suspicious of universal rules.[7] This approach is suitable for fictional narrative and historiography. In ancient Greek culture it allows the reader to find ethical matter in tragic drama as well as in philosophical enquiry. In Tragedy, norms of behaviour are examined through the complexity of individual lives. Each life should be taken as a whole, in order, through observation of act and consequence, to arouse terror and pity, ethical emotions, in the reader.[8] Since the Bible contains much story it, too, may be utilised for ethical reading, as with the story of David in the books of Samuel and Kings, which leads the reader to consider the ultimate morality of the man, from young lad to infirm old age. Barton's view is that "literature is important for ethics because literature is as complicated as life itself, and cannot be decoded or boiled-down. Ethical insight comes from reading it . . . *not* from trying to extract a 'message' from it ."[9]

At the same time biblical exegesis has its own contributions to make to reading the Bible ethically. These, too, relate to the connection between specific passages and universal rules. Philip Davies and David Clines argue, variously, for the need for a reader to stand back from text, not to take up a surface message therefrom, but to dialogue concerning the values which a text appears to be outlining. It may be necessary to resist the moral vision of the

6 Barton, J., *Reading forLife: The Use of Bible in Ethics and the Work of Martha C. Nussbaum*, in Rogerson, J. et al (eds) 1995.

7 Barton, J., *Reading for Life*, p. 69.

8 Barton, J., *Reading for Life*, p. 71.

9 Barton, J., *Reading for Life*, p. 75.

text.[10] The exegete needs to consider the content of any dogmatic requirement in the text and either agree with, or dissent from, it. Philip Davies focuses on the theme of resisting the text in the name of ethics in his article *Ethics and the Old Testament*, and takes Genesis chapters one to three as a basis for his argument.[11] He suggests that 'good/bad' actually infer "good/bad in the eyes of X".[12] In Genesis chapter three the woman makes a responsible choice in the light of her existing knowledge, but what is good in her eyes is bad in God's eyes, even though God acknowledges that she has made a valid decision. God's command becomes the only criterion of 'good/bad' here and God acts as a parent anxious to prevent the undermining of parental authority. The reader has to resist the surface level of the text, which endorses passive obedience to external commands.

Similar remarks could be made about the Deuteronomistic books where the ethics of the text are that: 'Your God has commanded and thus you shall do.' One of the problems about this moral style is that it is a cover for ethnic cleansing – the extermination of other national groups in the land which God gives.[13] By contrast the wisdom material in the Old Testament implies that human beings must be arbiters of their own conduct. Davies argues that the model of Proverbs, which requires human beings to take thoughtful responsibility for their own actions, offers a more mature methodology for would-be biblicists.[14]

The requirement to be a 'responsible reader' can lead not only to resisting text but also to listening carefully for the way in which texts can undermine their own apparent moral teaching. David Clines points out that texts have a capacity for deconstructing themselves and that this applies to legal texts as well as to other literary genres. Thus there are texts which delineate the role of a slave in Israelite society as being the property of the master, someone with no independent human rights.[15] At the same time, a text like Deuteronomy chapter twenty-three deconstructs that apparently fixed status by allowing that

10  Davies, P., *Ethics and the Old Testament*, in Rogerson, J. et al (eds) 1995.
11  Davies, P., *Ethics*, p. 166.
12  This topic has been dealt with extensively in recent scholarship. See, for instance, Brett, M. G., *Nationalism and the Hebrew Bible* in Rogerson, J. et al (eds), 1995. Mills, M. E., *Historical Israel: Biblical Israel*, London, Cassell, 1999, the section on ideological criticism. Also Prior, M., *The Bible and Colonialism*, Sheffield, Sheffield Academic Press, 1998, for a view on the significance of this material for modern politics and international affairs.
13  Davies, P. *Ethics*, p. 171.
14  Clines, D. J., *Ethics as Deconstruction* and *The Ethics of Deconstruction* in Rogerson, J. et al (eds) 1995.
15  Clines, D., *Ethics as Deconstruction*, p. 77.

an escaped slave shall not be handed up to the master, that he shall dwell as a free man and shall not be oppressed.[16] Clines says "I am, of course, not arguing that the abolition of slavery was the intention of the framers of this law; but simply that the wording itself stealthily undermines . . . the concept of slavery".[17]

What Clines discusses, then, is the complexity of meaning to be found in Old Testament ethical material concerning a single subject, in this case the position of slaves. Not to balance one text against another would lead to a partial and incomplete evaluation of Old Testament moral perspectives.

Rex Mason's book on propaganda in the Old Testament provides another strand here.[18] As well as examining very closely one particular passage in terms of its long-term meaning if translated into social action or balancing texts with apparently-conflicting viewpoints against each other, it is appropriate to consider the overall tendency of larger sections of biblical material. Mason compares Old Testament texts with that of *The Æneid*.[19] In both cases, he notes, there is an inbuilt political significance to the individual scenes. In the Old Testament it is possible, for instance, to trace the line of royal propaganda which views the early history of Israel as leading to the emergence of monarchy. The story of Abraham in Genesis shows signs of having been shaped to match the picture of David later on.

In terms of societal identity texts have been written to promote the status of a particular political leadership, it can be argued. This is a facet of Old Testament moral vision since it provides the reader with a focus for personal commitment, inviting him/her to share the ordered framework of a divinely ordained government. More than one such socio-cultural perspective can be found in Old Testament narratives, as Mason points out.[20] A modern reader who approaches this material as made up of timeless religious teaching will need to widen that understanding to include a sensitivity to the time-bound nature of some of the moral meanings she or he detects in the process of reading the Old Testament.

The survey, which has been conducted, of the possible links between the subjects of the Bible and Ethics indicates that any such links cannot be taken for granted. It may well be possible to move from moral philosophy to biblical morality, but only by paying careful attention to the parameters of

---

16  Deuteronomy 23 [15-16]
17  Clines, D., *Ethics as Deconstruction*, p. 80.
18  Mason, R., *Propaganda and Subversion in the Old Testament*, London, SPCK, 1997.
19  See Mason, R., *Propaganda and Subversion*, chapter 1.
20  This can quickly be identified from Mason's chapter headings. Mason, R. *Propaganda and Subversion*.

each area in its own right. At the same time biblical texts, which contain legal or ethical statements, must be subject to the same process of biblical exegesis as would be applied to other types of biblical material. Texts may well provide examples of moral vision or ethical behaviour and stories are of particular value here. But the route to identifying these examples is by the act of reading, of biblical exegesis, which in itself is not separate from any other act of careful reading of a narrative as a whole.[21]

## Ethical and Moral as Key Terms

Up to this point ethical and moral have been used as alternatives without absolute distinction but this does not mean that it is not possible to point to some shades of difference between the two terms. For the purposes of this study 'morality' is to be understood as the context within which ethical discourse takes place. Thus 'moral' is to be applied to the overall profile of a biblical character, or to the narrative frame of a particular tale or to an overarching theme. Within this setting 'ethical' measurements may be made. In the story of David, the king is portrayed as in God's favour and thus a moral person, but particular actions such as the taking of Bathsheba call forth ethical dialogue in which the royal action is evaluated negatively. The full picture of morality here requires consideration of action which is unethical in the light of the overall moral vision of the story of David, which does not abandon the view that David found favour in God's eyes.

In the Old Testament, it can be argued, morality operates at the cosmic level of the heavens and the earth as these are established as world boundaries in Genesis chapter one; it is a term which belongs with the origins of the universe. Heaven and earth belong together because they stem from the creative act of a single deity. The heavens become the home of God while the earth is the setting for the creature made in the divine image. Thus the context for human action is not simply earth but also the heavens; human acts are evaluated in the light of their impact on the inter-relationship between cosmos and human existence. Thus, when the biblical material examines Israel's social life, its framework of laws, in Exodus or Deuteronomy, it is not a question of rules created by humans to make society run more smoothly. But

21 God's speech in Genesis 3 may be read as an example of judgement/curse or as the recognition that an inevitable separation of relationship between God, world and human beings is the inevitable result of a disordered human choice. In either reading the long term consequences are the same, namely the human experience of being at odds with nature and remote from the deity.

rather social norms enable Israel to live within the bounds of order established at a cosmic level. The world is a moral place in which the details of ethical behaviour are worked out.


## The Framework of Narrative

So far space has been given to discussing the content of the term 'moral'. The title of this book links the concept of morality with one particular literary style, that of story in the Old Testament. It is time to turn to this second area and to establish some relevant boundaries in its regard. It has been demonstrated that careful consideration must be given to the manner in which the terms moral/ethical are employed in the reading of the Old Testament. The same rigour is necessary for the reading and interpretation of narratives at large.

Michæl Fishbane points to the use of repetition and inclusion in structuring Hebrew stories.[22] Thus, in Genesis chapters one to eleven, the repetitious use of genealogies links the individual incidents in one continuous framework. This allows the reader to focus on theological issues such as the recurrence of violence and bloodshed in the world, while preserving contact with the sense of time moving along, never simply repeating past events but bringing new generations into being.[23] Parallelism is another standard structure found in Old Testament stories, as Fishbane demonstrates in his chart showing the close linguistic similarities between the account in the third chapter of Genesis, of evil choices by human beings, and Cain's murder of his brother in chapter four.[24] Individual stories likewise share in patterns of inclusion and repetition, notably in the form of a chiasm whereby beginning and end of a story balance one another, revealing the key concept at the 'heart' of the narrative. An example of this is how, in the Tower of Babel story, in Genesis chapter eleven, verse one balances verse nine, verses three and four balance verses seven and eight, leaving verses five to six as the unrepeated, central element.[25] This pattern emphasises the dominance of God's control since the central motif is of God coming down to see for himself and then deciding to intervene to change human intentions.

A further level of understanding of narrative structures is obtained by seeking out the deep inner patterns by which stories operate. One example of

---

22  Fishbane, M., *Biblical Text and Texture*, Oxford, One World, 1998.
23  Fishbane, M., *Text*, pp. 28-9.
24  Genesis 4 [3-16], Fishbane, M., *Text*, p. 26.
25  Fishbane, M., *Text*, p. 6.

this stems from the work of Vladimir Propp who examined a wealth of European folk-tales in order to set out the paradigmatic structure of such a tale.[26] Aspects of Propp's thought can be useful for reading Old Testament tales. The reader might ask, for instance, why two very similar stories appear in Genesis chapters twelve to twenty-four, in both of which Abraham and Sarah go to a foreign place where Abraham, fearful for his safety, passes off Sarah as not his wife. Surely, by the second time Abraham might have learned that the device does not really work? From a Proppian perspective the problem is resolved by pointing out that here there are two versions of the same basic folk-story, the 'ancestress in danger'.[27] The focus, here, is not on the individual narratives but on the re-use of a single narrative style. This literary motif has its own internal logic and can be fleshed out variously, in terms of characters' names and details of action.

For the present study it is important to focus on the interpretative methods of Narrative Criticism. In this mode of reading, three areas are to be addressed: the text itself; the story (ie. the events that are the object of the narrative); and the narrating, the act of narrating with its spatial and temporal context.[28] In the field of biblical studies an influential work has been that of Alan Culpepper, where these three aspects of a narrative work are explored by developing a reading tool which moves from author [real and implied] to narrator, character, plot, style to reader [implied and real].[29] This kind of interpretive tool has been applied to the Old Testament by Shimon Bar-Efrat and David Gunn and Donna Fewell, and their studies will be drawn upon in later chapters of this present study.[30]

It is possible to link these ways of reading narrative with an enquiry into the moral vision of stories. Clarence Wallhout, for example, argues that the reader's interest in the lives of fictional characters "is an interest in the ethical relationships that are a necessary part of human interaction. The characters of fiction, like human beings in real life, form and discover their identities through their relationships with other characters."[31] In following the stories of 'other people's lives' and grappling with the complexity of literary persons and their stories the reader finds a way of reflecting on his or her own human

---

26  Fishbane, M., *Text*, p. 58.
27  See for instance, Westermann, C., *Genesis*, Vol. I, Minneapolis, Augsburg, 1984-6.
28  Bible Collective, *The Postmodern Bible*, Yale University Press, 1995, p. 83.
29  Culpepper, A., *Anatomy of the Fourth Gospel*, Philadelphia, Fortress, 1983.
30  Gunn, D. and Fewell, D., *Narrative Art in the Hebrew Bible*, Oxford University Press, Oxford, 1993; Bar-Efrat, S., *Narrative Art in the Bible*, Sheffield, Sheffield Academic Press, 1997; Walhout, C., *Narrative Hermeneutics* in Lundin, R., Walhout, C., Thistleton, A. (eds), *The Promise of Hermeneutics*, Grand Rapids, Eerdmans, 1999, p.123.
31  Walhout, C., *Hermeneutics*, p. 127.

experience. In this context moral vision and ethical behaviour gain a practical content based on an understanding of a commonality of human experience. It is through meeting and interacting with others that a human being explores the potential of self-identity and forms his or her own set of values and priorities. Narratives mirror this social process of meeting and interchange and thus achieve a moral dimension.

Walhout notes: "In comparing the stories of fiction with the stories of our own lives, we see more clearly the ethical dimension of narrative hermeneutics. Our personal life stories are always in process . . . Fictional stories, in contrast, provide a way of thinking about both the consequences and the purposes of actions. In fiction we can envision resolutions and completions in ways that we cannot fully achieve in our own historical odysseys."[32]

Stories may be said to have a mimetic function, in that they produce in their symbolic world of text, situations, which echo actual human experience of life in society.[33] Although these are 'fictional' situations, since they have emerged from the thought patterns of a particular writer, they have sufficient contact with what is experienced in daily life to stimulate the reader to transfer opinions about the textual events to parallel events in his or her own life. Conversely the reader views textual events through the spectacles of an already-developed viewpoint concerning the order and shape of the social world. The Bible Collective adds that "it is because fictional narratives have a mimetic relationship of resemblance to actual life and because the actions of life are fundamentally teleological and ethical that a hermeneutics of fiction is ultimately grounded in the ethical character of our living and thinking".[34]

It is important, then, to take time to read a given story carefully in order to identify the specific structures by which meaning is therein constructed as well as the surface level of linguistic use. From this act of reading a reader moves to integrate new information with that already held. The reading and interpretation of narratives challenges the reader to reflect on personally held beliefs and values. Thus, reading the book of Job as a narrative raises questions about how completely a human being can understand the inner structures of world order and so to what extent a human being can plan and carry through appropriate actions to ensure best fortune within their lifetime.

---

32  Walhout, C., *Hermeneutics*, p. 128.
33  Although the term mimetic is used simply here there is, of course, a huge body of scholarship relating to its use in hermeneutics. See, for instance, 1995, *The Postmodern Bible*, chapter 2. Also Auerbach, E., his classic work on Mimesis with its section on the narrative genre of the Old Testament.
34  Bible Collective, *Postmodern Bible*, p. 112.

The action of reading leads the reader out from the text to wider philosophical, cultural, religious matters. Conversely, it is appropriate to approach biblical texts from different methodologies of philosophy of language, sociology of language, psychology of language, for instance.

Barton asks "is not the nub of the structuralist/narratological challenge precisely this, to force confrontation between the Bible and theory developed outside it? Is the Bible to be truly 'at risk from a critical narratology', or does it dictate the terms of interpretation?"[35] It is valuable not only to read biblical text as a self-contained literature, which provides its own interpretive tools, but also to bring biblical literature into contact with extra-biblical modes of thought and to challenge readings of narrative text which align the voice of the text too dogmatically with one particular social or cultural or religious opinion. In this present study the methods of narrative criticism will be aligned with a search for moral perspectives within selected Old Testament narratives.

## Morality, Narrative and Hermeneutics

So far some extended consideration has been given to the subjects of morality and narrative; it is now necessary to bring these two areas together to formulate a hermeneutic for reading Old Testament narratives with an eye to their moral perspectives. The foundation of such a hermeneutic has already been laid in the references to John Barton's approach to story and ethics. In *Ethics and the Old Testament* Barton points out that about half of the Old Testament is composed of stories which rehearse the careers of specific individuals, no one story or character being the same as another. He also states that these stories are not simply moral fables; their moral vision is not obvious, nor is their meaning exhausted by a single reading.[36]

Waldemar Janzen also argues the value of Old Testament narratives as a source of moral guidance.[37] In the first chapter of his book he uses five story frames as his basis in setting out the parameters of Old Testament morality as he sees it. He believes that the bases of biblical morality in the Old Testament are the links which a person has with family and kinship. These links are explored within the pages of narrative, so providing the reader with material for building personal moral vision. Janzen acknowledges that aspects of these

---

35 Barton, J., *Reading for Life*, p. 20.
36 Barton, J., *Reading for Life*, p. 34.
37 Janzen, W., *Old Testament Ethics. A paradigmatic approach*, Louisville, Westminster John Knox, 1994.

narratives appear negative to the modern reader. In the story of Phinehas (Numbers chapter twenty-five) the murder by Phinehas of the Israelite and his foreign woman may be offputting and not regarded as ethical, but the Old Testament narrative applauds his action because he has put proper regard for loyalty to YHWH before any other consideration. It is thus that Phinehas becomes a 'hero' in the story and offers a model of right action. From stories such as this Janzen extracts paradigms for morality. He argues against laws and principles as the principal vehicles of moral teaching in the Old Testament and for the concepts of paradigms in stories. His view of paradigm is somewhat ambivalent, however, for it contains ideal behaviour which can be abstracted and re-enfleshed in a reader's own life, while, at the same time, not being reduced to abstractions such as loyalty or kindness. Rather his plan is that "instead of sacrificing the vivid characters and actions of our stories, we will try to combine their model aspects with larger, more comprehensive characters and patterns . . . we will search for Israel's inner image of a loyal family member, of a dedicated worshipper, of a wise manager of daily life, of a good ruler, and of an obedient proclaimer of the prophetic word".[38]

Janzen acknowledges that aspects of a story can throw bad light on a character, as in the David story, but he puts the spotlight on the 'ideal' model of a person, which he thinks the story illustrates. In the present study the emphasis, though taking up the value of story, will be different. It will include all parts of a character's behaviour or all aspects of a plot in its treatment of moral vision so aiming to press further the sophisticated and many-layered approach to ethics and story found in Barton's work. In talking of an ideal Israelite Janzen touches on a second important issue, the fact that the Old Testament is concerned not with individuals as such but as members of a social group, shaped by its values and committed to furthering its growth and well-being.

This aspect of Old Testament morality was touched upon above and will be central to the present work. Christopher Wright's chapter on 'The Social Angle' emphasises the need to engage on Old Testament moral discourse from social categories rather than individual, subjective interests.[39] Bruce Birch notes that "throughout the Hebrew Bible, Israel is understood and presented as a moral community . . . the existence of the canon itself implies that the story of Israel as a moral community in relation to God is intended to play a crucial role in the shaping of subsequent generations of moral community with the

---

38 Janzen, W., *Old Testament Ethics*, p. 20.
39 Wright, C., *Living as the People of God*, Leicester, Inter-Varsity Press, 1983, chpater two, especially pp. 34 f.

biblical communities themselves".[40] Birch himself applies this approach to
the Exodus event, which so importantly shapes the biblical identity of Israel.
His intent is to show how the moral community reflected in this Old
Testament material expressed its ethical principles through relationship with
its deity.[41]

Birch points out that scholars interested in the subject of ethics have, in
recent years, focused more on community and story as a means of expressing
moral views.[42] There is, across these several writers, a concern that the human
person as moral agent must be set into a social or community context, if a
fuller picture of morality or ethical behaviour is to be worked out. This
concern is reflected in two of the categories which will be used to comment
upon Old Testament narratives – that of community and person. The third
category is also clearly present in these several works of scholarship, that of
God, understood as the central pivot of the world order within which human
community and personal behaviour occur and against which they are
evaluated. This triangular context of cosmos, community and person is
present, for instance, in the several constructions of Old Testament morality
paradigms which scholars such as Emil Brunner have produced and which are
presented by Janzen in a diagrammatic form, with God at the head of each
flow chart.[43] It is this three-layered model which will form the basis of the
interpretative method employed in the following chapters.


## Cosmos

The level of Cosmos is to be understood as that which forms the ultimate
boundaries of morality and ethics. 'Cosmos' indicates the world within which
action takes place; estimating the importance and consequence of any action
involves measuring it against the cosmic framework. Such reflection results
in negative/positive evaluations of the events themselves. For the Old
Testament the fundamental aspect of 'world' is the existence of a creator God
from whose existence and through whose actions, world itself takes shape.
The biblical texts assume that the symbolic world of the book has a direct
connection with the daily world in which human beings live. But, at the same
time, this symbolic textual world operates as a defined space within which

40  Birch, B., *Divine Character and the Formation of Moral Community in the Book of Exodus*,
    in Rogerson, J., et al (eds), 1995, p.119.
41  Birch, B., *Divine Character*, see especially pp.134f.
42  Birch, B., *Divine Character*, p.122.
43  Janzen, W., *Old Testament Ethics*, pp.73f.

matters related to daily existence can be examined for their greater significance, thus opening up new vistas for the conduct of the human beings conducting the investigation. Within biblical space there is no attempt to separate religious issues from secular ones; all that happens stems from a cosmos which, by definition, is a religious site. Genesis chapter one sets the tone of the cosmos as a place of order and beauty when it states that God saw that what was made was good (*tob*).[44] The deity himself takes on the role of benefactor as well as critic, here, towards the world as harmoniously created.

The cosmic level of moral vision in the Old Testament combines positive views of God as a purposeful and powerful creator, with that of a negative dimension. A key matter is the critique of theodicy, how a good God created a world where evil arises; what is the source, then, of evil and what is its shape? A major answer to this question, in the Old Testament, is the responsibility of human beings for the distortion of created order. In Genesis chapter two the text suggests that human beings have a tendency to make disordered choices and this leads, in chapter three, to the breakdown of proper relationships between God and humans, between humans and humans, and between humans and the natural world of animals and plants. A parallel message can be found in Proverbs where the writer argues that human beings belong to one of two groups, the 'wicked and the righteous'; it is through his own choice of lifestyle that a man gains either reward or punishment from the Lord. This is the viewpoint, which Job's friends bring to his suffering, but Job himself offers another approach to evil. That it is the deity himself who brings pain to the innocent. Where only one powerful deity is acknowledged there is a problem with causation, especially if that deity is defined as basically constructive with regard to the cosmos. It becomes easier to attribute evil to the cosmic sphere if there are more powers in heaven. The beginnings of such a concept appear in the Satan's role in Job. Although the Satan is only God's officer he has an immense influence on the divine perspective thus causing the suffering of Job by persuading God that Job's loyalty needs to be severely tested.

In Daniel, in the genre of Apocalypse literature, the concept of a contest for world sovereignty between world powers and the God of Israel is clearly evident. In chapters one to six this takes the form of a battle between God and Daniel, on the one hand, and the 'great king', on the other. Great human kings set themselves up as 'gods' in their imperial settings. Chapter seven onwards extends this scenario into an ongoing war in heaven between the spiritual

---

44 The word *Tob* in Biblical Hebrew carries more than a sense of good as opposed to bad. It also has the sense of beautiful, perfect and so complete. This makes it a strong word, linking abstract notions of correctness with physical realisations of such ideas.

guardians of the different nations, which mirrors the to and fro of military success on earth as these nations confront one another. The kingdoms of the world, imaged as four beasts, emerge from the sea, a symbol of chaos, thus indicating their ambiguity as signs of absolute truth and power. The God of Israel vindicates his faithful followers by rewarding their faith and destroying human rulers in their arrogant pride.

One spin-off from this perspective of evil as a contest of power in the cosmos is the labelling of the people of Israel as God's kingdom, as Insiders, and those of different cultures and religious affiliations as Outsiders, people committed to a false interpretation of the universe, who would be destroyed when the truth about the cosmos was finally and fully revealed. This manner of defining the 'righteous' as 'Israel' and the 'wicked' as 'The Nations' is employed, for instance, in the first chapters of the Book of the Watchers in the first book of Enoch.[45] "The moral logic of a community that views the world under these images of . . . good and evil, brings pressure to . . . guard the boundaries."[46] Thus the cosmic level of morality gives the reader of the Old Testament a framework for evaluating both the nature of absolute power and the daily details of the political scene. Ultimately, morality involves choosing between good and evil at the cosmic level. These choices form the foundation for ethical behaviour, which can be regarded as a sub-set of morality here, since it entails discerning what a moral choice would look like at the practical level. Sin fits into these structure as a term to define human actions which separate the actor from the deity and which are thus an attack on God's own spirit of truth; 'sin' brings together morality and ethics. The cosmic struggle is engaged in, then, at the level of community existence.

## Community

In the Old Testament the concept of 'community' is attached to being 'Israel'. This term denotes a people related through kinship, a kingdom, a society united through shared customs and people with a common religious

---

45  I Enoch is an early Jewish work, not in the Old Testament canon, known through its Ethiopic form and from material found at Qumran in the 1950s. An English text can be found in Charlesworth, J. (ed.), *The Pseudepigrapha of the Old Testament*, 1985, volume one. An earlier version exists in the work of R. Charles, with which the later English text can be compared. The first chapters deal with the nations as the wicked, opposed to the faithful, who are viewed as the righteous.

46  Meeks, W., *The Origins of Christian Morality*, New Haven, Yale University Press, 1993, p.119.

affiliation.[47] It is the moral vision of this community, which occupies the Old Testament and to which are attached guidelines for ethical behaviour, as can clearly be seen in the Torah texts. However the God of Israel is viewed also as the creator of all the nations on earth, in Genesis chapters one to eleven, and much of the moral reflection found in wisdom material is shared with other Ancient Near-Eastern texts.[48] The Old Testament can, then, be described as offering not only an Israelite perspective of moral order but also as reflecting natural law, open to all reflective human beings. Barton's chapter on natural law provides a bridge between cosmos and community levels.[49] He presents two images of morality and scripture, one which regards biblical morality and ethics as the expression of God's commandments, revealed to those who choose to be part of a community of faith, and a second which takes a broader view and suggests that the biblical texts are evidence of a natural law system which is the context for all human groups and which can be explored both outside and within biblical texts.[50]

Wright also deals with the community level of morality in the Old Testament. His starting point, though, is at the other end of the scale, the link between the individual and the group. Wright argues that personal morality only makes sense within the context of the "social angle".[51] He notes that from Genesis chapter one onwards issues of morality are dealt with in relation to the broad sweep of humanity as a whole. Even the selection of one group, in Abraham, opens the possibility, in Genesis chapter twenty-two, that all nations will bless themselves through this person.[52] The importance of this point for our ethical understanding of the Old Testament is that we must take

47 See the references to Israel in earlier parts of this chapter.
48 It is commonly accepted among scholars that there is a cosmopolitan aspect to Old Testament wisdom material. For a recent survey on the Old Testament wisdom genre and related sources see Day, J., Gordon, R. and Williamson, H. (eds), *Wisdom in Ancient Israel*, Cambridge, Cambridge University Press, 1995.
49 Barton, J., *Ethics*, chapter four, and also Barton, J., *Natural Law and Poetic Justice*, in the *Journal of Theological Studies*, No. 30 Vol. XXX/1, 1979; and Barton, J., *Ethics in Isaiah of Jerusalem* in the *Journal of Theological Studies*, No. 32. Vol. XXXII/1, 1981.
50 Barton, J., *Ethics*, p. 59.
51 Wright, C., *Living as the People of God*. The social angle is the term which Wright uses to describe the manner in which the Old Testament deals with human beings not primarily as individuals but as members of a community. The social angle on Old Testament ethics has to do with the manner in which the Old Testament community lives out its identity.
52 In Genesis chapter twenty two there are signs that the text as extant is a late redaction, especially in that it does not limit its future concerns to the immediate family of Abraham, but looks to a time when Abraham will be known as a legendary founder in whose name a society takes shape. The founder represents that future in the Genesis passage and the blessing referred to will be for him and on his account.

account of the fact that so much of its ethical thrust is necessarily social.[53]

Thus, Wright argues, much of the Old Testament is taken up with the issue of what Israel was to do and be as a society.[54] If an indicator of morality in the Old Testament vocabulary is holiness then this term is always contextualised in group behaviour. It is as a nation or kingdom (Exodus chapter nineteen) that Israel is to reach its full identity as partner to its deity, aligned with world order. How that social profile works occupies a large part of Torah as well as Prophecy, moving from an overall moral hermeneutic for developing religious identity to detailed prescriptions of social relations within the daily lifestyle of group members.[55] It is within a land identified and gifted to Israel by God that the society of Israel takes its fullest form.

Morality here is expressed in the form of contract or treaty. Loyalty to the essential relationship between contractors requires Israel to trust in the name of its deity and so to act (ethically) in line with that trust. "Israel knew that they were the people of God because he had given them his land, and that gift verified the relationship written into the covenant with Abraham and the covenant made at Sinai."[56] 'Community', then, provides the middle level between universal reality and order, associated with divine existence, and individual understanding of the meaning of life and of human activity. It is as members of a society that human beings learn about the origins and boundaries of their social world; through taking on these 'sacred traditions' new members learn how to act appropriately in a community which has as its cultural base one particular religious understanding of the cosmos.[57]

## Person

Every community is composed of individual members and ultimately the strength or weakness of the group relates to the actions and views of individuals. This brings in the dimension of 'person', understood as a human being with the capacity for self-awareness and so the capacity for taking responsibility for individual actions, which impinge on other creatures and on

53  Wright, C., *Living as the People of God*, p. 34.
54  Wright, C., *Living as the People of God*, p. 40.
55  This links with the account of Israel as a moral social grouping, as set out by Wright. Wherever one turns in Tanach the same pattern of interest is to be found. The world is the creation of God, morally ordered, and human existence operates within that framework.
56  Wright, C., *Living as the People of God*, p. 53.
57  This term is drawn from the work of cultural anthropologists such as Clifford Geertz, Mary Douglas and social scientists such as Peter Berger. See especially Geertz, C., *The Interpretation of Cultures*, London, Fontana, 1993.

the world environment. 'A moral person' indicates not simply exterior human existence but the interior world of the understanding of the self as a being within which emotions, reason, will and inclinations are all active and sometimes in tension.[58] Thus the individual human being becomes a mini-world in him/herself in which value systems must be established and ethical or unethical activities measured against an overall moral vision of life and its meaning. The Old Testament traditions assume the need for the gathering together of inner energies to bring about action appropriate for that moral microcosm which is a human being. In Torah texts the people of Israel know their God to be on their side and they themselves to be a holy nation, as found in Exodus chapter nineteen, for example. Thus every Israelite must strive to align their hearts, the centres of their reason and life force, with those external perspectives.

In practice it was extremely difficult for the Israelite to follow this moral vision of the self, according to the Old Testament viewpoint. The book of Deuteronomy warns of suffering to come if God's ways are not observed and the prophets outline the nature of that suffering, which draws together individual death and injury with the fate of a nation abandoned to its military foes. Morality at this point absorbs the reality of suffering; it is through the pain and loss of a previous sense of identity that a remnant will be saved to restore a community in favour with its deity. Moral vision in this setting entails not only theological beliefs but also touches upon the life and death realities of human and communal existence.

The narratives of Genesis chapters one to eleven contain a tension between human beings in the image of God and separated from God. The hinge here is personal responsibility. Wisdom texts endorse this statement with their distinction between 'wise' and 'foolish', 'righteous' and 'wicked'. In Proverbs each person can choose which category to belong to, but only those who are 'religiously wise' as well as learned observers of the world will find reward for their behaviour in long life, many children and possessions.[59] The individual person must choose the appropriate moral vision in order to live ethically and successfully.

---

58 See Williams, R., *Interiority and Epiphany: A Reading in New Testament Ethics*, in Jones, L. and Buckley, J. (eds), *Spirituality and Embodiment*, Oxford, Blackwell, 1997.

59 This is the usual division of human beings into two categories, 'wise/fool' alongside 'righteous/wicked' which may be found in all three Old Testament wisdom books, for example, as well as in Psalms such as Psalm 1 which clearly defines humans and their fates according to this two-part model.

## Summarising the Field

Cosmos, community and person can be treated as separate topics, as set out above, but it must also be borne in mind that there is overlap between them. When all three are read together a subtle interweaving of meaning emerges in which the divine ordering of the world has ramifications right down to the level of individual human beings' experience of daily affairs such as health and prosperity. This thought is clearly present in all types of Old Testament literature. God is part of the everyday reality of living and is alongside the community and the individual, both watching and guarding; thus the term 'God' belongs to all three areas of existence. Community and person have to be taken together if the reader of biblical books is to understand the whole of the human dimension of world existence. At the same time the human dimension reaches into cosmic order. Each of the three major prophets in the Old Testament has visionary experiences which allow them to enter into a direct relationship with the deity and as a result of those experiences they incarnate the divine word, becoming God's mouthpiece to the rulers of his people.

In this discussion of biblical morality and ethics, foundational terms have been delineated and discussed. In particular a method has been set up for the reading and interpreting of Old Testament narratives which will occur in the rest of this book. Not that this present account is by any means all that could be said either in relation to general principles or to the details of relevant exegesis of biblical texts, but enough material has been explored to give a basis for a detailed examination of particular biblical passages. Content has been given to the three defining terms yet they remain capable of variety and flexibility. Further development of these terms will take place as they are utilised in the act of reading, leading to a critical re-shaping of their content. This preserves the standpoint taken in the section on biblical hermeneutics that there needs to be a balance between general theological hermeneutics and detailed investigation of biblical texts in any account of biblical representations of morality.

Cosmos sets the scene for all human thought and action, but the cosmic level contains not only good, not only God, but the problem of accounting for an evil which seems to be opposed to divine creation. Community is the focus for human response to life inside the cosmos. The community level offers a possibility of discussing and developing life's meaning; human beings who share a common religious or cultural setting can, through communication, provide a secure framework of ideas about the goal of world existence on which an ordered personal social life can be established. The person is the smallest social unit; societies need members to realise social goals and incarnate their ideals. Conversely, persons find their truest and fullest sense of self-identity when dialoguing with the social group to which they belong.[60] All three terms operate within the sphere both of morality and of ethics – at the level of moral vision and at that of a particular set of behaviour patterns.

### Character, Plot and Setting

To turn these terms around is to arrive at the order, which will be followed in the sections of this book. 'Person' will be explored through the presentations of three main characters of separate Old Testament narratives – Abraham, David and Esther. 'Community' will be represented through the area of plot construction in narrative since it is at this level of story that a communal picture emerges with the complex interaction of all the characters in the development of action and consequence. Here the stories of Ruth, Jonah and Joseph will be examined for moral perspectives. 'Cosmos' will be explored through the structuring of narratives in relation to time and space. The topics of world-order, the origins of evil and the role of suffering will be investigated in this section, via Genesis chapters one to eleven, the book of Daniel and the book of Job, respectively. It is in those areas that the symbolic world of the text deals with important human questions relating to those universal frameworks of existence, which themselves set the scene for the quest for appropriate social and personal ethics.

In all this the approach will be to start with the relevant narratives as those exist in Christian bibles. A range of scholarly comments on these stories will then be put forward in order to widen the reader's understanding of the issues raised by the text, including not only models of personal and community action but also broader-ranging matters relating to cultural aspects of interpreting the narratives. In all this it is intended that, by taking a literary approach to the subject of morality, the aim set out at the start of this chapter may be carried through. To broaden a reader's understanding of the concept of biblical morality by taking into account the whole presentation of moral/ethical material, not merely obviously legalistic snippets abstracted from their biblical moorings.

---

60  The work of cultural anthropologists such as Clifford Geertz is important here. See Geertz, C., *The Interpretation of Cultures*, London, Fontana, 1993.

# PART I:
# MORALITY AND CHARACTER

# Chapter Two

# Abraham

In the first chapter a brief definition of the term 'person' was given, identifying that term as one of three parallel terms, which this study would be using in order to evaluate moral perspectives in Old Testament narratives. 'Person' implies the individual human being who is capable of independent reflection and action and who is therefore able to take responsibility for the consequences of his/her acts. In Old Testament narratives the implied location of such a person is within 'Israel', as stated in the first chapter above. It is argued that the term person, as moral agent, can be explored through the fictional persons found in stories. Hence this chapter, together with the following two chapters, will focus on the nature of characterisation and on the particular characterisations of central figures in selected Old Testament narratives.

## Characterisation and Morality

In telling individual stories the narrator of a biblical book fleshes out personhood through actual individuals and their careers. Thus characterisation offers a method of exploration of moral meaning using the symbolic universe of the text as a setting for human beings and their choices, the consequences of those choices and moral commentary.[1] As Bar-Efrat notes: "the decisions they are called upon to make when confronted with different alternatives, and the results of these decisions, provide indisputable evidence of the narrative's ethical dimension".[2] This feeds through to the way characters are portrayed. Direct characterisation can include comments on the inner state of a character's disposition. Bar-Efrat says "if a person is defined as being righteous, wicked, wise or foolish, this constitutes both characterisation and judgement".[3] Thus Noah is categorised as a blameless man who walked with God, a comment which

---

1  The topic of a 'sacred universe' was originally discussed by Peter Berger and then became an established concept in biblical studies. A recent survey of the usefulness of this methodology for biblical exegesis is found in Horrell, D., *Converging Ideologies: Berger and Luckman and the Pastoral Epistles* in *Journal for the Study of the New Testament*, Volume No. 50/93, pp. 85-103, 1993.
2  Bar-Efrat, S., *Narrative Art in the Bible*, Sheffield, Sheffield Academic Press, 1997, p. 47.
3  Bar-Efrat, S., *Narrative*, p. 53.

gives moral value to Noah as well as defining his role in the Flood Narrative of Genesis chapters six to nine.

Information concerning the development of a character in a story is provided by the narrator, by other characters in the same story, and by the words of the character him/herself. Using this information the reader constructs a picture of the character as a person with motives, sometimes clear and sometimes hidden, and as shaped by the consequences of personal action and the activities of others. Gunn and Fewell describe this as "a reading of biblical narrative that probes beneath the surface of speech enables a reader to build a much richer story world".[4] One aspect of this deeper investigation, they suggest, concerns the balancing of different elements in the story against one another. Gunn adds that "we may also seek to fathom characters by measuring what they say against what they do . . . in effect we are comparing and contrasting the voices of character and narrator . . . when there is incongruity we often find that the narrator's report of action is a more reliable indicator of character than the character's speech".[5]

Characters emerge from narrative as complex constructions with the possibility of being both predictable and unpredictable in different scenes within the single story. It is this diversity of opinion which a reader may have about a character in a biblical narrative which makes the moral evaluations of personhood offered by the presentation of a given character itself diverse and multi-faceted. Great men such as Abraham and David emerge as acting in an ethical manner, yet not without shadows lying across their overall behaviour. In dealing with their emotions, desires and fears these men reflect the moral tensions which relate to the very nature of human existence and which help define the moral standing of a human person.

It was pointed out in chapter one that the worth of an individual is determined in biblical thought in relation to social and cosmic context. It is the interplay between these three levels of cosmos, community and person, which produces ultimate meaning. However, what the reader usually encounters first, when reading a biblical story, is the level of the individual actor in the text; thus characterisation is a key pointer to the overarching values carried in the story. The first stage of reflection on moral meaning and so of ordering and evaluating is at the level of an individual person's experience of life events. The message to be extracted from reading may

---

4  Gunn, D. and Fewell, D., *Narrative Art in the Hebrew Bible*, Oxford, Oxford University Press, 1993, p. 69.
5  Gunn, D. and Fewell, D., *Narrative Art*, p. 71.

emerge from the long-term harmonies created by a sequence of events related to the story; events may dovetail with one another thus revealing an ordered purpose to human behaviour. Equally, however, the narrative may reveal the incoherence of daily existence, a person's uncertainty about the moral value of experience since that experience is itself chaotic and variable. In this second situation it is through the very disorder that meaning will emerge.[6]

With regard to Abraham as a character in Genesis chapters twelve to twenty-four, both versions of pursuing meaning can be illustrated. The delineation of Abraham as a man of faith evidences an ordered world where ethical behaviour is possible, because there is a long-term harmony to events. God promises a son who eventually comes to birth and whose life is saved from destruction. Yet, behind this interpretation lurks the issue of incoherence. Abraham's promised son does not arrive until chapter twenty-one and both Abraham and Sarah have, meanwhile, attempted to put their own order on to family events in relation to creating an heir for the patriarch, via Eliezer as heir or Ishmæl as son. Viewing Abraham as a person, with several levels of response to events, offers the reader further characterisations of Abraham, as a coward who abandons his wife to other men, for example, in the Egyptian scene, or as passive agent, allowing his wife to act on his behalf, in the first Hagar scene. These other evaluations of the patriarch's worth present a contrast with that of the man of faith interpretation and will be examined further in the course of this chapter.

## Genesis Chapters Twelve to Twenty-Four

The section of Genesis from chapter twelve to twenty-four contains both the story of Abraham itself and stories about Abraham. This comment relates to the composition of a single narrative from several separate ones. John Goldingay creates a single story of Abraham, composed of the scenes between these markers. Thus the story can be described in a chart as follows:

6   For an example of this, see Barton, J., *Ethics*, pp.12-13, where he points out that deeper meanings can be found when viewing the disagreements between Old Testament texts as differences of opinion inside a shared framework of assumptions.

Call of Abraham (migration)
Abraham and Sarah in Egypt
Abraham and Lot
God promises Abraham a son
Sarah and Hagar (one)
COVENANT
Abraham and Lot ( Sodom/Gomorrah)
Abraham and Sarah in Gerar
Sarah and Hagar (two)
Call of Abraham (sacrifice)

This pattern leaves the covenant of God with Abraham through the promise of a son at the heart of the overall narrative. In this approach the story of Abraham concerns the God of Abraham's demands of his worshipper (submission to the deity's will), while a subplot also highlights the link of trust between two males (Abraham and God). This is achieved by contrasting the behaviour of the males with that of the females in the story, especially Sarah who tries to produce a child by her own means, sending her maid to her husband in her place. Sarah's plan is not the divine one and her efforts cause her and her maid much pain.

Further reading of the text, however, deconstructs that view, since the God of Abraham appears also to be on the side of Hagar, a woman, appearing to her, a mere female slave, in the wilderness and making promises to her which parallel those made to Abraham. At the same time Sarah's attempt to find another route to a child can be viewed against Abraham's insistence that Eliezer and Ishmæl are his heirs, in his dialogues with God in chapters fifteen and seventeen. Noting these textual elements leads the reader to further considerations about Abraham himself. What was going on in Abraham's mind between the scenes narrated? What did Abraham really think about the divine promises? Abraham, as well as Sarah, behaves in a normal human fashion, trying to find short term solutions to problems that press in, such as how to achieve safe travel in foreign parts.

It can be noted here that the voice of the narrator is only partially helpful to the reader. Each scene narrated, through the dialogue between the characters, gives some clue as to the intentions of the main characters, but the narrative voice between scenes contents itself with largely geographical and temporal bridging. The narrator does not greatly intrude on the reader's understanding. Moreover God appears less frequently than in Genesis chapters one to eleven. The emphasis in the story, then, falls on the human characters for the progress of the plot: a structure which also allows the reader the opportunity to consider the part played specifically by a variety of human behaviour, with all its complexities, in the movement of affairs. Cohn says that "God does not compel Abraham and Sarah. They make their own decisions and he redeems their situations . . . the omniscient narrator has moved farther from heaven and closer to earth in the Abraham cycle".[7]

There are silences in the narrative, which give the reader scope for personal interpretations. Even where there is dialogue it is terse and an aura of silence hangs over the character of Abraham especially. When God speaks Abraham does not always reply. He acts, as God wants, but offers little comment on what that action implies. Jack Lindblom comments on this narrative style, referring back to Auerbach's classic comments on the Old Testament: "Feelings and thoughts of persons are not externalised, that is, motives are lacking and purposes remain unexpressed . . . in the Genesis chapter twenty-two passage we meet with that 'heavy silence' between Abraham and his son as they walk to the mountain of sacrifice."[8] These literary features allow the reader to fill in the gaps, explain the motives and so develop 'the story of Abraham' along different, and even opposing, lines of thought.

## Text and Structure

Although the literary critic tends to read the text synchronically, as one whole book with overall meanings, historical criticism has pointed out these chapters are in fact composed of a number of separate narratives which are now joined together by the over-arching theme of 'the promises of God' – of a son, descendants and a land.[9] This construction makes Abraham into a great figure of Israel's distant past, founder of the line of patriarchs, which would eventually lead to the development of Israel into a nation in Egypt.

7   Cohn, R., *Narrative Structure and Canonical Perspective in Genesis 18* in  Rogerson, J. (ed.), *The Pentateuch*, Sheffield, Sheffield Academic Press, 1996.
8   Lundblom, J., *Parataxis, Rhetorical Structure, and the Dialogue over Sodom in Genesis 18* in Davies, P. and Clines, D. (eds), 1998, p. 137.
9   Although the narrative is now continuous the critical tools of Source and Form methodologies show that the text is a composite of earlier sections have been melded together. See, for instance, Westermann, C., *The Promises to the Fathers*, Philadelphia, Fortress, 1980.

J. P. Fokkelman has noted the way in which references to Abraham's age structure and contain the narration of this story of Abraham: "These verses form a pattern by which this cycle . . . is divided into three sections . . . the central panel . . . chapters seventeen to twenty-one, covers the hundredth year of his life, precisely the period in which God makes the concrete and definite announcement of the arrival of Isaac."[10] This use of repetition builds up suspense in the narrative and allows the reader to compare Abraham's behaviour in the stories of the 'ancestress in danger' with the viewpoint he expresses when he dialogues with the deity, as well as with the divine perspective on human affairs.[11] God's final vindication of his promise that Sarah will become pregnant by Abraham comes, in temporal terms, long after human beings would have believed conception possible.

David Clines points out that the divine time-frame as presented in the Pentateuch is even longer than that of Abraham's lifespan.[12] Even by the end of Genesis, Clines states: "The vision of descendants as many as the stars of heaven (chapter fifteen, verse five) or the sand of the sea (chapter twenty-two, verse seventeen), and of Abraham as father of a multitude of nations (chapter seventeen verse five) has yet to be realised."[13] As to the land itself, "on the whole patriarchal narratives take place outside the promised land, as much as inside it, the possession of the land remains a hope".[14] The cosmic level of evaluating life events can only be seen in its totality when the reader examines the Pentateuch as a whole and goes even beyond this into the Former Prophets. From the long-term view, Clines suggests, readers can identify the moral purpose of the deity, which is based on divine promise and its fulfilment: "The promise of the blessing is both the divine initiative in a world where human initiatives always tend to lead to disaster and are an affirmation of the primal divine intentions for humanity".[15]

---

10  Fokkelman's commentary on Genesis can be found in Alter, R. and Kermode, F. (eds), *The Literary Guide to the Bible*, London, Harper Collins, p. 48.
11  This is the scholarly code title given to this scene, an indication of the fact that the stratagem is repeated in several forms in Genesis, and not only in the story of Sarah. It is argued that the idea for such a story belongs to the oral world of folk tales.
12  Clines, D., *The Theme of the Pentateuch*, Sheffield, Sheffield Academic Press, 1997.
13  Clines, D., *Theme of the Pentateuch*, p. 49.
14  Clines, D., *Theme of the Pentateuch*, p. 49.
15  Clines, D., *Theme of the Pentateuch*, p. 30.

## The Man of Faith

It at this level of the overarching structure of the Pentateuch and the topic of a promised son that Abraham can be described as 'the man of faith'. This is because, at this level, the reader encounters him as part of a larger story, the first of the founding fathers of Israel. What is immediately accessible is Abraham's contribution to the origins of Israel, his role as ancestor supreme. It is possible to build up a picture of a noble, dignified Abraham who does not cry out loudly and continually against his lack of the promised child but goes on with the daily business of living in silent trust that, when the time comes, God will redeem his promises.

The textual silence on Abraham's motives could be read to indicate Abraham's depth of religious commitment. Abraham goes in search of the God he has heard speaking and of his own human destiny. Similarly, the repetition of the command to go in chapter twenty-two, and Abraham's acquiescence to it, allows for Abraham's motive to be a continuing search for religious meaning even in life's appalling paradoxes. These interpretations of the beginning and end of the Abraham story create a picture of a solemn man, self-possessed, silent, resourceful, taking risks in the certainty of personal belief. This character is not necessarily an easy companion but he can be respected for his integrity and his keeping faith with his understanding of God and God's requirements.

But it is equally possible to produce a critique of this picture of Abraham. If the reader does not immediately pull the whole story together but takes seriously its construction from independent stories each of which has its own beginning, middle and end, and if the reader then examines each of these stories individually, a different view of the character, Abraham, can emerge.

The overall text proceeds from a promise of a child to his birth to his near death, but it does so in a cyclical mode, whereby the sub-themes are introduced and then interwoven with one another. Some of these sub-themes are one-off presentations, such as that of Abraham the military leader. Others, such as Abraham's allowing foreign kings to take his wife, are repeated, and others again, such as the triangular relationship of Abraham, Sarah and Hagar, are developed further in the next repetition of that theme. It is in this interweaving of short scenes that the image of Abraham as a moral person gains its complexity and depth.

For when each separate scene of Abraham's story is examined, a somewhat different picture emerges from the unassailable model of faith. Despite God's promise, Abraham puts his wife Sarah into another man's hands in chapter twelve. God has to make it clear to Pharaoh that Sarah is married to Abraham and Pharaoh's reproof is endorsed by the text, which leaves Abraham silent in the face of reproach. Despite this lesson, Abraham is to repeat the manoeuvre with regard to Abimelech, at a time when, in the text's chronology, Sarah was already pregnant with Abraham's child. Although Abraham does not initiate his sexual relationship with Hagar, he easily complies with the scheme and then washes his hands of the consequences when Hagar is pregnant and Sarah decides to ill-treat her. Even when the scene is repeated with Ishmæl, now a grown lad, Abraham allows his doubts to be overcome, albeit by a message from the deity.

There are scenes where Abraham seems to act with integrity, as when he beseeches God on behalf of the just persons in Sodom and Gomorrah, for instance, although this apparently disinterested concern for the innocent must have been linked with his knowledge that his own relation, Lot, was among the inhabitants of the cities. Abraham's battle scene carries the same concern, the need to rescue a kinsman, from enslavement to an enemy this time. Perhaps the most ambivalent scene here is the Binding of Isaac. To sacrifice a child must either be the height of moral vision and ethical behaviour or the most corrupt and unethical action possible. The scene turns on Abraham's trust in God, an inclusion with chapter twelve. But is this dependence on what the deity appears to want true moral vision? How far did Abraham's imagination suggest to him that God needs humans to sacrifice someone beloved by them in order to demonstrate a total commitment to the divine?

## Models of Abraham as a Person

These two levels of the text, the broad range of the whole Abraham narrative and the immediate short scenes of which it is composed, make several different moral interpretations possible. Abraham may be viewed as:

> A pious man.
> A comic character.
> A trickster.
> A character in a Tragedy.
> A savage parent.
> An unworthy husband.

And it these profiles which will now be discussed.

The model of great piety picks up on the presentation of Abraham as a man of faith. It is one which places great value on Abraham as a paradigm of a proper moral perspective on existence and for ethical action. By contrast, the titles of 'comic figure' or 'ambiguous figure' suggest a critique of the view that Abraham's character is totally exemplary. In Comedy the plot line moves towards happiness, despite difficulties on the way, and that is how, it can be argued, Abraham's story works, overall. Genesis chapter twenty-two gives this movement in miniature. An event occurs which could be a dreadful tragedy but which is converted, within the story, to a positive note of life and blessing. Yet there are really tragic aspects to the Comedy of the chapters twelve to twenty-two and some of these reversals cast a moral light on Abraham's character. In particular it is the domestic scene which is shadowed by unhappiness and which offers the reader a picture of moral ambiguity. Not all Abraham's responses can be wholeheartedly accepted as positive, so at best he emerges as ambiguous in terms of moral evaluation and at worst he can be judged to be a man of false values and uncaring towards others within his social setting.

## A Pious Man

This is the key model for most mainstream commentaries on Genesis,[16] and is expressed very fully in a recent book by Karl-Joseph Kuschel.[17] Kuschel summarises the Abrahamic material in Genesis early on in his book and from that produces a description of Abraham as a person of high moral worth. For, not only did that person act ethically in his own life circumstances, he also showed the way to later generations as to true values and so, for Kuschel, Abraham enshrines the key aspects of Judaism as a religious system. Here one particular model of a biblical character is being aligned with the foundational values of a world religious system. Kuschel says that "more than any other figure in the Pentateuch, Abraham stands for this twofold aspect of trust in God and . . . trust from human beings in return . . . the theology of Genesis is fundamentally a narrative anthropology of faith. It relates what human beings do if they really

---

16 Mainstream commentaries, such as that of Westermann's two volume work, bring out the dominance of this mode of interpretation. A short example of the style is to be found in chapter 3 of Moberley, R., *Genesis 12-50*, Sheffield, Sheffield Academic Press, 1995.

17 Kuschel, K.-J., *Abraham. A Symbol of Hope for Jews, Christians and Muslims*, London, SCM Press, 1995.

believe. They trust in God's word and promise – through all doubt, all scepticism and all hesitation."[18]

Although this image of Abraham makes of him a foundational figure for religious belief it is not, for Kuschel, a simplistic or static view. Abraham develops his own faith through a series of life events, which open up before him: God has to be made sense of in each of the new events, which Abraham encounters. And mixed into these scenes are flawed human situations, such as the fact that, as Kuschel notes, "hardly have his sons and heirs been born than there were jealous scenes between his wife and his concubine, which can only be resolved by a brutal expulsion".[19] Kuschel argues that though he is a model of piety Abraham is not a model of perfection.

Kuschel, however, is not interested in Abraham as simply a figure of piety among Jewish readers of Torah. He desires to create, from this character, a channel of cultural harmony in the modern era. Abraham, the pious man, is the paradigm for pious behaviour among others, and that shared piety could bring these other human beings into a much needed bond of mutual understanding and toleration. This is possible because the three major world religions, which Kuschel is concerned with, Judaism, Christianity and Islam all have, in their sacred writings, a version of the story of Abraham. In all three versions it is Abraham's piety which is to the forefront, for in Judaism, Christianity and Islam Abraham is revered for his faith in a single deity.

But, although all three religions allot Abraham a significant role in their religious traditions, historically they have often been divided by war and violence. In the modern period there is a greater mood for dialogue across religious borders, especially where they co-exist in the same geographical region, so there is a need to find a common symbol through which dialogue might be engendered. Kuschel argues that Abraham offers such an ecumenical paradigm: "In all [three] traditions Abraham shows what is most important for human beings before God: not legal religious achievements, but dedication to the will of God, a well-tried trust in God."[20] This paradigm respects the particular stance of each of the three religions, taking as its centre the role of Abraham as originator of all three religious communities, either directly, through Isaac and Ishmæl, or by derivation, through the ancestry of Christ. If Jews, Christians and Muslims can accept one another as sharing an interest in Abraham, "then they will constantly

18 Kuschel, K.-J., *Abraham*, p. 26.
19 Kuschel, K.-J., *Abraham*, pp. 27-28.
20 Kuschel, K.-J., *Abraham*, p. 28.

deepen this ecumenical fellowship by reflecting on the meaning of faith in the one true God: the God whom Abraham did not give up", Kuschel argues.[21] Here moral vision is the equivalent of a religious worldview. Readers of the Abraham story can make that vision their own, choosing to live by its content.

## A Comic Character

This is, of course, only one possible moral perspective on the character Abraham. Other interpretations present Abraham to the reader more as one man among others, within the literary context, possibly offering a more indirect commentary on human behaviour generally. It is to this manner of reading that the comic model belongs. Referring to Abraham as a comic figure does not mean that his character is trivial or frivolous, of course, but rather that he is a character in a comedy – a story of human life, which ends hopefully. As W. Whedbee suggests, "whatever trials and threats the hero must endure, Comedy usually ascends from any momentary darkness and concludes with celebration, joy and at least the promise of new life".[22] J. Magonet picks up that idea in his book *The Subversive Bible*: "The Bible is not just a 'pious' document to be handled with kid gloves . . . even a cursory glance at the Bible shows that it covers too many areas of human life and experiences, is composed of too many different styles and modes, to fit very comfortably into conventional religious forms."[23]

One of Magonet's worked examples is that of the subversive role of the Abraham story in relation to justice. Magonet, for instance, contrasts the Abraham who pleads with God over justice in the case of Sodom/ Gomorrah with the Abraham who is willing to suppress justice when he offers Isaac as a sacrifice to God. Does that mean that Abraham is a fragmented person or are the contradictions the work of "the subversive hand of a single author"?[24] Positing that these come from a single view on the hero allows for ambiguity to become a recognised trait of character and extends the thought-world of the text.

Genesis chapter eighteen shows God choosing Abraham to be the source of a great nation and to educate them in the principles of righteousness and justice. Because of this vocation God has to teach Abraham about the

21 Kuschel, K.-J., *Abraham*, p. 203.
22 Whedbee, W., *The Bible and the Comic Vision*, Cambridge University Press, 1998, p. 7.
23 Magonet, J., *The Subversive Bible*, London, SCM Press, 1997, p. 3 f.
24 Magonet, J., *The Subversive Bible*, p. 21.

nature of good and evil, by revealing to him the verdict on Sodom/Gomorrah. But Abraham's response questions divine justice itself; should the innocent be punished with the guilty? And this represents a challenge to God, which accompanies a new moral vision, as Magonet notes: "In a culture where gods are supreme powers and human beings are totally subordinate...[this] is an outstanding reversal of roles."[25] Abraham now stands in free equality with God enshrining the need to fight for justice against whatever powers stand in its way, up to and including God.[26]

Yet this same character is willing to sacrifice his own son to God without arguing his case for justice and mercy. Read literally, the event contradicts the image of a man of moral vision found in chapter eighteen. Only by shifting the divine context of the scene can Rabbinic tradition harmonise these pictures of Abraham. It is only a test after all. God never intended a real sacrifice. Thus Abraham's acquiescence is laudatory for it would never lead to death. The use of two terms for God in the story also allows for flexibility. Whereas Elohim tests Abraham it is YHWH who stops him.[27] These reading tactics let both God and Abraham off lightly. Yet the essential difficulty remains. Magonet says "Abraham remains a riddle in the complexity of his character captured by these accounts", and adds: "At the moment when we might domesticate Abraham . . . we find his dark side, the single-minded fanaticism . . . that would allow him to sacrifice his son."[28]

The moral perspective offered by this reading of Abraham ultimately raises a question mark over the moral worth of a person. Was Abraham a moral person? If so, was he only moral in some of his actions? Can his personality be broken up in this way? Must the reader not take all Abraham's actions into account and finish with a riddle, an unresolved mystery relating to personal morality? William Whedbee, too, raises questions about a too-solemnly pious approach to the character, Abraham. He states that "in my view, the gap between promises and their fulfilment creates the context and conditions for the emergence of comedy . . .

---

25 Magonet, J., *The Subversive Bible*, p. 23.
26 Magonet, J., *The Subversive Bible*, p. 23.
27 Genesis texts variously use two terms for God, Elohim and YHWH. While it is likely that this is to do with the historical development of the individual traditions now combined in a single work, it gives readers the chance to separate out the nature of God according to two 'faces'. This is a technique used especially in the recent work by Miles, J., *God – A Biography*, New York, Simon and Schuster, 1995.
28 Magonet, J., *The Subversive Bible*, p. 36.

comedy loves to exploit the incongruity between promises and their partial or failed fulfilment".[29]

## A Trickster

From comedy it is possible to move to trickery and illusion. Whedbee remarks that certain stock characters are to be found in comedies: "Buffoons, clowns, simpletons, rogues and tricksters, incarnate the human."[30] Here it is worth noting the role of Abraham as trickster in the story of Abram and Sarai in Egypt. There is always laughter within the text, though that laughter, says Whedbee, "is often complex and ambivalent, ranging from sardonic and subversive to joyous and celebrative".[31] It is this gap between expectation and reality, which makes a space both for laughter and for grief. The stories of the 'ancestress in danger' offer an account of trickery which invites the reader to laugh, albeit ironically, at Abraham's success in extricating himself without personal loss, from a problematic event. Likewise, the presentation of Abraham in Genesis chapter fourteen as a warrior-hero operates in the manner nowadays called a 'spoof'. Whedbee argues that "the utter unreality of the dramatic success of the rescue mission against the overwhelming odds presents a larger-than-life heroic character".[32]

But comic presentation has its dark side. The birth of Ishmæl is a parody of the 'proper' birth and underlines the uncertainty of divine intervention. The appearance of God in chapter seventeen to make further promises is met by implied laughter on Abraham's part – can Sarah really be expected to have a child? – and in chapter eighteen by real laughter on Sarah's part. Can the divine words have any real impact on human experience? Human laughter here encapsulates human perspectives on the value of life. Only what actually happens, what is accessible to human forethought and planning, has any reality; the rest, though pious, is just wishful thinking. But practical human attempts to impose meaning on life are not without grief. Sarah's worry over childlessness, the enmity between Hagar and herself, Hagar's dread of death and rejection twice in the narrative, show that human beings do not have knowledge of the effects of their present acts, do not have total vision with which to evaluate what goes

---

29 Whedbee, W., *The Bible and the Comic Vision*, p. 65.
30 Whedbee, W., *The Bible and the Comic Vision*, p. 7.
31 Whedbee, W., *The Bible and the Comic Vision*, p. 9.
32 Whedbee, W., *The Bible and the Comic Vision*, p. 71.

on.  From a human, day to day, perspective life is ambiguous in terms of how events will proceed and how they will conclude.

Ambiguity thus becomes part of moral perspective.  It may not be ideal but it is the reality.  Philip Davies' account of 'Male Bonding' is further evidence for this style of reading Abraham.[33]  In Davies' view both God and Abraham are complex characters who are engaged in the kind of contest which leads to male bonding in society.  God offers Abraham a relationship, which Abraham is prepared to go along with, if only to see what will happen.  So he sets out from home – but quickly chooses his own route and ends up in Egypt in an arrangement that he appears to be happy with.  Davies points out that it is God who is displeased with events, in Genesis chapter twelve.  Neither Abraham nor Sarah is depicted as frustrated by the choices available.  P. Davies says "Abraham is beginning to display himself as an unscrupulous entrepreneur", and adds: "YHWH cannot, or will not, directly control Abraham, though he can bring about his own plans by guile and by the divine powers he has."[34]

This contest of strengths and interests carries on throughout Abraham's story, according to Davies.  In particular, God keeps stringing Abraham along with promises of descendants and land and Abraham is prepared to see if God will carry these through but is busy setting his own life in order in case they are empty words.  At the end Abraham has two sons and no land; he has to buy the cave at Machpelah for Sarah's tomb.  Perhaps he was right to put less than total belief in God's proposals!  The sacrifice of Isaac is yet another example of the struggle for prime place between two males.  God calls Abraham's control of affairs into question but Abraham reckons that God is more involved in Isaac's existence than he himself is.  After all, Isaac is God's winning hand in the contest of strength so far, since his birth proves the power of the deity over events.  Abraham can afford to call God's bluff and of course wins the trick.  Neither God nor Abraham comes out of this with untarnished reputation, unlike Isaac who behaved with loyalty and integrity.  Davies comments that "rather like Abimelech, he found himself suffering at the expense of a game of bluff going on between two old tricksters".[35]

Davies' approach here is similar to that of Whedbee.  It offers a comic vision of the world and of a man's life in which the overall morality is that of flexibility, craftiness and guile.  God and Abraham can laugh together

---

33  Davies, P., *Whose Bible is it Anyway?*, Sheffield, Sheffield Academic Press, 1995, chapter five.
34  Davies, P., *Whose Bible is it Anyway?*, p. 101.
35  Davies, P., *Whose Bible is it Anyway?*, p. 111.

having called each other's bluff, once Isaac is released from the altar, and can call it quits. Laughter covers both the guile and the open celebration of a friendly rivalry worked through in a series of gaming moves. Behind the laughter, however, the rivalry and competition is still sharp and earnest with each contender seeking pride of place at the expense of the other.

In this reading, Abraham's worth as a person is constructed consciously around the flaws and the gaps in the story. He is a figure whom human beings can identify with in his mixture of hope in the unseen work of the deity combined with human manoeuvres to survive in an everyday world, which frequently presents him with complex and dangerous situations. In the measurement of value Abraham tips the balance into positive for his story is structurally comic and not tragic, but the seamy side of life with its pull towards compromise is ever present.

## A Character in a Tragedy

The balance between tragic and comic elements in the stories about Abraham may ultimately resolve themselves positively but this interpretation is partly coloured by the fact that Abraham's career is interwoven with the adult life of Isaac and his life with that of Jacob. The line of generations continues from the making of the heavens and earth through the successive waves of human births and deaths in the rhetorical structure of Genesis and this line of continuity leads the reader to place life before death in the Abraham narrative.

Read another way, though, this cycle on its own has some very deep shadows. Even with relation to the laughter the shadows persist, as Jack Miles argues.[36] In Abraham's story the humour is sometimes bitter laughter on the lips of an Abraham to whom the divine promises have seemed worthless currency.[37] Miles describes these stories as scenes in which God struggles for mastery over life with Abraham. The vehicle for this conflict is the human power of procreation, which God had freely given to his creatures in Genesis chapters one to eleven. Now Abraham may only have a true line of descent if God allows it and Abraham has to submit first. Although Abraham appears to agree (he migrates) he shows his displeasure by 'handing over' Sarah to Pharaoh and by focusing on humanly achievable heirs such as Eliezer. God could be read here as a

---

36 Miles, J., *God – A Biography*, where Miles plays on the two names for God as devices for displaying God's double nature.
37 Miles, J., *God—A Biography*, p. 50.

volatile and tyrannical figure, unsure of what he really wants from human beings. The very fact that he makes promises of a son reflects divine insecurity and is ominous in terms of their ever being fulfilled. Finally God demands the submission of human potency. J. Miles suggests that "the Lord's demand for a piece of Abraham's penis is vividly consistent with all the ambivalence he has previously shown towards human potency", and says "God is demanding that Abraham concede, symbolically, that his fertility is not his own to exercise".[38]

In parallel, Abraham's own attitude to God is potentially hostile. His response to the deity's revelations about the judgement of Sodom and Gomorrah in chapter eighteen is aggressive, full of satirical undertones and falsely-insinuating flattery.[39] The Gerar incident shows that Abraham is still angry. The climax for both characters is Genesis chapter twenty-two where God finally knows what he wants, an absolute human submission over the powers of life and death and Abraham is prepared to call his bluff (would he have ever actually killed Isaac?). Both God and Abraham admit defeat here, without an actual death, but a very heavy shadow hangs over the scene and Isaac appears to be a tragic pawn in the battle of two males. In this reading, Abraham almost achieves tragic hero status as an embattled human being facing a jealous and vindictive deity.

Phyllis Trible takes the sacrifice scene one step further, in tragic terms.[40] She points out the repetition of the verb 'take' (*Laqach*) in the chapter and how the dialogue encapsulated by the action of taking shows Abraham evading truth, both to his servants in the first dialogue and to his son in the second.[41] It can be argued that although the final use of 'took' is Abraham replacing his son with the ram and the third dialogue is God's speech stopping the death and blessing Abraham, and although Isaac is still alive in chapter twenty-three, there is an aura of tragedy here. An anomaly in the text stresses this. For Abraham comes down from the mountain on his own, gathers his servants and departs. Trible comments that a reader may well feel that Abraham somehow just *had* to have sacrificed his son. This comment implies that the last section of the story is a glossing over of the tragic ending.

Within Jewish tradition the haggadic fleshing out of the text by Rabbinic commentators led to an acceptance, in *Genesis Rabbah* for

---

38  Miles, J., *God – A Biography*, p. 52.
39  Miles, J., *God – A Biography*, p. 55.
40  Trible, P., *Genesis 22: the sacrifice of Sarah* in Bach, A. (ed.), *Women in the Hebrew Bible*, London, Routledge, 1999.
41  See Trible, P., *Genesis 22: the sacrifice of Sarah*, pp. 274-6.

instance, that Isaac did die and that this was a willing sacrifice on his part; and even that his death was overseen by angels. As Yæl Feldman points out the Akedath (Binding) of Isaac then became part of Jewish culture.[42] He explores its impact on Isræli culture in the Zionist movement. He notes the paradoxical use of sacrifice of Isaac motifs alongside aggressive resistance motifs. In ancient Greek culture such sacrifice was usually made by a daughter and signified the normal female role of submission.[43] Inter-generational conflict is also carried by the Oedipus story. But that is not a story of a son's passivity but rather of his aggressive violence to a parent.[44] Isræli culture in the 1960s combined these elements in an uneasy paradox. For Zionist pioneers, military prowess and aggression were allied with a passionate willingness to die for the fatherland.[45]

In later generations, however, the armed struggle and its consequences were viewed with less pleasure. Fathers might expect their sons to be willing, as they were, to fight, but the sons might well be looking for a peaceful settlement and were now prepared to be aggressively resistant to their fathers' demands. Feldman suggests that, in this setting, the death of Rabin may truly echo the 'death' of Isaac in Genesis chapter twenty-two, a 'son' sacrificed because of his desire to look for peace against the wishes of an older generation. The reader is aware, here, of this scenario as a tragic end to the Abraham story as a model for moral vision, in which all parties are caught up in sorrow and bewilderment, fathers and sons alike. This is a tragic 'reading' of Abraham's story. Feldman comments: "Behind a knife there is an aggressive father, a real flesh and blood father, whose aggression is matched by his ideological self-righteousness and by his unbending principles . . . wreaking havoc around them these fathers destroy their families."[46]

## A Savage Parent

These tragic themes open up yet another vista on the personhood of Abraham. In Miles' version Abraham is potentially a heroic role-model,

42  Feldman, Y., *Isaac or Oedipus? Jewish Tradition and the Isræl Aqedah* in Exum, J.C. and Moore, S. (eds), *Biblical Studies: Cultural Studies*, Sheffield, Sheffield Academic Press, 1998.
43  Feldman, Y., *Isaac or Oedipus?*, p. 169.
44  Feldman, Y., *Isaac or Oedipus?*, p. 164.
45  Feldman, Y., *Isaac or Oedipus?*, pp. 173 f.
46  Feldman, Y., *Isaac or Oedipus?*, p. 181.

resisting a hostile deity with human resources, but, in Feldman's account, the Abraham/Isaac pairing tips over into an evil model of personal behaviour – that of a villain. So Abraham becomes a model for unhealthy behaviour at the level of community, based on his misguided though sincere beliefs concerning the cosmic level of existence, a view developed by Carol Delaney.[47]

The image of Abraham as religious founder imposes on believers in these religions the necessity to model themselves on Abraham's behaviour. But in each case this carries violent undertones, including, in Islam, overt violence as the father substitutes the animal sacrifice for the life of a child. Delaney argues that Abraham's legacy for twentieth century readers is marked by this darker side. She then shows how that religious legacy has influenced ordinary Christians by recounting a modern version of this story from real life, where a man has religious hallucinations in which he was told to cut his daughter's throat, an action he duly carried out. Is this insanity, murder, proper religious faith, a crime against world order, or what else? The issues raised at the court hearing ask the essential questions about moral vision and ethical action and allow Delaney to focus in on this particular profile of the character, Abraham.[48] She discusses the way in which the Binding of Isaac/Ishmæl has had continuous influence on Judaism, Christianity and Islam.[49] Delaney goes on to say: "In all three monotheisms ... the story has been a primary structuring force . . . on the psychological level, it has figured in notions of faith and steadfastness, sacrifice and love, authority and obedience . . . On the stage of history, it figures in conflicts over territory, cities and shrines."[50]

Thus the impact of Abraham as a model for human beliefs is negative. Abraham was prepared to kill a child for God. The sacrifice of Isaac/Ishmæl becomes a foreshadowing of the theme of sacrifice in Christian liturgy and an actual animal sacrifice in Islam. In each case it is male authority and power which is endorsed.[51] Even secularised society in Europe shares this inheritance. Delaney argues that Freudian psychology is itself an instrument of furthering the oppression of son by father. Freud,

---

47 Delaney, C., *Abraham on Trial*, Princeton, Princeton University Press, 1998.
48 Delaney, C., *Abraham on Trial*, Part 1, chapter two.
49 It is interesting to note that the sacrifice of Isaac in Jewish versions of Abraham's sacrifice is balanced by the sacrifice of Ishmæl in the Qu'ranic texts. Since Ishmæl is the ancestor of Islam in these texts it is right that it is he who is the object of Abraham's devotion to the deity.
50 Delaney, C., *Abraham on Trial*, p. 184.
51 Delaney, C., *Abraham on Trial*, p. 180.

despite his Jewish background, did not address the role of Abraham in Jewish tradition. When Freud explained the social myth of 'God' as a projection of societal needs, he had recourse to the archetype of the murder of the Father by the Sons but omitted to deal with the social and psychological effect of Abraham's model of murder of a son by a father. Delaney says "although Freud thought that the concept of God was a projection of the feared and admired qualities of the human father . . . he appears to have put fathers, or at least the idea of the father, on a pedestal".[52]

This is, for Delaney, a narrow male vision of the roots of social behaviour. In this failure to examine a primal crime of the Father in murdering his son, Freud produced a social and psychological model, which failed to take account of male domestic violence.[53] The impact of Abraham as a male authority figure in religious tradition was not critiqued, and so secular thought joined religious thought in imposing a cultural paradigm of violence which leads to the crying out of children against their domestic abuse. Delaney notes that "through the ages, the theologians and, more recently, psychoanalysts have tried to drown out that cry as over and over children are sacrificed to the will of the father(s)".[54] She also suggests that it is the voice of the mother also, which is wiped out by the Abrahamic model of faith. In her real life case, the mother was not consulted by the father about the act of killing a child. In Genesis chapter twenty-two Sarah suddenly dies. She is not consulted in Genesis chapter twenty-two – was the shock of the event too great for a mother to bear?

## An Unworthy Husband

Thus the reader arrives at a major source of criticism of Abraham as a key figure for human beings to identify with, which comes from feminist readings of the text. The two main women in the picture are both wives of Abraham, women whose histories are determined by their domestic status. Moreover, their stories are told from a man's position. The reader hears

---

52 Delaney, C., *Abraham on Trial*, p. 224.
53 Delaney adduces from Freud's own relationship to his father that he had problems about father/son relations which he suppressed and which he did not wish to approach. These seem to have had to do with an affair, which the father had with a woman who then disappeared and whom he might have killed. See Delaney, C., *Abraham on Trial*, p. 220 for more information.
54 Delaney, C., *Abraham on Trial*, p. 229.

what Abraham proposes but does not always hear how Sarah responds and Hagar's viewpoint is subordinated to those of both Abraham and Sarah.

David Clines, for instance, points out that the phrase 'ancestress in danger' may more suitably be re-titled 'ancestor in danger'.[55] For what motivates Abraham in Genesis chapters twelve and twenty is the thought of saving his own skin. If Abraham dies in Egypt there will be no son. So Abraham may be allowed to take thought for his part in God's plan. But, when the reader re-reads chapter twelve from the overall perspective of Genesis twelve to twenty-four, s/he knows that Sarah is the key to the divine plan and that, therefore, Abraham is lacking in real understanding of the divine promises. This is a reading for describing Abraham as lacking in moral vision and as acting unethically. Fewell and Gunn state that "the narrative demands from us an ethical judgement on Abraham here".[56] Clines notes that "for his refusal to accept the divine prediction or to imagine what the consequences of the move to Gerar might be, if Sarah could . . . be pregnant after all".[57]

A reader may want to know how Sarah felt about being passed off as Abraham's sister but the text is silent. Fewell and Gunn comment: "Thus Abraham sacrifices his wife, for his safety perhaps, but assuredly for economic gain."[58] Does this mean that Abraham is callous and self-concerned? Then there are the scenes where both Abraham and Sarah are told yet again that Sarah will conceive. Both characters respond with secret scepticism but the man's doubt goes unrebuked whereas Sarah is severely reprimanded. Do Abraham and God, two males, collude to keep Sarah in the subservient mode? The final crunch comes when Abraham takes Isaac for sacrifice without the consulting the boy's mother. But what does this tell the reader about Abraham? As Trible asks, "how far will Abraham go when self-preservation is at issue? Perhaps God needs to see if there is *ever* a point when Abraham is willing to sacrifice himself rather than his family. He has sacrificed the other members of his household; will he go so far as to sacrifice the son of promise?"[59]

---

55 As remarked upon earlier in this chapter, Rabbinic readers interpreted Sarah's sudden death, unprepared for in the text, as the result of events in the previous chapter.

56 Fewell, D. and Gunn, D., *Gender, Power and Promise the subject of the Bible's First Story* Nashville, Abingdon, 1993, p. 53.

57 Clines, D., *The Ancestress in Danger: But not the Same Danger* in *What Does Eve Do to Help and Other Readerly Questions?*, Sheffield, Sheffield Academic Press, 1994, pp. 76-7.

58 Fewell, D. and Gunn, D., *Gender, Power and Promise*, Nashville, Abingdon, 1993, p. 43.

59 Trible, P., *Genesis 22*, p. 286.

Abraham comes across in this style of reading the text as self-serving and unethical in his dealings with women. He is content to use and abuse his wives, in order to save his own life and to achieve his own goals. Sarah is a matriarch in her own right, according to Genesis chapter seventeen, but she is ignored in chapter twenty-two and is written out in chapter twenty-four. Trible argues that "patriarchy has denied Sarah her story, the opportunity for freedom and blessing. It has excluded her and glorified Abraham . . . after securing the safety of Isaac, it has no more need of Sarah, so it moves to eliminate her."[60] Abraham himself is the arch-patriarchal figure, identified with the male perspective of the narrator; even God seems to be on his side, sharing his perspective. What Fewell and Gunn note is that "the final outcome is that Abraham is relieved of responsibility. Abraham is always the one who wins. Abraham has been conditioned to bank on his chosen status."[61]

So much for Abraham as Sarah's husband, but what about his second wife? Hagar is further down the scale still. The story does not relate whether she was happy to be sent in to Abraham and it could be suggested that her contempt for Sarah later in this scene proceeds from her distress at being exploited by another woman, forced into sexual relations with her master. Certainly she can be regarded as an abused woman since she is twice cast out and left to die in the wilderness. Here, too, Abraham appears as vacillating and weak, owning Hagar, the slave woman, and her son, but unable fully to name them as his. In this reading Abraham is a flawed model of a head of household to offer to a community seeking guidance on means of resolving domestic problems.

Other readings suggest that God is the problem here as well. Abraham, not Sarah, might be the cause of infertility; incapable of being sexually aroused by Sarah he is nevertheless able to operate sexually with the Egyptian woman.[62] God is uncertain which woman to support. He promises a child to Sarah but allows Ishmæl to be born and offers some support to Hagar in her rejection. Finally, however, he opts for Sarah and has a major part to play in her pregnancy since her human partner cannot act potently on his own. At this stage Hagar is written out of the text in terms of its major concerns and, ultimately, the homosocial bonding of the circumcision motif excludes both women. The two males have finally got

60 Trible, P., *Genesis 22*, p. 286.
61 Fewell, D. and Gunn, D., *Gender, Power and Promise*, p. 54.
62 Rulon-Miller, N., *Hagar: A Woman With an Attitude* in Davies, P. and Clines, D. (eds), *The World of Genesis*, Sheffield, Sheffield Academic Press, 1998, pp. 61-80.

together and solved the tensions, which have rumbled on in the household for so long.[63]

Hagar now functions as a symbol of the 'outsider' and her son will found a wild, intractable nation which will be hostile to Sarah's descendants.[64] Enmity is thus established between the sons of Ishmæl and the Israelites. Since Islam has chosen to favour Ishmæl in its cultural traditions the scene is set for a real life conflict of insider/outsider between Jews and Arabs, which persists to the present day.[65] As against Kuschel's reading of the Abraham story, this reading offers little hope that the model of person found therein can assist in the solution of problems at the community level of inter-cultural relationships which stem from allegiance to two separate deities at cosmic level, YHWH and Allah.

## Abraham under the Microscope

We have seen that Abraham's characterisation is multi-faceted. His value for models of morality at the community level of cultural tradition is extensive. But are these models good or bad influences on the reader? For the interpretation of his character varies from great acclaim as a man with true faith in God to condemnation of one whose behaviour impacts badly on his own household, especially his women and his son. Abraham's story opens out, then, to the topic of moral person on two opposed fronts – the cosmic and the community. In cosmic terms, both narratively and theologically, Abraham is an example of a benefactor to human beings who come after him; but, in community terms it is less clear about his role as a paradigm of fruitful behaviour. As founder of a nation there is still high acclaim for him, but his relationships with women are suspect in terms of lack of real concern for their views. His parental status is also ambivalent, though he is presented as a useful relative for Lot to have. Thus the moral vision concerning Abraham includes a mixture of helpful and unhelpful actions.

Of major significance in estimating Abraham as a moral person is his role in broader cultural issues. It is important to review how generations of readers, up to the present time, have developed their own cultural behaviour under the influence of the Abraham traditions. It has been shown that these projections have the power to deepen social harmony or to

---

63  Rulon-Miller, N., *Hagar*, p. 78.
64  Rulon-Miller, N., *Hagar*, p. 76.
65  Rulon-Miller, N., *Hagar*, p. 61.

undermine it. The line is not always clear. Kuschel views Abraham's piety (including Genesis chapter twenty-two) as a model for religious dialogue; but Delaney argues that an obsession with piety, wrongly interpreted, has been a destructive force in human social groups. These are clearly readings of the text going in different directions but both are developments from the same narrative. It is not easy to prioritise one reading and thus one possible cultural re-incarnation of the ancient text.

If Abraham is a biblical figure worthy of a reader's attention, then some difficult matters have to be addressed. He may, for instance, appear as the model for values, which a new generation of readers no longer hold to be important or even believe to be bad. He may be described as unethical, lacking in insight about the communal dimension of life, and hence doubt may be cast on his importance as role model for more global matters. Those who work from within one of the three religions, which revere Abraham's memory, are more likely to have the perspective of him as a moral person who does what the deity requires. A reader approaching from a different angle, may have a perspective in which Abraham is a moral person who exemplifies the strengths and the weaknesses common to human beings, or may even hold the view that Abraham as a moral person reveals a good deal of what is to be avoided in human affairs. Abraham as a full character must include all these reading possibilities. The concept of moral personhood is likewise broad enough to contain both the positive and the negative – Abraham as a saint in his piety and as a savage in his parenting, for example.

# Chapter Three

# David

Like Abraham, David has a high profile as a character with positive features. But, unlike Abraham, this has more to do with God's choice of David to be the ruler of all-Israel than with David's own faithfulness to God.[1] As with Abraham, readers may find elements of his story a challenge to an ideal view of David as a man and as a figure of authority. The most positive version of David's identity is found in the account of his reign in the books of Chronicles, where little reference is made to David the man and much to David as a prudent and favoured ruler. Psalms eighty-nine and 132 echo a similar viewpoint with their references to David's loyalty to the God of Israel, and that deity's favourable response to David's line. David's story, as presented by the first and second books of Samuel, however, evidences much ambiguity about the significance of his life. In this version David's own actions as a man offer a commentary on the theme of divine support. The chief example of this two-sided presentation is in the account of David and Bathsheba, where David "does his own thing" thus earning divine displeasure and judgement, despite God's statement that the king's own death is remitted in the face of royal remorse.

The basic outline of David's story is the same in Samuel and Chronicles, namely that he is chosen by God to be king of the relevant territory, that having established control, he brought the Ark of the Lord to Jerusalem and envisaged building a permanent home for God there. To this fundamental outline of royal history the first and second books of Samuel adds issues relating to David the man. The drawn-out history of David's relationship with Saul, his love for Jonathan, his adultery and murderous contrivances, the disastrous record of David's children are added on to the outline of royalty, offering a means of reflection on his performance as a man who seeks and obtains power.

---

1  David does remain loyal to YHWH but his story in the first and second books of Samuel does not contain the element of extended waiting for the fulfilment of God's favour in the same way as is present in Abraham's story in Genesis chapters twelve to twenty-four. David's rise to power is effected fairly rapidly within the time-frame of the first book of Samuel.

## Personhood and Character

These several characterisations of David create him as a human being with
different faces.  In particular the narrative voice in Chronicles and in
Samuel fashions the reader's understanding of David.  By what is said
about David, as much as by what David himself says and does, the reader is
led towards particular perspectives on David as a character.  When, for
instance, the narrator states, in the second book of Samuel chapter ten, that
the time of the year for campaigning arrived and the army went out to battle
*and* David stayed in Jerusalem, a hint may be found that David is already
set on a slippery path which leads him to adultery and murder.  For it is
when he stays at home, not sharing the rigour of campaigning, that he sees
Bathsheba bathing.  If he had been on campaign – as kings should? – he
would not have met with temptation.[2]  Here the 'and' of the Hebrew needs
to be translated by 'but'.

The different characterisations of David in the narratives of the first and
second books of Samuel and the books of Chronicles open the way for
varying values to be attached to David as an example of moral personhood.
It is possible, for instance, to argue that David is a prime example of
someone who struggles with his passions and, ultimately, lacks true
control.  In David's contest for leadership with Saul he displays self control
when refusing to kill the king when opportunity arises to do so in order to
seize control of Israel.[3]  Instead of cutting off a life David cuts off part of

2    This comment allows for the translation 'when kings campaign', i.e. David did not act as
     one would expect kings to do. W. Brueggemann *David's Truth in Israel's Imagination and
     Memory* Philadelphia, Fortress, 1985 states that the text is indeterminate here, allowing for
     this reading but not making it clearly the intended reading. M. Perry and M. Sternberg, *The
     King through Ironic Eyes: The Narrator's Devices in the Biblical Story of David and
     Bathsheba, and Two Excursuses on the Theory of the Narrative Text, Hasifrut* 1968 argue
     for deliberate irony here. These varied interpretations of the text's meaning are discussed
     by Moshe Garsiel, who provides another reading in his article *The Story of David and
     Bathsheba: A Different Approach,* in *Catholic Biblical Quarterly* Volume 55, No. 3, 1993.
     Garsiel highlights the dangers accruing to kings who go on campaign and suggests that it
     was not shameful for David to remain in Jerusalem.  Garsiel allies this thought to an
     interpretation of the second book of Samuel, chapter eleven, which involves a specific
     temporal marker of a year after the Syrian alliance in aid of the Ammonites against Israel
     had failed. This reading removes the dramatic irony from the continued residence of David
     in the city.
3    It is possible to argue for an opposed meaning here whereby David continues to manipulate
     events.  It did not suit him to kill Saul, but he turned this fact to his own practical advantage
     by claiming respect for Saul's office. See Noll, K., *The Faces of David*, Sheffield,

Saul's garment and displays this to Saul as proof of his basic loyalty to the Lord's Anointed. By contrast David shows little self-control with regard to sexual passion in the Bathsheba incident. Even towards the end of his story, David's passions threaten his sense of purpose when he grieves for his son, Absalom, rather than uplifting the morale of his forces.

David's career is also evaluated within the theme of covenant. He is introduced as part of God's contract relationship with his people. God made Israel into a people through the events of Exodus and Sinai and then gave them a land.[4] Leadership emerges out of this setting. God meets Israel's demand for a central ruler by the choice of Saul as war-leader. David is therefore presented as the man whom God prefers to Saul. At the heart of David's story is the scene where God promises to make an agreement with David's son and his sons after him, whereby they remain rulers in Israel so long as they maintain the divine commandments and ordinances.

Yet despite this theme of blessing, David is involved in suffering. In the early part of his story in the first and second books of Samuel, David faces Saul's volatile madness and persecution. He fears for his safety and flees from the king. But David's troubles never detract from the inevitability of the working out of divine purpose. David will not die before he has become king. In his later years David suffers again. His first child by Bathsheba dies, his son rapes a half-sister, her brother kills the sibling rapist. All these events should perhaps have caused suffering to a king who knows the proper behavioural rules for an Israelite but David appears hardly to be shocked or worried.[5] The revolt of Absalom, however, and Absalom's own death produce real signs of grief and desolation in David. Maybe he finally absolves his own acts of arrogant pride in his power through his grief. He lives on, however, to become a weak old man, lacking sexual power, manipulated by his family and court officials in their attempts to secure a future ruler who would meet their differing needs and alliances. David's suffering here is the common lot of humankind when

Sheffield Academic Press, 1997, pp. 81-83.

4    This comment assumes the Torah narrative as an ideological background whereby Exodus brings a nation to freedom, and Sinai creates an identity for that people, in terms of their own religious culture.

5    This statement assumes biblical David to be operating within biblical Israel. By biblical Israel is meant here the coherent presentation of Israel's past across the generations which results from the manner in which the texts have been edited together. In this framework David would have inherited the tribal sacred traditions which include the Mosaic Law. Biblical Israel had received the Decalogue from Moses at Sinai so would have had an absolute ban on adultery and murder.

age and infirmity render them passive. It is not a suffering which, by itself, is ennobling of a person, though it may cause the observer to have compassion on the pitiable state of fallible human nature, in this guise hardly appearing to be a creature made in the divine image. But how far is David *ever* a human being who witnesses to divine nature, in himself? Or, is it rather that David witnesses to God's own power to create a reflection of divine glory in weak and unstable human beings?

## David and Dimensions of Tragedy

The discussion of the function of suffering in the delineation of David's personhood in the first and second books of Samuel raises the possibility that David should be viewed as a type of tragic hero. This is to posit that the material here fits a specific literary style, that of Tragedy, thus making the text a contrast to the perception of possibly comic elements in biblical vision. That David is a hero for Israel emerges at the surface level of the story from his role as military commander and source of authoritative leadership. That profile links with the concept of tragedy through the fact that David's achievements so often lead to evil and destruction rather than a happy ending. He might, in this context, seem to be a person whom evil fortune dogs, clouding his vision and distorting his actions. But David cannot totally be exempted from responsibility for the negative impact of his own choices. Surely he could have avoided adultery, naming it as plain sexual desire not romantic love? Surely he could have disciplined his own children so preventing a cycle of tragic events?

Cheryl Exum states, with regard to tragedy and biblical narrative, "the tragic hero is the victim of forces she or he cannot control and cannot comprehend, encountering on all sides unresolved questions, doubts and ambiguities . . . The tragic vision isolates the hero over against an arbitrary and capricious world."[6] This description can be partially applied to David since, at some level, David is at the mercy of fate and of actions other than his own – Saul's madness and hostility for instance. It may be that parents cannot be held responsible for their children's choices. Something of that approach may appear valid since David's line is said to be under divine cursing.[7] But the reason for the curse is David's own choice of another man's wife. It is an arguable point as to whether this act is the stuff of

6    Exum, J. C., *Tragedy and Biblical Narrative*, Cambridge University Press, 1992, p. 5.
7    As stated in 2 Samuel 12 [10].

Tragedy since David cannot but know that such an act is contrary to the laws of Israel.

On the other hand it might be said that tragic figures achieve their status through an inbuilt flaw and that this choice is David's flaw, since it stems from a self-centred approach to his newly formulated royal authority. Exum remarks: "At the core of tragedy lies the problem and mystery of evil . . . The tragic protagonist is caught up in a situation not entirely of her or his own making. At the same time she or he is also responsible, a guilty victim."[8] This may validly be used to describe David on his forced departure from Jerusalem in the face of his son's rebellion. At that point David is both bearing the brunt of past guilty action and its consequences and experiencing a disorientation caused by feeling the consequences of the actions of other human beings in the narrative. Exum asserts that these complexities build up the reader's perception of a tragic story rather than a tragic hero.

But is the hero worthy of the story? In contrast to Saul, David remains a self-contained character. Saul is visibly driven by passions, suffers from spiritual torment in the face of divine silence and the burdens of kingship. David remains an unknown quantity, even his reasons for taking Bathsheba are withheld by the narrator.[9] This makes David less impressive as a hero than Saul. He does not appear to struggle against fate. When his child dies he abandons mourning, much to his courtiers' amazement. When he is told of Amnon's sin against Tamar he does nothing. Exum remarks that "David's failure to take any outwardly appreciable measures to avoid his fate suggests the absence of genuine inner struggle".[10] Only David's lament for Absalom reaches the extremities of human passion in the face of a perverse destiny.

As will be shown in this chapter, David's profile is an ambiguous one. He is portrayed both as noble leader and as crafty, cruel and selfish. The role of suffering in David's career exemplifies the ambivalence of his reputation. Though there are some aspects of Tragedy in David's story it is hard for the reader to embrace fully the image of David as a tragic hero, ennobled by suffering, without some qualifications being made. Nonetheless the presence of tragic elements in the first and second books of Samuel's account of the king contributes to the possible presentation of him as a moral person and adds depth to the reader's grasp of the concepts of moral vision and ethical action. It can be argued then, that, while not

---

8   Exum, J. C., *Tragedy and Biblical Narrative*, p. 10.
9   Exum, J. C., *Tragedy and Biblical Narrative*, p. 142.
10  Exum, J. C., *Tragedy and Biblical Narrative*, p. 143.

amounting to Tragedy proper, the story of David in the books of Samuel has many tragic aspects to it. This is in distinction from the presentation of David in Chronicles where his profile is positive, and, to that extent, the story is comic.

### David as Founder of the Jerusalem Temple-State

In the first book of Chronicles David is consistently presented as a public benefactor. He begins his reign because he is the people's choice "even when Saul was king it was you who led out and brought in Israel",[11] and because he is seen as God's choice also.[12] David then makes a covenant/ contract between himself and Israel, the background to which is his role as public benefactor in his military successes against Israel's enemies. There follow the tales of David's mighty deeds and those of his armies. The successes build up to a triumph over all enemies and peace for Israel. The Ark of the Lord comes to Jerusalem as a final signal of YHWH's approval and forms the foundation for a state religion. David now prepares plans for his son to build God's house just as God has prepared a house of future kings for David. David's farewell speech at the end of 1 Chronicles ties all these themes together.

Walter Brueggemann has labelled this "theological-ecclesial truth".[13] The core Davidic story has been formulated to meet the needs of a new generation, that of the post-exilic province of Judah.[14] Brueggemann states that "now the texts think primarily of a community of faith gathered around a future derived from David; but this David is no concrete help for politics and no concrete threat to the Babylonian or Persian overlords".[15] He argues

11　I Chronicles 1[11].

12　I Chronicles 11 [2].

13　Brueggemann, W., *David's Truth in Israel's Imagination and Memory*, Philadelphia, Fortress, 1985, p. 88.

14　Brueggemann here acknowledges that the Davidic corpus as a whole, including Chronicles, belongs to a post-monarchical Judah. This is clearly valid since Chronicles acknowledges the event of the exile in 1 Chronicles chapter 9. Brueggemann is prepared to argue for stages in the composition of these texts back to a tribal Israel from within which monarchy emerged. Current scholarship is very divided on the subject of how much pre-exilic material can be found in the Old Testament. For example, see: Davies, P., *In Search of Ancient Israel*, Sheffield, Sheffield Academic Press, 1992; Whitelam, K., *The Invention of Ancient Israel*, London, Routledge, 1996; Lemche, N., *Israel in History and Tradition*, London, SPCK, 1998.

15　Brueggemann, W., *David's Truth*, p. 88.

that the story in Chronicles focuses on cultic and worship matters, pointing out the many references to cultic officials and their roles in the worshipping Assembly.[16]  He states that the Chronicler's account is "the most consistently *ecclesiological* presentation of Davidic hope in the Old Testament".[17] Liturgy makes it possible for Israel to envisage an alternative world to that of its provincial status in the Persian and Hellenistic worlds.[18] Judah can reconstitute its own identity within the alternative Davidic world created by the narrative text.[19]  Brueggemann concludes "this David is a completely obedient man without self assertion or moral ambiguity. This is the David that is necessary for the authorisation of a faithful religious community".[20]  Insofar as the Chronicler finds a medium for Judahite identity in the theme of YHWH's personal commitment to 'Israel', 'David' is created as a tool in the service of this ideological end.[21]

David here is an ideal figure, a model for community action. As such he appears as benefactor and protector of Israel in 1 Chronicles – in being named as shepherd, for instance.[22] David's own actions fit into this image; he acts responsibly as mediator between the community and God.

## David in the First and Second Books of Samuel

It is now time to return to the story of David told by the books of Samuel and 1 Kings, since it is this version of David's career which has aroused the most scholarly concern and speculation.  As Philip Satterthwaite remarks, David's rise is highlighted by being set against Saul's decline.[23]  Saul is delineated in a way which attracts sympathy: "The narrator suggests the

16  Brueggemann, W., *David's Truth*, p. 105 f.
17  Brueggemann, W., *David's Truth*, p. 99.
18  Brueggemann, W., *David's Truth*, p. 99.
19  Brueggemann, W., *David's Truth*, p. 90.
20  Brueggemann, W., *David's Truth*, p. 105.
21  This is to take 'Israel' to refer, not to the northern kingdom or the tribal federation which left Egypt and settled in Palestine, but as a generic title for all those people who, in biblical texts, claim to be part of the nation which made covenant with its God in the desert.
22  See here I Chronicles 11 ², where this title is attributed to David.  More generally the concept of shepherd as a royal term, signifying beneficial rule of subjects was widespread in the Ancient Near East.  For other biblical references see, for instance: Psalm 23; Isaiah 40; Jeremiah 31.  For an overall description of the range of the term see *The Anchor Bible Dictionary*, Volume 5, New York, Doubleday, pp. 1187-1190.
23  Satterthwaite, P., *David in the Books of Samuel: A Messianic Expectation?* in Satterthwaite, P., Hess, R. S. and Wenham, G. J., *The Lord's Anointed*, Carlisle, Paternoster, 1995.

complexity of a character driven to pursue his rival, but on occasions reduced to weeping and remorse over his actions."[24] This mode of telling the story adds extra weight to the importance of David.  Saul is fighting against his own destiny in pursuing David.

David's rise climaxes with the death of Saul and Jonathan in battle, a sequence of events having already shown that David succeeds while Saul fails because YHWH has transferred his favour from one to the other. Although this narrative can be read to show David's simple-hearted trust in his God and his attempts to be loyal to his leader, aspects of the narration leave scope for doubts as to David's simplicity.  When he flees from Saul is it really because he is afraid of being killed?  Or is it because David now openly allies himself with Israel's enemies, the Philistines, as a way of countering Saul's greater military might in their personal competition for the throne?[25]

When David becomes king in Jerusalem he might well believe himself to be invincible, a ruler who 'owns' his own personal benefactor deity.  The account of David's desire to build a Temple home for YHWH bears out this argument.  But God's response makes the point that David is not in fact in charge of God, rather God is a free agent who chooses David's line.  It is not absolutely clear how much God offers David in the second book of Samuel, chapter seven, but the very distinction God makes between his control of cosmic and community affairs and David's own royal power casts a shadow forward over the rest of David's life and beyond.[26] Satterthwaite argues that "Chapter seven, coming as the climax to the account of David's rise, sets out a vision of how God can bless Israel through his king.  The following account of David as king (second book of Samuel, chapters eight to twenty) shows how the later years of his kingship in many ways failed to realise this vision."[27]

The uncertainty of David's record as king in the first and second books of Samuel is largely produced by the interaction of the parallel roles of David as human being and as ruler.   David Gunn remarked on the structuring of the Samuel narrative with regard to this.[28]  On page ninety-

24  Satterthwaite, P., *David in the Books of Samuel*, p. 48.
25  For the hidden messages in the account of David's rise to power see Noll, K., *The Faces of David*.
26  Lysle Eslinger wishes to argue that God in fact gives David very little in this covenant-making scene.  See Eslinger, L., *House of God or House of David; The Rhetoric of 2 Samuel 7*, Sheffield, Sheffield Academic Press, 1994.
27  Satterthwaite, P., *David in the Books of Samuel*, p. 56.
28  Gunn, D., *The Story of King David: Genre and Interpretation*, Sheffield, Sheffield Academic Press, 1978.

one of his study he offers a diagrammatic picture of the links between the twin themes of power in state and in family. David as king acquires a kingdom and establishes a dynasty. He does this by acting as a usurper of royal power; but his power is usurped in turn in a rebellion. This rebellion is linked to dynastic matters since it is David's son who is the rebel. The lynchpin here is the issue of David's claim to be a 'son of Saul' interwoven with his own role as father. Through family relationships the matters of state are worked out. On the private front there is a balancing image. David as a man becomes husband and father. With regard to his sexuality David usurps another man's role as husband, while his own son later usurps his father's role as partner to a number of wives. This sexual activity impinges directly on the public domain since David the king attempts to cover his tracks by issuing royal commands to his officials which basically amount to murder. Absalom's coupling with David's wives is likewise a political move to stress that his power is now greater than his father's.

A key term of Gunn's, here, is that of usurpation. David usurps the public rights of Saul and the private rights of Uriah. His greedy grasp of power and sexual benefit is balanced by the usurpation of David's own rights in these spheres by his children, especially by Absalom, who seizes both throne and wives, kingship and male dominance. Thus two central issues emerge, that of power and sexuality. David's sexuality cannot be separated from the record of his use of royal power. The intermingling of these themes have raised various models for David:

> David the human being.
> David the male.
> David as son and brother.
> David as husband.
> David as parent.
> David as king.

In the playing out of these models the extremities of David's character are revealed. According to Noll, "David is the quintessential winner, the mighty warrior, the faithful Yahwist, the opportunist, the hoodlum-like strongman, the exquisitely smooth manipulator of other persons, the cunning killer, the lusty voyeur, and the anguished father".[29]

K. Noll's study of *The Faces of David* explores the complexities by contrasting the approach of the author with that of the narrator, of David's

---

29 Noll, K., *The Faces of David*, p. 128.

story.[30]  The author, it is envisaged, is the one who is responsible for the
story as a whole, with all its contradictions and innuendos; the narrator is
the one who actually leads the reader through the story at surface level.
The narrator can choose what order to tell the events in and what to
emphasise or pass over.  By observing the gap between author and narrative
voice, the reader may learn more than one message about the subject of the
narrative.  Noll argues that "David's character emerges, at least partially, by
means of the opposing perspectives provided by the narrator's and the
implied author's differing explanations of him."[31]  The image of David as a
'good character', a model for the reader in a moral universe, encouraging
him/her to adopt the stance of Yahwistic ideology, is carried by the
narrator, while the author's role tends to deconstruct that profile.  Noll says
that: "Ideologically, the narrator is an apologist for Yahweh and for human
characters whom the narrator believes to be devout Yahwists", and adds:
"The implied author is an apologist for nothing."[32] The author's
undermining of the narrator prevents the text from acquiring a moral or
didactic tone.  With this structural insecurity in mind it is appropriate to
turn to the several models of David outlined above.


## David the Human Being

David is first mentioned as a young boy, the son of a named father.  The
reader watches the growth of this boy from early manhood to full maturity
to infirmity and death, through the chapters of the Samuel narratives.  One
question which can be asked is, does David develop as a person?  Leo
Perdue discusses David in the context of a distinction between dynamic or
static characters, in an article published in 1984.[33]  His portrayal of David
relates to the succession narrative and concentrates on the concept of

---

30  Noll, K., *The Faces of David*.
31  Noll, K., *The Faces of David*, p. 35.
32  Noll, K., *The Faces of David*, p. 36.
33  Perdue, L., *Is there anyone left in the house of Saul . . . Ambiguity and the Characterisation
     of David in the Succession Narrative*, in Exum, J. C. (ed.), *The Historical Books*, Sheffield,
     Sheffield Academic Press, 1997.

ambiguity.[34] The grounding for this reading of David is the nature of the narrative itself.

Reading David as a dynamic character allows for the path of human development. David's prime role is to govern Israel but will he do so by brute force or by compassion? Perdue outlines a characterisation in which David begins his rule by using compassion, as when he shows mercy to surviving Saulides such as Mephibosheth and when he refuses to condemn Shimei for cursing him. Absalom's death, however, is a turning point. David's innate desire for mercy towards enemies is stifled and, now, as an old man, David uses the cynical brute force he had resisted earlier on, as in the order to Solomon to find a means of executing Shimei.

Reading David as a static character, a human being whose attitudes are from the beginning fixed for life, Perdue delineates a person who is consistently deceitful and ruthless. The key term here is *hesed* or loyalty. David uses this term publicly but in a deceptive manner, which enables him to seek out potential enemies – as when he looks for survivors of Saul's house in order to show loyalty to Jonathan. He does indeed feed and house Mephibosheth but is this really not self-interest? Keeping the man as a semi-prisoner in David's own household prevents enemies gathering round a rival to the throne. Perdue asks whether all David's actions are not in fact examples of a rooted self-interest rather than an altruistic regard for those around him. David's deathbed commands to Solomon to exterminate all major political figures from the 'ancien regime', such as Joab and Shimei, are of a piece with this consistent self regard.

In the first picture, the dynamic David, there are some potential moral lessons to be read, even though these are ultimately negative. The early promise of disinterested use of power by a human being fades with the hardening experience of years of rule and authority. By his death David becomes a ruthless manipulator who is prepared to use lies and treachery for his personal ends. The picture is one of degenerating moral integrity but there is at least an initial social concern. In the second picture there is only a hard personality, which, from youth to death, is totally self-involved and prepared to act in defiance of any real loyalty to fellow human beings.

---

34 The title Succession Narrative has generally been attributed to the text from II Samuel 9 – I Kings 2 which deals with the Davidic court and the accession of Solomon. For a short account of the style of previous scholarly discussion of this material see the entry under *Court Narrative*, in *The Anchor Bible Dictionary*, Volume 1, New York, Doubleday, pp. 1172-1178. An offspin of this delineation of material as a separate item within the books of Samuel is that it can be treated fairly as an independent literary structure with its own inner organisation and ideologies.

Given that the life of human beings is dealt with inside a cosmic setting, the reader may well ask how God could ever have chosen this man to rule over his people.

Jack Miles, by contrast, centres his view of the deity, in the David episode, on the love, which God developed for this particular human being.[35] Miles argues that a new stage in the relationship between God and human beings comes about in this covenant. God has been the god of the fathers but now "he is announcing a real change in his relationship to this one real human family, namely David's".[36] This comes about because of David's own exuberant loyalty to YHWH. Although YHWH asserts his independence he nevertheless makes David the promise of intimate family loyalty. Miles sums up his view in the comment that "David is not just a ruthless killer and a visionary leader; he is also a passionate lover, an ardent and loyal friend, and a poet and musician of melting tenderness and soaring lyricism. Why should God not fall in love with David? Everyone else does!"[37]

How should this fatherhood of God be read? Miles argues that it must be read through David's own role as father. Just as David, despite all the difficulties, remains proud of his son, Absalom, and falls into deep grief at the young man's death, so also God remains forever devoted, by paternity, to Israel. Like a father, he will experience anguished grief when his 'sons' abandon his ways and bring on themselves the disaster of exile. In this reading, David the human being provides a means of accessing the God who is both cosmic ruler and community protector. David's very ambiguities serve as a foil to highlight the several faces of divine constancy and concern for the community.

## David the Male

David is, of course, not just a human being but one who is gendered male. The masculinity of David has its own possibilities of meaning for readers. David is portrayed in relationships both with men and women and the quality of these relationships can be explored. Clines argues that the major aspects of maleness in the Ancient Near-Eastern world are to be found in David's story. He is a fighting man, a man who is persuasive with words, who is beautiful to behold, a musical man; most importantly David is a man

35  Miles, J., *God – A Biography*, New York, Simon and Schuster, 1995.
36  Miles, J., *God – A Biography*, p. 171.
37  Miles, J., *God – A Biography*, p. 172.

who bonds with other men and treats women not as companions but as objects of male desire. On male bonding Clines remarks that "according to Hammond and Jablow, the function of male friendship . . . was to provide a source of support that was freely chosen".[38] It contains the elements of "loyalty to one another, a dyadic relationship with an exclusive tendency, a commitment to a common cause".[39] David and Jonathan clearly form such a relationship in the first book of Samuel. There is an intimacy about their relationship, which is not achieved in David's relationships with women. His liaison with Michal is marked by bitterness and separation and Bathsheba David simply summons to his bed.[40] Clines states that "we have to conclude that David does not actually like women very much, and certainly has no fun with them".[41]

Clines argues that this male David acts as a role model for other males in the Samuel narrative. He then investigates how far that paradigm still works for modern male readers. Certainly success in war, in communication and in love affairs are still held in esteem by modern male readers. Beauty and close male to male relationships find less regard in modern eyes since they impinge on modern debates about defining masculinity. At the same time, although David acts heterosexually with women, there is little discussion of the role of sexuality as such, compared with modern concerns for proving maleness through sexual activity. Clines argues that, overall, David's depiction in modern commentaries as 'good' stems from male commentators' ability to identify with him as a male and then to create images of the man David after their own masculine preferences.[42] This may be regarded as the creation of moral worldview in the broadest sense, namely the establishment of paradigms of behaviour, which other male human beings can imitate, not necessarily in every detail of a narrative, but in its general contours. This is to keep moral vision to social matters rather than cosmic and, indeed, to one particular human gender.

---

38 Clines, D., *Interested Parties: the Ideology of Writers and Readers*, Sheffield, Sheffield Academic Press, 1995, p. 224.
39 Clines, D., *Interested Parties*, p. 225.
40 The final scene recorded is that in which, in II Samuel chapter six, Michal watches David, dancing before the Ark, and then criticises his action.
41 Clines, D., *Interested Parties*, p. 226.
42 Clines, D., *Interested Parties*, p. 243.

## David as Son and Brother

But can this paradigm of human sexual identity be widened to include other social relationships? The issue of Jonathan's relationship with David offers scope for a complex reading of David's sexuality in its social setting. Clines argues that this relationship is not homosexual, as does Mark George.[43] George promotes the view that the David/Jonathan alliance is a homosocial one, "because men promote the interests of men. The 'love' between these two men flows into the actions taken to promote the interests of these same men".[44] The homosocial bond allows David to take over Jonathan's social identity, becoming the heir apparent in Jonathan's place. George suggests that "by raising up a lament for Saul and Jonathan, David acts as Saul's son, performing the duties of a son for his dead father. Such actions are appropriate for David on the basis of his relationship with Jonathan".[45] The love of David and Jonathan is the way by which male power is handed on from person to person in the public world of male activity.

Donna Fewell and David Gunn, by contrast, argue for a homosexual reading of the relationship. The key term is 'love'. What Jonathan displays is a deep affection for David in which he strips himself, offering clothes and weapons.[46] In what follows Jonathan puts David before his own father and unites himself to David in loyalty before all other social ties. Jonathan may thus be viewed as David's lover; but what about David? There is no sign in the text of a consummated affair. Is David not using Jonathan and his love as a tool against Saul? Fewell and Gunn argue that this becomes evident in David's lament over Saul and Jonathan. David acknowledges that Jonathan's love for him is more than the love of women but this serves only to focus on David as suitable material for such devotion.

Fewell and Gunn note that "David's move here is characteristically astute. Having enjoyed every advantage of Jonathan's attachment, he now finally capitalises on it. He publicly acknowledges what was no doubt rumoured . . . but he seizes the opportunity to define the relationship in a

---

43  George, M., *Assuming the Body of the Heir Apparent; David's Lament* in Beal, T. and
      Gunn, D. (eds), *Reading Bibles, Writing Bodies*, London, Routledge, 1997.
44  George, M., *Assuming the Body of the Heir Apparent*, p. 169.
45  George, M., *Assuming the Body of the Heir Apparent*, p. 171.
46  Fewell, D. and Gunn, D., *Gender Power, and Promise: The Subject of the Bible's First
      Story*, Nashville, Abindgdon, p. 149.

way that is highly favourable to himself."[47] In both these versions David's sexuality and male-relatedness is a means of obtaining social and political control of Israel. As Fewell and Gunn ask "has David ever really loved anyone?".[48] David might, here, be a model for maleness which includes homo- as well as hetero-sexuality. But further investigation raises the matter of David's exploitation of other people's regard for him and the doubt over David's capacity for positive feelings for others.

By acting as a brother to Jonathan, David succeeds in inserting himself into the house of Saul, thus strengthening his claim to the throne. The relationship between David and Saul is a chequered one in which Saul frequently distrusts and threatens David, while David, though claiming loyalty to Saul, in fact allies with Saul's foes, the Philistines, and takes guerilla warfare into Judah in their cause. One question, which can be asked here, is how far is David really acting as a son to Saul? David's first appearance in 1 Samuel already contains the two possibilities – that he might act as loyal subject to Saul or that he might conspire against him. David is anointed to be ruler and must have had an awareness that this would mean supplanting Saul and, at the same time, David is the young musician who alone can drive the evil spirit from Saul. It is Saul who first threatens David in the aftermath of the Goliath affair, as well as offering him marriage into the royal family, only to withhold the gift. David twice spares Saul's life in the wars that follow. Thus Saul appears to be the source of trouble rather than David. But how far is this the case? David has from the beginning been able to rely on Jonathan, knowing that he will cede him the throne of his father. So how far is David a cunning manipulator whom Saul is right to fear?

W. Brueggemann argues that in the story of David's rise to power the narrative voice deliberately plays on David's innocence and Saul's guilt. The story is written to endorse David as legitimate ruler of Israel and to undermine any claims from the Saulide perspective. "One may understand this narrative to be hopeful, because it tells, generation after generation, that the marginal ones can become the legitimate holders of power."[49] In the first book of Samuel, chapter twenty-four, this contrasting of two claims to monarchy is brought to a climax. Brueggemann states that David's speech here has "a tough and uncompromising nobility that puts David completely in the right and leaves Saul in a morally and politically

---

47 Fewell, D. and Gunn, D., *Gender Power, and Promise*, p. 151.
48 Fewell, D. and Gunn, D., *Gender, Power, and Promise*, p. 148.
49 Brueggemann, W., *David's Truth*, p. 23.

exposed position".[50]  David had a chance to kill and did not take it; Saul admits his failures with regard to his parallel treatment of David.  David is more righteous than Saul.  As Brueggemann admits, there are hints in the first book of Samuel that this is not the whole story of David's and Saul's relations but it is the message which is pushed to the fore.  David could have been a good son but Saul was a rotten father.

Joel Rosenburg's comments about David's childhood are relevant here.[51]  He points out that what the first book of Samuel tells us about David's own family raises the question about David's father: "His father views the lad indifferently or over-protectively" and his brother has little regard for him.[52]  Rosenburg argues that David has little chance of a meaningful life in Jesse's household and naturally turns to non-kin for warmth and affirmation.  He suggests that "the homage David pays the house of Saul, almost to the end of his own rule . . . bears much of the aura of medieval chivalric romance, seems wholly sincere".[53]  It is possible to view David's lament in the second book of Samuel, chapter one, as the full flowering of that homage and to view David as a real son to Saul whom he though of as his true father.  Since Jesse disappears from sight in Samuel, says Rosenburg, "we cannot escape the feeling that a certain coldness or emotional remoteness governs David's relations with his parents from the earliest days of his public career".[54]

Linking Rosenburg's viewpoint with that of Brueggemann above it is possible to argue that David could have been a good son if he had had a proper paternal role to emulate.  Both Jesse and Saul, however, let him down in this regard and David's failings as a son may be attributed to these experiences.  That the pattern of bad father/son relationships repeats itself with regard to David and his own sons is par for the course.  Noll, on the other hand, plays on the contrasting views of narrator and author to bring out David's own lack of real reverence for Saul as father.[55]  Noll suggests that David entered Saul's circles as a deliberate act of careerism.  He realised the gains to be made from military valour, with his eyes already set on the throne.  Noll adds: "He is clearly an opportunist.  Even as a youngster his ears perk up at the potential for fame and fortune."[56]  Even

50  Brueggemann, W., *David's Truth*, p. 37.
51  Rosenburg, J., *1 and 2 Samuel* in Alter, R. and Kermode, F. (eds), *The Literary Guide to the Bible*, London, Fontana, 1997.
52  Rosenburg, J., *1 and 2 Samuel*, p. 130.
53  Rosenburg, J., *1 and 2 Samuel*, p. 130.
54  Rosenburg, J., *1 and 2 Samuel*, p. 131.
55  Noll, K., *The Faces of David*, p. 36.
56  Noll, K., *The Faces of David*, p. 52.

his apparent humility in refusing the first offer of a royal bride is a calculated act of simplicity to ingratiate himself further.[57] If this profile is followed the reader learns to view David as Saul's fate: a cunning and ruthless man whose actions will destroy Saul and his descendants. Did Saul deserve such a son (in law)?

## David as Husband

A parallel obscurity lies across David's relationships with women. David certainly has relationships with a number of women, in the narrative, from Michal to Abigail to Bathsheba to Abishag: to say nothing of the rest of David's harem who are not individually named. In particular David's attitudes to Michal and Bathsheba have raised issues for commentators. Michal can be viewed as David's possession, as wives were in the ancient world.[58] She was won by David from her father's hand and then taken away to be given to someone else before being returned to David. The scene in which Michal scorns David at the entrance of the Ark to Jerusalem could then be read as rebellion against her proper husband. Whereas Michal did well to help her husband escape Saul's anger in an earlier scene, she is now of less worth as she rejects David because of his dancing in the streets. Exum argues that "sexual jealousy, lack of the proper religious enthusiasm, royal ignorance – these are all ways of neutralising Michal's outburst".[59]

Michal's worth is measured, here, by that of David. David has blessed the people but receives in return his wife's scorn. But David has the last word. Fewell and Gunn suggest that "he is YHWH's gift to women and if Michal does not appreciate that he can do without her. He no longer has any use for her".[60] The story itself conspires with the character, David, to dispose of Michal, for the line of Saul is destined, in the ideology of Samuel, to disappear and be replaced by the house of David. Michal

---

57  Noll, K., *The Faces of David*, p. 54.
58  This touches upon the patriarchal nature of Old Testament texts, an attitude, which in turn comes from writers and readers. These were likely to be males of the elite classes in the Ancient Near East and whose culture was one in which males dominated the public world and females operated in domestic spaces in the household. There is a long series of feminist writing on this topic; scholars include Schussler-Fiorenza, E., *In Memory of Her*, London, SCM Press, 1983 and Redford Ruether, R., *Sexism and God-talk*, Edinburgh, T. and T. Clark, 1983.
59  Exum, J. C., *Plotted, Shot and Painted*, Sheffield, Sheffield Academic Press, p. 60.
60  Fewell, D. and Gunn, D., *Gender Power, and Promise*, p. 154.

cannot, theologically, be allowed children. As Fewell and Gunn remark, "Michal's subjectivity is swallowed up in the ongoing drama of David the great king, the man whom YHWH has chosen to rule".[61] Cheryl Exum points out that Michal's story is framed by two windows. In the first she gains worth by lowering David to safety; in the second she is devalued, trapped by the great king's interests into childlessness.[62]

Bathsheba might appear to be better off than Michal. She comes into the story as the object of a king's desire, becomes the mother of his children and eventually negotiates the succession of her son Solomon to the throne. But Bathsheba's career, like Michal's, is subordinate to that of David. He takes what he wants; we do not hear whether it is what Bathsheba wants. As in Michal's case commentators have shown tendencies to place blame on the woman for the difficulties of her marriage to David. Surely she should not have been bathing in 'public view'? Exum comments: "Because Bathsheba was seen bathing, she was sent for. It is thus the woman's fault that the man's desire is aroused."[63] Both Cheryl Exum and Alice Bach respond to this proposal with the thought that this is a male response.[64] Bach, however, argues for a move beyond this stance to one which allows Bathsheba freedom to move outside the male narrational gaze: "We may figure Bathsheba as an openly constructed character . . . perhaps in lamenting for her husband, she is lamenting her own helplessness."[65]

Maybe David 'loved' Bathsheba, whereas Michal loved David, and this balances his treatment of the two women. But the over-riding emphasis in the story is not on a man's relationships with women so much as a king's need for wives and sons. Certainly David shows little intimate affection for the women in his court life. Although this attitude may be attributed to a general male approach to women in patriarchal societies, it does not offer much in the way of an acceptable paradigm for women readers in the modern community. They may be able to align themselves with Michal or with Bathsheba but David's responses to these women in the story do not provide a useful moral vision which positively aids the construction of female behaviour paradigms. At the cosmic level something may be on offer in the rebuke that God delivers to David through Nathan. David has

---

61  Fewell, D. and Gunn, D., *Gender Power, and Promise*, p. 155.
62  Exum, J. C., *Plotted, Shot and Painted*, chapter three.
63  Exum, J. C., *Plotted, Shot and Painted*, p. 47.
64  Bach, A., *Women, Seduction and Betrayal in Biblical Narrative*, Cambridge, Cambridge University Press, 1997.
65  Bach, A., *Women, Seduction and Betrayal*, p. 136.

seized an innocent creature and devoured her. But even here it is not clear that it is the treatment of a woman, which is criticised so much as the crime against another male whose property has been stolen.[66]

The ambiguity of David's relations with men and with women raises the question of David's overall sexuality. Although there is little of intimate description in the text, nonetheless the issue of sexual activity comes in and out of David's story and contributes generally to his downfall. Jonathan Magonet draws attention to the ambivalence of David's sexual prowess.[67] He notes that the angry exchange between Michal and David raises questions about the state of their married life: "Were we to read the story as marriage guidance counsellors we would quickly find ourselves wondering about the state of sexual relations between the two of them that leads her to interpret David's dancing before the Ark as a mere sexual display before the women of Jerusalem."[68]

This exchange sits beside a dramatic day for David, one on which he brought the Ark to Jerusalem, having learned through Uzzah's death that the Ark cannot be manipulated but must be approached humbly in awe of the deity it represents.[69] Michal appears to trivialise David's religious ecstasy with her sexual innuendos but Magonet argues that she has hit a right note: "For Michal has rightly pointed to the sexual energy that is part of this enormously complex man . . . Paradoxically in the ecstasy of this moment of entry into Jerusalem, that sexual drive has been channelled into a deeper religious awareness and joy."[70]

For Magonet this symbolises David's ambivalence. Physical energy and religious experience could go several ways but, sadly, will go badly. Michal sees David and scorns him, David sees Bathsheba and goes down to her. Magonet notes that "at the moment when he must choose what to do with that energy she has evoked, he makes a wrong decision".[71] Sexuality touches upon the general field of emotions and passions, a topic raised earlier. It is clear that David's story offers a nuanced model with regard to

---

66 This can be read from the oracle where Nathan's emphasis is on the poor man rather than on the one little ewe lamb and where the stress is on a man's right to his own property, without fear of seizure by a powerful neighbour.

67 Magonet, J., *The Subversive Bible*, London, SCM Press, 1997, chapter eleven.

68 Magonet, J., *The Subversive Bible*, p. 127.

69 A reference to II Samuel 6 [6-13], where Uzzah steadies the Ark and is killed for his trouble. The power of the Lord is random and self-willed and cannot be manipulated. David is afraid to take the Ark home, leaving it in another man's house until he sees that it can indeed bring blessing.

70 Magonet, J., *The Subversive Bible*, p. 128.

71 Magonet, J., *The Subversive Bible*, p. 128.

this area of human behaviour. David could have used his passionate nature for cosmic ends, as in the sublimation of sexual energy involved in dancing for the Lord, and so become a model of appropriate passion-control for readers, but, instead, he allows himself to be driven by feelings into adultery and murder. Ultimately David can serve as a warning of what fragmentation can occur when passions are not under intellectual control, but his profile has little to offer the reader of a positive use of sexual passion within the community and the cosmos.

## David as Parent

From that time onwards the consequences of David's sexuality touch his family's fortunes. David's lack of self-control is mirrored in Amnon's rape of Tamar and in the traumatic relationship, which David has with Absalom. David's sexual activity offers a paradigm for his children's behaviour which is disastrous. Mark Gray comments on Fokkelman's description of Amnon "as a chip off the old block", pointing out that this sums up the approach of many commentators to the link between father and son.[72] They are "birds of a feather, concupiscent characters cut from the same cloth, who, when visually stimulated by a beautiful woman, invariably 'become a prey of sexual lust'".[73] Gray discerns, however, a difference between father and son. David's taking of Bathsheba is a terse, swift affair bluntly narrated while Amnon is described as having an obsessive fixation. David represents the old guard who were too perpetually on the run to have time for self-indulgent, dilettantish violence, whereas Amnon symbolises the rise of the decadent court elite, with too much time on their manicured hands to devote to excessive self-gratification.[74]

The reader may ask, however, who set the tone for this court elite. Hans Jensen picks up the concept of mimetic rivalry, based on the phenomenon of *desire* as an interpretation of Davidic fortunes.[75] In David's and Amnon's cases this desire is sexual. With Absalom the desire is for power, but he uses sexuality in support of that desire when he publicly possesses his father's wives. Since Absalom wants to *be* David he acts David's part

---

72  Gray, M., *Amnon: A chip off the Old Block? Rhetorical Strategy in 2 Samuel 13:7-15* in *Journal for the Study of the Old Testament*, Vol. 77, No. 98, 1998.

73  Gray, M., *Amnon: A chip off the Old Block?*, p. 39.

74  Gray, M., *Amnon: A chip off the Old Block?*, p. 46.

75  Jensen, H., *Desire, Rivalry and Collective Violence in the "Succession Narrative"* in Exum, J. C. (ed.), *The Historical Books*, Sheffield, Sheffield Academic Press, 1997.

in the household. In a parallel way, in the first book of Kings, Adonijah seeks to marry the dead king's wife. In each case desire leads to rivalry and to collective violence, suggests Jensen. "For the pestilence is done away with by King David's victimisation of himself; the famine is driven away by killing seven of Saul's sons and grandsons; and the war between Absalom and David is ended by the death of Absalom, the king's son."[76]

In these instances David's actions serve as a model for those of his children who seek to become new Davids through taking on the paternal persona. But this Davidic world brings about its own destruction. Each son is killed by the next in a competition for David's role. The monarchical framework thus deconstructs itself since ultimately David's worth as parent interweaves with his profile as ruler. As Gunn suggested, David's government is marked by grasping desire for gratification, and this usurping tendency binds David's dual roles in the first and second books of Samuel together.[77]

## David as King

The final judgement on David's role as king, then, cannot be separated from the presentation of David as human being, as male, as sexually active, as husband and as parent. On the surface of the text, David's kingship is established without shadow. The covenant of the second book of Samuel, chapter seven, also seems to offer a positive light: "God has chosen not only David, but David's line 'forever', and the covenant is an unconditional one . . . [and] once it is granted that a certain line has permanent dynastic rights, much more power is centralised in the king of the day."[78] Here Rex Mason comments on this line of political argument as royal propaganda, which asserts that, whatever the obstacles, God continually works to support his chosen regime.[79]

A more sober reading of the text reveals the David so favoured to have been little more than a local guerilla captain who operated, according to Mason, as "the leader of a gang of mercenaries who acted very much in their own interests. He took service under the Philistines but two-timed them by carefully larding the way to popular support in Judah with . . .

76 Jensen, H., *Desire, Rivalry and Collective Violence*, pp. 202 f.
77 Gunn, D., *The Story of King David*, p. 101.
78 Mason, R., *Propaganda and Subversion in the Old Testament*, p. 43.
79 Mason, R., *Propaganda and Subversion in the Old Testament*, p. 45.

generous bribes".[80]   Moreover, King David continued to function much in the style of a self-designated ruler, taking Bathsheba, wiping out Uriah, as Mason remarks.[81]

Mark Brettler picks up these two layers of David's story in the first and second books of Samuel in his interpretation of these texts as ideological documents, written for the promotion of royal authority without too much regard for original historical details.  The story of the local war-leader largely disappears under the controlling theme of royal concerns such as legitimacy, hegemony and succession.[82]  Brettler compares this with royal propaganda in Mesopotamian texts where, for instance, Sargon's letter to the god Ashur can be viewed as an ideological reconstruction of historical events.[83]  This ideological literary style consciously creates a paradigm for readers who are meant to see here an exemplary figure insofar as the ruler is a chosen partner for a deity in relation to a given community. In this approach person, community and cosmos are three harmonious levels, which have to be read together for the reader to arrive at the ultimate moral vision, which the text is purveying.  In Noll's study it is the narrative voice which transmits this royal ideology, offering David as a mediator between deity and subjects, and focusing on the central worth of David's cultic action of bringing YHWH to Jerusalem and proposing a permanent home for the deity there.[84]

## Cosmos, Community and Person

Throughout the above account it has been argued that David's profile as a person is ambivalent, leading to a reader-response varying between acclaim and condemnation.  David's positive side is most clearly seen in his role as cultic mediator.  It is through Ark and Temple that the David's dynasty will exercise power and represent their subjects before YHWH; it is this cultic role which is endorsed by the Davidic covenant, the promises of the deity to David and his son.  But religion and secular affairs are not separate.  By control of cult David also gains political clout, setting the seal on his rise to

---

80  Mason, R., *Propaganda and Subversion in the Old Testament*, p. 40.
81  Mason, R., *Propaganda and Subversion in the Old Testament*, p. 40.
82  Brettler, M., *The Creation of History in Ancient Israel*, London, Routledge, 1995, p. 101.
83  Brettler, M., *The Creation of History in Ancient Israel*, p. 95.
84  Cf. Noll, *The Faces of David*. Chapter One deals with Noll's methodology, which involves the interplay of these two sources of information in the story, namely the author and the narrator.

power through military endeavour. In this context the three levels of cosmos, community and person are sewn together in a symbiosis which supports a total worldview of the readers as a congregation of worshippers and political subjects.

By contrast David's negative, shadow side emerges from the evidence of David as a human being and active in male sexual roles. If David is gay then he uses his lover's concern to safeguard his own future and the lament over Jonathan becomes an empty hyperbole. If David is heterosexual then he has little regard for his women as persons in their own right rather than as adjuncts to his property. As parent David does little to promote healthy role-modelling by his sons, though his grief for Absalom strikes the reader as a note of genuine affection and anguish at a son's loss. Cosmos, community and person come apart in this reading for David the person has little to offer for constructive social action which harmonises human existence with the cosmos.

Yet the story of David does not leave the reader cold to its central character. Despite all defects David remains a fascinating source of reflection on human behaviour, the meaning and purpose of human existence. Gunn describes the story of king David as "serious entertainment".[85] Can such a work provide moral vision though, especially since its main character behaves unethically? It would appear that the answer is affirmative, perhaps because David has one stable element in this story. He remains throughout loyal to his God. Moreover, God has chosen David and remains favourable to him, never displacing him as king with any finality. The overall shape of the David story, then, is loyalty of a sort: God's perseverance with the flawed human being he has favoured and David's perseverance with the deity in whose name he was anointed to rule Israel.

Thus it can be asked of David whether he is 'golden boy' or an abusive male, head of a dysfunctional family. The title golden boy yields a constructive content to the concept of moral vision. It involves a harmony between a cosmic deity and a chosen human being, who pledges loyalty to that deity and to his commandments. At its height it covers the idea of a covenant, a commitment, between cosmos and person. But this title is balanced by its shadow side. Golden youth becomes husband and father

---

85 Gunn, D., *The Story of King David*, p. 61. Here Gunn indicates his view that the primary function of the Davidic narrative in Samuel is not propaganda or royal ideology but simply entertainment – what might be described as a 'good read'. But he also indicates that this is literature with depth, intended also to offer food for reflection on human behaviour and value systems.

and here there are many indications of the kinds of behaviour to be avoided. But it is not easy to separate out good from bad in this context, when the whole of a narrative is taken up and serious attention is given to looking at a biblical character in all his/her aspects. The final messages to be taken from the David story can only include both boundaries in its assessment of the moral perspectives of the narrative – golden youth *and* abusive male. Room for both extremes exists at cosmic level since God presides over the story and still values its hero. At community level the story provides a model of the need for discernment over the choices facing human beings. A person can so easily contribute negative energies to communal living and can distort the next generation's vision of its own identity. Certainly, what emerges here is the variety of, and contradictory nature of, the readings that are possible from the profile of a biblical character with regard to moral vision and ethical behaviour.

# Chapter Four

# Esther

So far this section of the present volume has looked at two stories about great male heroes in the biblical history of Israel, Abraham and David. It has been shown that Abraham can be read across a range of meanings, which offer differing views on his moral vision and on the ethical nature of his actions. The full content of these readings has been revealed by examination of Abraham's role in post-biblical religious and cultural traditions. David's story already, within the Old Testament texts, provides the reader with a complex picture of the variety of human behaviour. The focus now turns to a female character, who can offer the reader yet another insight into the subject of moral personhood. The book of Esther provides an easily accessible narrative about a woman who helped to save her people, the Jews, from great danger.

## The Esther Story

The story of Esther is found in the Hebrew Scriptures and tells the tale of an 'anonymous' Jewess who became Queen of Persia and who, in that position, was able to safeguard her own people whose lives were threatened. In this role Esther is supported by Mordecai, her guardian, opposed by Haman the courtier, and urgently in need of her royal husband's approval.

Salvation, in this story, turns on the king's power of decree. It might be expected that, in a biblical book, salvation would issue from the divine throne, but God is absent from the Hebrew version of the story. It is up to the human characters to settle the fate of individuals and of whole social groups. Much depends, in this narrative, on the Persian governmental system and especially on the authority of written texts, public decrees, which establish an unalterable law.[1]

---

1  The text both revolves around the Persian system of government and, at the same time, satirises it. Persian law is unalterable. Thus the decree against the Jews cannot be directly rescinded, and hence the need to find another legal way of preventing the attack with the recourse to a further decree allowing the Jews to stand to arms, legally, to defend themselves. The assumption is that no one is going to want to move against an armed and defended group.

The book of Esther found in the Hebrew Scriptures is, however, not the only version of Esther's story in existence. The book, in the Greek versions, has a number of additions. It is possible, indeed, to trace a text history of the story through a number of different stages, beginning with the Alpha Text.[2] Looking at each version of the story a reader can spot the differences in meaning which are created by shifts in narration. Especially in later Greek versions, there appears to have been a deliberate attempt to bring God into the story as both Esther and Mordecai make long petitionary prayers to the God of Israel in a time of distress. As well as considering what each version adds to the overall 'story' of Esther, each one can be read as its own story: each with its particular plot development and its presentations of characters.[3]

While the main storyline concerns Esther, several sub-plots interweave to create complexity. Thus Vashti's story appears unconnected to the main plot, except as a preface, but in fact has a deeper influence than that, explaining, for instance, Esther's great reluctance to enrage the king by disobeying court etiquette. The rivalry between Mordecai and Haman spills out from a personal conflict to affect Mordecai's people, then Esther herself and the king, since Haman plans to take revenge against Mordecai by attacking all Jews. The means to meet this threat comes through the sub-plot of Esther and Mordecai's family connections. The Jews, many of whom are a long way from the centre of power in the court, nonetheless have their fates woven into the story of court intrigue.

## Esther and Moral Vision

The story of Esther involves characters who give concrete substance to certain ways of behaving. Haman's story, for instance, is one of blind arrogance, of a man content with his own aggrandisement, whose life ends in summary execution with one turn of the wheel of destiny. The story of the Jews is one in which the fate of a whole people depends on the decisions of a few powerful persons whom they have not met, illustrating the powerlessness of the majority of citizens in determining their own lives. The king, who does hold such power, nevertheless comes across as a man

---

2　See here the short notes on versions in Levenson, J., *Esther*, London, SCM Press, 1997, pp. 27-34 and the longer, seminal, work by Clines, D., *The Esther Scroll*, Sheffield, Sheffield Academic Press, 1984.

3　See here Day, L., *Three Faces of a Queen*, Sheffield, Sheffield Academic Press, 1995. This work will be discussed in greater detail later in this chapter.

who is not in control of himself, someone who is always reacting to the lead taken by others and who does not perceive the manner in which his position is being exploited by members of his court. The reader can, then, construct a moral vision from reflecting on these diverse characterisations and the behavioural patterns, which they indicate.

Clearly there are some general points of evaluation to be made here – the positive effects of noble courage and clever thinking, the weakness of pride, the persistence of loyalty and its reward, for example. Esther can, therefore, be labelled a morality tale or a wisdom story; but this title is earned in a special manner in the Old Testament setting where the wisdom concerned has often a religio-cultural face.[4] William Whedbee has paralleled Exodus and Esther as two narratives of 'liberation and laughter'.[5]

It can, for instance, be shown that in both books the Isrælites/Jews face extermination at the hand of a great ruler and that the leader who brings them to safety is, in both cases, initially reluctant to take up that responsibility. Moses tells God in Exodus chapter three that he cannot be a leader and Esther tells Mordecai that she cannot risk upsetting the king. Sandra Berg, meanwhile, has discussed the links between Joseph and Esther, showing that there are similarities not only in language, but also in settings and events between these texts.[6]

While both stories reflect on the varying fortunes of their key figures at court, the solitary figure of Joseph is balanced by the paired characters, Esther and Mordecai. Also, although Joseph's story includes a banqueting scene of importance, much more attention is given to domestic drinking parties in Esther.[7] It is probably true to say that the writer of Esther had the general tone of the Joseph narrative in mind and that both works are examples of literature exploring the possibilities, in the time of the Persian Empire, for successful Jews at foreign courts and the cultural identity required for such success.[8] Joseph and Esther imply the validity of a cross-cultural personal identity, despite the threats and difficulties posed by such a lifestyle, thus offering a new perspective on community values.[9]

---

4   Michael Fox offers a discussion of the reasons for and against labelling Esther by differing genre titles. See Fox, M., *Character and Ideology in the Book of Esther*, Columbia, University of South Carolina Press, 1991, chapter four.

5   See Whedbee, W., *The Bible and the Comic Vision*, chapter three; See also Sasson, J., *Esther*, in Alter, R. and Kermode, F. (eds), *Literary Guide*, p. 339. Also Miles, J., *God*, p. 361.

6   Berg, S., *The Book of Esther*, Missoula, Scholars Press, 1979.

7   Berg, S., *The Book of Esther*, p. 127.

8   Berg, S., *The Book of Esther*, p. 141.

9   Berg, S., *The Book of Esther*, p. 145.

Jon Levenson suggests that the text is "best seen as a historical novella set within the Persian Empire".[10] Although it clearly deals with historical matters it seems likely that the work was not intended to be a documentary chronicle of actual events in Persia so much as a tale to endorse the value of keeping to a proper social identity in a foreign culture. Although there is a question mark over the violent revenge of the Jews the text as a whole supports good relationships between Jews and Gentiles.[11] Esther is married to a foreign king and immersed in court life and Mordecai is a faithful supporter of the king who helps to foil a plot on the royal life.[12]

On another level Michael Fox puts forward the argument that there is a moral vision to be gained by reading the text in relation to specific historical experience.[13] He points out that Esther is of great significance for modern Jews. Known by the Rabbis as The Scroll (*Megillah*) it is the text which underpins the Jewish festival of Purim. A *Pur* is a lot, and, in Esther, the fate of the Jews is caught up with the casting of lots. At the carnival time of Purim, Jews dressed up as the characters of the book and acted in a satirical fashion, copying and mocking the bluster of Ahasuerus or the villainy of Haman and, most of all, the frequent and extended drinking scenes at the Persian Court. This is farce with a serious face, for European history has frequently thrown up a challenge to Jewish existence. Fox specifies here the twentieth century in Europe. In the real life context of ethnic cleansing of Jews (and of other minority groups in a host culture) the story of Esther has a special moral perspective to offer.

The fate of the Jews in Esther moves from death to life, a movement structured in the text by the recurrent pattern of feasts, which mark the progress of the plot. This structuring by reversals defines the story and

---

10 Levenson, J., *Esther*, p. 25.
11 The extremity of the attack by the Jews on subjects of the Persian Empire has led to a dislike of the book of Esther as a work of Jewish imperialism. Beal notes that Martin Luther disliked it on the grounds that it was too Jewish, and, in the 1950s, Christian commentators struggled to find the text acceptable in the post-holocaust context, which demanded a generous spirit towards Jews (Beal, T. K., *The Book of Hiding*, London, Routledge, 1997, pp. 6 f.). The Greek B text is more aware than the other versions that it is not proper for Esther to be married to a foreigner and thus be unable to keep to Jewish laws of purity and food preparation.
12 Fox, M., *Character and Ideology*, pp. 11 f.
13 See eg. Levenson, J., *Esther*, Introduction. This matter is also addressed by Berg, S., *The Book of Esther*.

links it to the comic vision.[14]  For the procession of repetition and reversal leads ultimately to rejoicing in the festival of Purim.  The Scroll of Esther, the Megillah, is mirrored by the historical repetition which creates a vision of destiny as positive rather than negative, of a hope for survival which overcomes short term threats to existence.  This is achieved by the literary genre of fantasy in the book and by the event of carnival behaviour in everyday life.

Here there is a definite link between the fantasy literature, Esther, and the tradition of clowning within Jewish spirituality.  Judith Kerman remarks "in fact, hasn't sacred clowning had a crucial place in Judaism for a long time? . . . Purim, probably has always been a festival in which the whole community clowns."[15]  This clowning parodies community values, with cross-dressing, funny plays, a special Purim Rabbi and a celebration of wine and drunkenness.[16]  Yet, says Kerman, the Jew-as-clown is "clownish *because* he's concerned with the moral, because he insists that the universe is not morally chaotic".[17]  The bizarre, the impossible happens; Job puts God on trial, for instance, but at the end acknowledges the sovereignty of a God who is to be worshipped as the guarantee of moral boundaries.[18]

Timothy Beal also notes the historical significance of the work.[19]  Although it is a piece of historiography rather than a documentary record, as a "socially symbolic act . . . it provides insights into Jewish political self-representation in that context".[20]  In a time when Persian Jewry had been separated from their religious and cultural roots by exile, the text examines the enduring reality of 'Jewishness', which is situated rather in social loyalties than in common adherence to a transcendent deity.  Mordecai is not stridently Jewish but when so defined by his opponent Haman, he owns his ethnic roots and his membership of a common tradition, both by mourning the decree against the Jews and by exhorting Esther to intervene.  Esther, too, has openly to claim her Jewish kin and, in defining herself,

---

14  Kerman, J., *A Teshuva on Sacred Clowning, from Reb Kugel* in Pippin, T. and Aichele, G. (eds), *The Monstrous and the Unspeakable*, Sheffield, Sheffield Academic Press, 1997, p. 64.

15  Kerman, J., *A Teshuva on Sacred Clowning, from Reb Kugel*, p. 65.

16  Kerman, J., *A Teshuva on Sacred Clowning, from Reb Kugel*, p. 72.

17  Kerman, J., *A Teshuva on Sacred Clowning, from Reb Kugel*. See esp. p. 73 for a discussion of this theme in Jewish tradition.

18  Beal, T., *Hiding*, is a work which starts from and constantly revolves around the topic of Diaspora Judaism and Jewish self-interrogation according to issues of identity.

19  Beal, T., *The Book of Hiding*, p. 111 f.

20  Whedbee, W., *The Bible and the Comic Vision*, p. 172.

brings safety to her social group of origin. Here community and person are
extensions of one another and stand and fall together.

## Characterisation in Esther

It is the tension between life and death in Esther which gives the book its
ultimate shape. As Whedbee points out, the work is in fact a Comedy, with
shadows to it. More than this, the book is nearly a farce at times, a
burlesque which satirises human behaviour, especially that of 'great
people'. It is possible to argue that the characters are used fairly
superficially in order to convey this satirical mode of thought. Thus, he
says, "we see such stock characters as a foolish, fickle king, a beautiful,
wise heroine, a loyal courtier and a wicked villain".[21]

Michael Fox, however, has put forward the view that the characters
deserve deeper examination.[22] Fox argues that readers' reactions point to
the depth of characterisation. Different readers produce competing views
of the nature of the main characters, and thus the characters provide a
parallel to real life events in which a reader can reflect on matters of moral
vision. He suggests that "like living persons, they can call forth conflicting
opinions among different acquaintances".[23]

This characterisation is achieved, nevertheless, by the story line.
Whereas the Davidic narrative contained enough speech for the reader to
form a picture of Saul and David from the character's own voice, the book
of Esther has little speech and so the characters have to be reconstructed
from the plot. Frequently devices such as dramatic irony offer a means of
analysing character. Haman, for instance, is executed with the equipment
that he had set up for Mordecai; this irony provides the reader with a means
of evaluating Haman's arrogance, when this is set against his sudden loss of
confidence at his swift change of fortune.

## The Role of the Narrator in Esther

It is, therefore, largely through the eyes of the one who tells the story that
characters are endowed with meaning. The narrator is in fact a character
who tells the story since the narrator operates within the textual world; this

21  Whedbee, W., *The Bible and the Comic Vision*, p. 173. See also Sasson, J., *Ruth*, p. 141.
22  Fox, M., *Character and Ideology*, p. 1 f.
23  Fox, M., *Character and Ideology*, p. 3.

style of character is a party to events and so is a reliable witness to the truth of the symbolic world of texts.[24] However, the narrator can still withhold information from readers, leave gaps in accounting for events, as well as offering direct comment on a character.[25] In Esther the narrator knows a good deal about Persian court life and administration, as well as knowing about the characters and their thoughts; to that extent this narrator is omniscient, knowing more than the surface level of the narrative tells the reader.

Narrators can offer description and evaluation of characters. Esther is described, for instance, as strikingly beautiful, a title which identifies her initial role in the story as a desirable young woman. Evaluation offers information concerning the personality of a character, both with regard to traits and to mental states.[26] Mordecai has traits of loyalty and perseverance, which are manifested by him in a constant manner within the narrative. Esther's reply to Mordecai's demand for assistance against Haman, quoted by the narrator, reveals her mental state of distress at the risks involved in this for her.

The narrator influences the depiction of characters as rounded (capable of change and development within the narrative), or flat (not changing), or even stock (types of behaviour, personified, rather than persons as such). Whedbee noted it is possible to fit the characters in Esther into flat or stock categories, but David Gunn and Donna Fewell warn against too rigid or simple an approach to characterisation in Esther.[27] For example, Esther herself is, apparently, the central figure but, say Gunn and Fewell, "some commentators insist that, to the contrary, Mordecai is the major figure and Esther but part of the supporting cast. Both cases can be argued cogently from the text."[28]

To use Alan Culpepper's terminology here, narrative usually throws up a main character (a protagonist) around whom the others revolve.[29] Theoretically, Ahasuerus ought to be a lead figure but, as was pointed out earlier, he actually does the revolving rather than the centring. Esther and Mordecai could be viewed as joint protagonists here, though for a time Haman takes the lead.

---

24  Gunn, D. and Fewell, D., *The Narrative Art in the Hebrew Bible*, p. 53.
25  Gunn, D. and Fewell, D., *The Narrative Art in the Hebrew Bible*, p. 59.
26  Bar-Efrat, S., *Narrative Art in the Bible*, p. 53.
27  See Whedbee, W., *The Bible and the Comic Vision*, chapter three.
28  Gunn, D. and Fewell, D., *The Narrative Art in the Hebrew Bible*, p. 76.
29  Culpepper, A., *Anatomy of the Fourth Gospel*, Philadelphia, Fortress, 1983.

## Character and Moral Perspective

Like Fox, Bar-Efrat regards characters in narratives as channels for the
expression of values.   He notes that "characters can . . . transmit the
significance and the values of the narrative to the reader, since they usually
constitute the focal point of interest".[30] Their function is to crystallise
readers' views on daily life by gathering into an individual person within a
range of persons the possible human reactions to life-events.  Fox points
out that characters are selves; they have thoughts, feelings and even
subconscious minds.[31]  There are personal boundaries in that they cannot go
beyond what the author has attributed to them; they do not exist outside
what is said about them by the story.  But that still offers the readers much
scope, including speculation about how such characters would act if
circumstances changed.  The reader reconstructs literary selves by putting
together their words and actions to form a coherent personality.  Fox states
that "finally, when the narrator is omniscient (as in Esther) we are allowed
direct access to the characters' thoughts, feelings and motives – even
unconscious ones".[32]

From this basis it is possible to create rounded profiles for most of the
characters in the book.  Vashti, for instance, comes alive as a woman and a
Queen who feels that her dignity and worth are being undermined by the
king's command, as if she were a mere concubine.   The reader can
speculate as to what she thought afterwards, in her relegation to obscurity.
In a second example a character becomes ambiguous.  Mordecai stays loyal
to his adult choice of loyalty to the king and to his family ties, but why
does he continue to linger by the palace once Esther is set in place?[33]  The
Greek text has felt the necessity to explain this via Mordecai's original
dream of a future crisis.

Haman, by contrast, is open to the reader because the narrator tells so
much.  Fox argues that "devious though he is, Haman is allowed no
mysteries.  His motives, drives, and attitudes are transparent, his twisted
soul laid bare to all."[34] This does not make him superficial even if a reader
can guess his typical reaction.  Rather he is an object of scorn for his self-
concern, and an object of pity on account of his self-delusion, and for his
suffering through the king's misperception of his intentions to Esther.  As

---

30  Bar-Efrat, S., *Narrative Art in the Bible*, p. 47.
31  Fox, M., *Character and Ideology*, p. 6.
32  Fox, M., *Character and Ideology*, p. 8.
33  Fox, M., *Character and Ideology*, p. 196.
34  Fox, M., *Character and Ideology*, p. 178.

such, Haman can serve as an example of personality traits to be avoided, but also as a type for all those who find that their personal wisdom is totally inadequate for the situation they find themselves in. Such a moral perspective could be gained by any reader and then applied by them to their own situation.

## Fictional and Non-Fictional Stories

In this book it has been assumed that Old Testament narratives can be described as 'fictional' stories, although Narrative Criticism as a whole deals with fictional and non-fictional writings separately. Non-fictional stories are biographies and similar works and it might seem right to classify Old Testament stories in this way. But it is difficult to put them into this category since it is not clear how far any story offers an exact account of an historical figure. This is even more the case with Esther, which appears to deal with recognisable character-types from folk-tale genres – with supposedly good and bad figures being clearly identified as such by the narrative voice. However, such stories still have a mimetic function, as discussed in chapter one.

In order to identify and illustrate the moral perspectives which, it is argued, these narratives convey, tools drawn from Narrative Criticism are being used. This is being carried out by focusing not on the use of all these tools in connection with a single narrative, but by taking a tool and examining what utilising that tool over several narratives produces in the line of moral attitudes. In taking this line of singling out one tool at a time this study fits within a postmodern approach to the method of narrative criticism, which allows for a narratological approach while also holding to diversity, the presence in a text of more than one message. Rhoads suggests that "narrative critics will do well, therefore, to acknowledge the complex nature of narrative . . . narrative critics will continue to look for patterns of coherence and at the same time be more aware of what we notice and also learn from reading against the grain".[35]

In this task of reading against the grain, one matter which emerges, is the link between narrative reading and ideological criticism. More especially it is a matter of spotlighting the power positions which male and female characters occupy in Old Testament narratives. Esther, for instance,

---

35 Rhoads, D., *Narrative Criticism: Practices and Prospects*, in Rhoads, D. and Syreeni, K. (eds), *Characterisation in the Gospels*, Sheffield, Sheffield Academic Press, 1999, pp. 264-266, p. 270.

starts as a powerless girl but because she finds favour with the man who has absolute power she herself comes to have a public political role. This is a story line, which carries mixed messages to historical audiences. It can lead readers to endorse, implicitly, a male-dominated public sphere; it can cause readers to reflect on the opportunities which a woman can make to break into a male world. Whichever way the message is read, the text, though fictional, has a clear impact on a historical readership and on their attitudes to their own socio-cultural systems.

## From No-One to Someone

This title expresses Esther's career in a nutshell. She begins as a Jewish girl, without even her own family, an orphan taken in by a relative, and she ends as the Queen of Persia, authorised to seal documents with the king's own seal. Beal considers that the book of Esther sets its story into the frame of concentric circles of belonging, from outside through marginal to inside to centre.[36] On one level this model has the Persian court at its centre, with the king at the very heart of life. Thus Esther progressively moves from outsider to insider as she physically moves through the palace gates and then the palace buildings till she reaches the royal chamber. This plot sequence fits into the topology of 'rags to riches'. As a girl Esther has no real stake in shaping events, rather it is she who is shaped – by Mordecai, by the palace eunuch. At this point Esther could be defined simply as 'pretty woman', admired and desired by men, and open to their proposals for her future.

It is her beauty, which brings Esther inside, placing her at court where she can now be part of the political scene. Once inside, Esther begins to develop her own inner traits. How does she win the favour of eunuch and king? Is it just a matter of appearance or are there other reasons? Is it, perhaps, because they sense her innate intelligence and potential assertiveness? It is these traits, anyway, which Esther will display as she now responds to Mordecai's appeals and sets herself a political role to win over the king to the support of her people and condemnation of Haman's attack on them. Esther is alone in this political battle of subtle scheming; Mordecai can only wait and see, outside the palace. And Esther pulls it off; a king mellow with drinking, an enemy lulled into self-content, provide the opening she needs. It is, of course, providential that the king has been

36 Beal, T., *The Book of Hiding*, This picture emerges as Beal explores the narrative. See especially the section entitled *Threshold Identities* in chapter four.

sleepless and has been consulting the annals, only to hear of Mordecai's loyalty and so to remember his debts to a good man. But, nonetheless, Esther has a major part in the reversal of fortune, which sees Haman dead and Mordecai brought inside, into the intimate inner circle of king, queen and trusted courtier.

Esther is honoured in the festival of Purim as a saviour of her people. Thus it is not just a woman who moves in from the margins of society, it is a Jewish woman, through whose memory all Jews can find a hope of moving from social margins to social centres. In this Old Testament narrative a key character provides material for the creation of a moral vision of personhood which focuses on person as a microcosm of community. What one person shows in the way of courage and intelligent manoeuvring can be emulated by all those persons who can identify with that figure. In this instance it could be women and it could be Jews, especially, who can make that identification.

The depiction of Esther painted above draws largely on the Hebrew text but there are, of course, several versions of the story across the Hebrew and Greek Old Testaments. Isolating each strand of the story and telling it in its own right produces several parallel models of the character, Esther, as Linda Day has established.[37] Day works with a model of characterisation drawn up according to Chatman's models of paradigm traits.[38] The qualities which she identifies are: "authority; passivity; emotions; religious belief; relationships with Jews, king, Mordecai, adversaries; existence in the Persian Court; sexuality".[39] These traits can be illustrated from all the versions and are the pieces from which the reader constructs his/her understanding of Esther as a person.

Day argues that there is enough common ground here across all versions to allow for the differences of each text to be visible. She then defines the versions with which she will work as three – the Masoretic Hebrew text (M), a short Greek text, labelled the Alpha text by scholars (A) and the longer Greek text which she labels (B). Using Day's findings two main paradigms of Esther can be constructed – a secular Esther and a pious Esther. The secular is based mainly on the M text and the pious view on the A and B texts (though these each have their own version of piety).

---

37  Day, L., *Three Faces of a Queen*, Sheffield, Sheffield Academic Press, 1995.
38  Day, L., *Three Faces of a Queen*, p. 21.
39  Day, L., *Three Faces of a Queen*. The topics are set out on p. 169 and then discussed at length in chapter three.

## A Secular Esther

The Esther of the M text, notes Day, "lives primarily in the secular world, not the religious . . . As neither her relationship with God nor her piety in personal actions is recorded, we know nothing about that aspect of her character."[40]In this model, Esther is presented largely as a balanced and self-possessed woman. Emphasis is given to her Jewish family origins and to her beauty, with its sexual side of giving great pleasure to the king. Once established as queen, Esther takes easily to her regal role; faced with the decree against Jews she draws on her royalty and is supremely confident in her approach to the king. In what follows she usually appears calm and rational, intelligent and regal, only once breaking down into tears.[41] When her plans come to fruition Esther takes charge of affairs in a suitably royal manner.[42]

This model offers an interesting reading of moral vision from a specifically human perspective. Faced with the workings of absolute power (as in the deposition of Vashti) Esther acknowledges the boundaries created by such power structures but then works to make that power support her cause rather than that of Haman. In this Esther does not fall into 'self seeking', rather she is prepared to take a risk for those whom she owns as her people. Here is a model for a humanistic world where, without the urgings of supernatural forces, human beings can act naturally for the good of others even at cost to themselves. To this extent a secular Esther allows humanism its own space in the arena of religions.

## A Pious Esther

In this model the story line remains the same but a major difference is the role that God and religion play in Esther's characterisation. In the Alpha text Esther is presented as pious; she has a personal religious commitment involving prayer and fasting as religious activities. This different slant on Esther is mostly deduced from prayers which she makes, which are absent from the Hebrew text. This religious profile is woven into a depiction of Esther in which she shows the greatest development as a person across all three versions. In the early stages of her career at court she is dependent and passive and this climaxes in her fear and anxiety when she has to

40 Day, L., *Three Faces of a Queen*, p. 179.
41 Day, L., *Three Faces of a Queen*, p. 150.
42 Day, L., *Three Faces of a Queen*, p.163; p. 173.

approach the king. But her successful ability to operate at the heart of public affairs produces a new woman, a maturely-confident person whose position is secure and who herself is a guarantee of justice.[43]

This picture of Esther shows her discovering her innate qualities and developing deeper and stronger relationships with her husband. Through her dependence on her God, Esther finds the courage to extend her personality and in so doing she has a positive impact on the male world of high affairs. In this version also, then, Esther finds her personal vision rooted in her community identity. Whereas, in the M text, this leads the queen to engage herself more fully in the Persian administration, in the A text Esther expresses her community bond with the Jews through a thorough-going demand for rooting out their enemies by physical resistance. In the A text God is part of the picture which includes such retributive violence; the cosmic level can be viewed as endorsing this style of behaviour.

### Esther – A Covenant Partner

This model emerges from the Greek B text which is close to the A text in many ways, especially in relation to the inclusion of God as part of the story at a cosmic level. There are some particular emphases in the B text, however. Esther is presented throughout the story as much more self-conscious about being Jewish. Here the narrator shows awareness of how cultural behaviour differs between Jewish households and those of Gentiles; these differences make inter-marriage, for instance, very difficult, yet Esther is married to a gentile ruler. Thus Esther comes across in the narrative as not happy at the Persian court. Though she brings pleasure to the king she herself does not really enjoy intimacy with him – she is playing a part. According to Day, Esther keeps more things secret from the court in the B text, certain actions that she must hide on a daily basis.[44]

At the same time Esther relies more heavily on Mordecai in this version. She does this in the events leading up to her appearance before the king, but also in the last sections where Esther joins Mordecai to herself in the administering of public affairs. Esther's piety, in the B text, takes the form of covenant remembrance. Day states that "practising piety, not revealing her origins, and obedience to Mordecai are all connected to her attitude and

---

43 Day, L., *Three Faces of a Queen*, p. 147; pp. 194 f.
44 Day, L., *Three Faces of a Queen*, p. 191.

relationship with God.  Esther also views her own religiosity in terms of her people and her religious tradition."[45]

This model makes Esther into a specifically Jewish figure of salvation. In this model the individual human being, a kinship group and that group's patron deity form a harmonious and closed circle of existence.  The individual finds identity precisely through this circle of being.


## Esther the Woman

This model of Israel, consisting of person, community and cosmos, brings the reader back to the manner in which the story of Esther functions as a wisdom tale and to the similarities between it and the story of Joseph. Klara Butting takes this similarity into a new line of interpretation connected with Esther's being a female character.[46]  She points to the similar traits between the characters such as their initial passivity in allowing others to shape their lives.  Both Joseph and Esther meet a crisis, which pushes them into a new dimension of existence. For Joseph this is the pursuit by Potiphar's wife, which leads to imprisonment, whereas in Esther's life the threat is rather more to her people although she does have to brave the king's wrath.  Both characters then take on a royal/semi-royal role at a gentile court and deploy great political powers.  Each, from this position, takes on a protective function with regard to their own kin. Butting makes this link between Esther and Joseph in order to stress Esther's role as a woman, that is a woman filling the male role of saviour/protector.  She argues that, in Esther, it is a specifically male political world, which is the social context for the story of personal growth and communal liberation.[47]

For Butting the emergence of Esther from within this male world of tyranny speaks of a re-creation of social systems more generally.[48]  As Butting, among others, has noted, Esther maintains a general aura of obedience in spirit to the king while in fact disobeying him.[49]  She presents herself before the enthroned king without being sent for (and in the Alpha

---

45  Day, L., *Three Faces of a Queen*, p. 178.
46  Butting, K., *Esther: A New Interpretation of the Joseph Story in the Fight against AntiSemitism and Sexism*, in  Brenner, A. (ed.), *Ruth and Esther*, Sheffield, Sheffield Academic Press, 1999.
47  Butting, K., *Esther: A New Interpretation*, p. 242.
48  Butting, K., *Esther: A New Interpretation*, p. 245.
49  Butting, K., *Esther: A New Interpretation*, p. 246.

and B texts the king is initially furious) and then refuses to present her real petition when asked to do so by the king. Esther does these things knowingly thus using royal, male power against a world-order structured by men, relying on her favour as a beautiful woman with her husband. This behaviour is manipulative and can be approved of or denounced. Esther could be justified in taking the only path open to a woman in this male world, therefore her actions are validated by their motives of protection of her own people. But women who trade on sexual favour are often attacked in Old Testament narrative as subversive of male strength and rational control, as with Delilah in Samson's story in Judges. Yet, as Butting notes, Esther is not really a model of a totally free agent.[50] At the end of the story the male world of politics is largely unchanged. Esther is exploited by that male world in order that it may continue to flourish.

## Esther and Social Location

This topic is the focus for Timothy Beal's study of Esther, where he works around the ambiguous and ambivalent forces in the text. Esther, he suggests, is a 'book of hiding' where characters are written out and written in by writing over others.[51] Thus Vashti is written out in the first scene. Her role as queen and woman is written over by the writing in of Esther. Yet, to understand Esther's character fully it is necessary to look back to Vashti and to see her presence still hidden in the narrative. For Vashti, disobeying the king led to annihilation, but her spirit of autonomy lives on in Esther who, in her turn, also disobeys the royal protocol – and survives. This underlying connection between the characters, their pairing and the exploration of their identities by these devices, is dwelt upon also by Athalya Brenner and Alice Bach. Here use is made of Alice through the Looking Glass themes to discuss the use of repetition and reversal in characterisation.[52] Vashti, it is suggested, escapes through the Glass by her refusal to accept to be the object of the male gaze whereas Esther is caught

---

50 Butting, K., *Esther: A New Interpretation*, p. 248.
51 Beal has already indicated the importance of this concept by including it as the title of his book, before examining it in detail in his commentary on Esther.
52 Brenner, A., *Looking at Esther through the Looking Glass*; Bach, A., *Mirror, Mirror in the Text: Reflections on Reading and Rereading*, in Brenner, A. (ed.), *A Feminist Companion to Esther, Judith and Susannah*, Sheffield, Sheffield Academic Press, 1995.

in the Mirror and has to stand before her male audience and work for her liberation.[53]

Beal prefers to use here the language of hiding and 'coming out'.[54] Vashti's refusal to come in, and so come out before the men of the court, leads to her removal as she comes out, in the sense of asserting her autonomy as a person. Her style of coming out threatens to blur the social boundaries of behaviour and causes her marginalisation in the story. Yet she still exists in the margins and 'comes out' indirectly in the character, Esther. Vashti's disobedience and Esther's obedience form a mirrored pair of presentations of women. Vashti becomes the symbol for all women when Memucan turns her behaviour into an attack on male/female roles in all households. Esther replaces her as the model of passive femininity but herself disobeys by opposite behaviour to that of her predecessor. Esther comes out as a Jew, and that is acceptable to the narrator; but it is as a woman that she does so, raising shades of the earlier royal woman. At this point, Beal argues, "convergences with Vashti, the Old Testament her-woman, also begin to appear, so that her revelation is a coming-out not only of the other Jew but also of the other woman".[55]

Beal argues that the whole book concerns the ambiguity of the concepts of 'self' and 'other' as terms for locating people in a social field. Esther is the other woman to Vashti and the other Jew to Mordecai but she is also acceptable Persian wife and disobedient, foreign partner. Beal argues that "it is impossible to fix her in a particular social location within an order marked by oppositional differences".[56]

Beal concludes that an essential moral message of this book is that of the ambiguity of, and blurred boundaries between, self and other. As such the book questions the stability, in absolute terms, of any human social system. Beal argues that "in Esther no whole-hearted resolve or final solution can be certain, not even the tidy reversal of fortune for the Jews in the later chapters . . . the subversive possibilities opened by the book's representation of public power cannot be undone simply because that power has gone through a new Jewish consolidation".[57] In this open-ended

---

53  Bach, A., *Mirror, Mirror in the Text*, pp. 85 f.
54  Cf. *Coming Out*, used by Beal as a title for one of his chapters. This is drawn from gay vocabulary as in the opposites Closet/Come Out. Beal justifies his use of it as a theological term on pp. 111 f.
55  Beal, T., *The Book of Hiding*, p. 100.
56  Beal, T., *The Book of Hiding*, p. 100.
57  Beal, T., *The Book of Hiding*, p. 121.

perspective to the moral vision of the text(s) of Esther two cultural issues stand out, the matter of gender and that of ethnicity.

## Ethnicity and Moral Vision

The ethnicity, which is in question, is that of the Jews. The book of Esther reflects the ambiguity attached to their existence. On the one hand they fit into the Persian Empire where they are one subject people among many. On the other hand their individuality and ties of loyalty to each other can mark them out as a source of subversion. It is interesting to note that Haman himself is a foreigner, being an Agagite and not a Persian.[58] What is at stake is a competition for acceptance and the rivalry between ethnic groups threatens the peace and order of the empire as a whole. The narrative voice in Esther views the Jews as a marginalised group whose existence is deeply challenged. The fact that they turn then into aggressors themselves, killing ninety-five thousand Persian citizens, is not understood as anything but the spin-off from their justified fight to ensure their own future. However, Christian commentators have sometimes picked up on the aggression. The moral vision, it is suggested, is that of validated aggression and a forcible take-over of other people's culture. Beal, for instance, notes how Luther's hatred of the book has been followed in later centuries and has spilled into violence against European Jewry.[59]

## Women and Morality

A second, wider issue related to the book of Esther is that of the place of women and their readings of text. This is not totally separate from the ethnicity issues raised above since it can be argued that here men are the dominant culture and women are the minority one. One of the deeper issues addressed in Esther is the nature of power, its sources and its uses, and one side of that is how women stand in relation to power. In relation to texts a reader can ask where the balance of power exists in relation to the characters in a story. Thus more general matters of power structures can be

58 The term Agagite links Haman to the Amalekites, through a biblical genealogy. The Amalekites were great enemies of biblical Israel in the time of Saul, so an older rivalry is taken up into the post-exilic diaspora context of Esther where the foreign empire is, in some ways, only the context for ethnic fighting, not an active player in this field.

59 Beal, T., *The Book of Hiding*, p. 6.

debated through the interaction of characters in a narrative. In Esther the picture of power relations is a subtle one, as Beal has argued. The role of queen is an important one but it is subordinated to the male power role both by Vashti's removal and by a court protocol, which governs even the relations between a happy royal couple. However, Mordecai, another male, exists largely only at the margins of the story, at the palace gate, and can only gain access to power through another figure, thus taking on a female role. The one who stands in for him is, of course, a woman. Thus it is reasonable to ask what broader values the book of Esther offers women readers.

Elizabeth Schussler-Fiorenza has argued for the need to provide a woman's method of reading biblical text. In *Bread not Stone*, she suggests that this would be a form of Liberation Theology insofar as it rescues the biblical vision of liberation.[60] It does so by widening the interpretations of textual meaning and so offering more than one, normative meaning to texts. Whereas Schussler-Fiorenza seeks an intellectual method of asserting women's readings as mainstream interpretation in a male-dominated culture, Elsa Tamez seeks the voice of women in the 'here and now' readings of ordinary women.[61] In the contemporary Latin American culture where misery, malnutrition, repression and torture are rampant, "a reading from a woman's perspective has to go through this world of the poor".[62] This leads the woman's reading to a deep suspicion of the ideology of the text and its male-centred values. In Esther this would entail looking at the manner in which Esther brings hope to the 'poor' of the story. Itumelung Mosala adds to this Latin American approach an African viewpoint in which women's readings operate from the basis of gender, national and class struggle.[63] For him this means reading Esther against the background of the feudal and tributary nature of Persian government, as a survival text which nonetheless allows the exploitation of women for patriarchal ends. Esther stands back to allow Mordecai the 'glory of victory' in this reading.

60  Schussler-Fiorenza, E., *Bread Not Stone*, Edinburgh, T&T Clark, 1984, pp. 265 ff.
61  Tamez, E., *Women's Rereading of the Bible*, in Sugirtharajah, R. (ed.), *Voices from the Margin*, London, SPCK, 1995.
62  Tamez, E., *Women's Rereading of the Bible*, p. 55.
63  Mosala, I., *The Implications of the Text of Esther for African Women's Struggle for Liberation in South Africa*, in Sugirtharajah, R. (ed.), *Voices from the Margin*, pp. 173-177.

## Moral Perspectives in Esther

A wide range of possible moral attitudes has been illustrated in the commentary on Esther. These range from viewing the text as a simple comedy with stock characters, told to support religious customs, to exploring the narrative as the channel for boundary crossing and boundary blurring in which there is no simple answer to how a person shapes an identity. Esther herself is at the heart of these parallel interpretations, being a character expected to support a number of separate roles – as wife, as fellow-Jew, as model for Persian households. The study of three individual versions of her story serves to illustrate how a reader can create Esther's personality anew depending on which role is given centre stage. And behind the text loom the ongoing cultural debates, which shape the readers themselves in any given age. No single harmonious vision of ordered existence emerges here. But each interpretation of meaning circles around the links between person and community, viewing these levels as intimately interwoven and as sharing common ideological interests. The link between these two levels and that of the cosmos is somewhat less certain in Esther. Yet the nature of the crisis in the book, the ultimate issues of life and death, touch on the area of absolute meaning. If the term cosmos takes the transcendent as part of its meaning then the matter of God cannot be wholly absent from the mind of a reader. However, it may well be that the content of the word God can only be supp;ied by human observation of, and reflection on, what actually happens in this world. The rest is silence.

## Morality and Character: A Summary

*Persons*

Abraham, David, and Esther exist in a separate narrative with its particular scenes, recounted by its particular narrator. Thus each character gives rise to independent images of cosmos, community and person. Abraham and David, for example, are very often defined through relationship with God, whereas this relationship is missing, in any direct form, in the story of Esther. Yet the nature of the story in each case offers the possibility of reading all three characters heroically, that is, as models of the attitude to cosmos and community, which a person should have. Thus Abraham trusts God's promises and so secures the future existence of his community. David also trusts God is on his side and so provides strong leadership for the community in war and worship. Esther puts her energies not into personal goals but into securing her people from annihilation.

As has been pointed out many times, plurality of meaning comes from reading about these characters, and part of this breadth is itself the unheroic aspect of the three figures. Abraham may not have been so trusting after all and his relations with Sarah run counter to the divine plan in several scenes. David may have been largely self-seeking in his relations with Saul and he gives his children a poor model of respect for others. Esther may have been forced into action by Mordecai's ominous statement that she would be the loser in the end if she did not throw her lot in with the Jews. It is interesting to note here that Esther gets off more lightly than Abraham or David. This is possibly because of the circumscribed nature of her social roles. Being a woman she has less access to the public sphere, therefore carries less responsibilities in the public areas of war and worship. At the same time, she is not a head of household, either. Esther's sphere of authority is that of queen-consort only. But she makes the most of the influence that social role offers.

## Cosmos and Community

Cosmos stands for the absolute levels of meaning, the ultimate in world order. But, in these narratives, the divine is linked to the variable nature of human existence. Just as Abraham or David can be viewed as clear-cut or as ambiguous characters, so God shares in that two-sided perspective. God is, on the one hand, the guarantor of the community's future and, on the other, remote, unhelpful, or even cruel. Here human evaluations of the nature of the deity rank highly. Abraham goes along with God, in Philip Davies' article on *Male Bonding*, but takes his own measures for the future at the same time. David depends on God for military success, but is at heart a 'careerist', who makes use of a divine patron. In Esther, God is visible at all only through the activities of a set of human beings in action.

The value of the characters is frequently expressed in terms of their usefulness for the community to which they belong. At the heart of this value is their enhancement of family fortunes, as has been stated above. But, beyond the family, lies the community of the nation, the people (*Am*, in Hebrew). These three characters all have value for the society of Israel, a social unit defined in the introductory chapter. Abraham's ploys in Egypt and Gerar remind the readers of the social gap between 'them and us', our people and the foreign nation. The same is true on a grander scale in Esther, though, in both texts, the foreign ruler is viewed positively overall.

David operates in relation to Israel's internal structures, being the ruler whom Israel's God has chosen as leader.

This wider scale of community leads also to the ongoing social, cultural role of the biblical characters. In each case it has been shown how readers continue to relate to the character as a model of a moral person. In the latest scholarship the spotlight is often on those gaps and silences, on the margins of the narrative. It is from those margins that the reader looks in on the central character and finds new messages concerning moral vision.

# PART II:
# MORALITY AND PLOT

# Chapter Five

# The Story of Ruth

The previous section explored biblical perspectives on morality relating to cosmos, community and person, from the perspective of the concept of the moral person. This investigation was carried out by examining several main characters in biblical texts, against the backdrop of the nature of characterisation in narrative. The present section continues the exploration of biblical models of moral vision and proper behaviour – this time through the subject of community. In the social world of the biblical texts an individual gained his/her personal identity through integration into the family or wider kinship structure. The content of personal morality is thus defined by the values held by that social network or community. The self was a collectivist reality rather than one created by the autonomous activity of an isolated human person.[1]

The means to studying community within the biblical world will be that of returning to stories, but this time examining the nature of the interaction between the characters, with a focus on the way in which plot operates. It is through the movement of action and reaction on the part of characters in a narrative and through the balance of action and dialogue that the message of the storyteller is encountered. The diversity of responses to a given situation on the part of several characters and the influence of each character on the final outcome of a situation are major resources for examining the relevance of events for a social group.

## The Function of Plot

The plot is the structuring force in a story, that which gives each individual event its fuller meaning. Bar-Efrat notes that "the plot serves to organise events in such a way as to arouse the reader's interest and emotional involvement, while at the same time imbuing events with meaning".[2] Each

---

1   A good deal of research has been carried out on the subject of collective or corporate understandings of identity. One of the major areas of biblical scholarship to deal with this topic has been that of socio-scientific New Testament research. See, for instance, Esler, P., *The First Christians in their Social Worlds*, London, Routledge, 1994, which posits a Mediterranean self based on family and kin groupings and Malina, B. and Neyrey, J., *Portraits of Paul* (Louisville, Westminster John Knox, 1996), chapter one.
2   Bar-Efrat, S., *Narrative Art in the Bible*, p. 93.

incident in a story is not evaluated for its immediate meaning but "the incidents are like building blocks, each one contributing its part to the entire edifice . . . the removal of one may cause the entire structure to collapse".[3] In Hebrew narratives the reader is frequently left to fine tune the meaning within a given story, since the usual connecting word in Hebrew is *and*, without further subordination of one event to another, in terms of cause and effect.[4]

Essentially, each story has a beginning, a middle, and an end. An initial situation is established which leads through unfulfilled desire or incompleteness to conflict. The middle parts of the story highlight the conflict, which reaches a climax only to be resolved in the final scene. This sequence is parallel with human experience in life, though narrative closure may be more complete than the real life ending of a series of related happenings. The book of Ruth exemplifies this narrative paradigm since it begins with an initial event, famine and migration, which leads into one family's life in a foreign land as Elimelech and his wife and sons emigrate to Moab. The story of this new life produces narrative tensions when the householder dies. The readers' hopes are then raised by the marriages of Elimelech's two sons, only to be dashed by the deaths of the two brothers who leave their widows childless. The tension in the story builds to a new level as Naomi and her two daughters-in-law set off to return to Bethlehem to make yet another new life there and Naomi persuades Orpah to turn back, to her own people. Ruth's refusal to abandon Naomi moves the narrative to a new focus, that of the future in Bethelehem, paving the way for the scenes in the harvest field where Ruth goes to seek food for the two women and where she encounters Boaz. The theme of harvest is the backdrop to the resolution of the story and the fullness of barns holding reaped corn mirrors the human fullness of two women through the birth of a child. But first Ruth has to lay claim to Boaz more formally and the reader is left wondering whether her night visit to the threshing floor and her intimacy with Boaz will bring her the needed security of marriage. Even the next scene at the Gate of the town contains tension since Boaz has to deal with the prior claims to land and woman of a nearer kinsman to the dead Elimelech. Finally, all is well with the ceding of land and Ruth to Boaz and the marriage of these two characters bringing new life to birth in Naomi's grandchild.

Bar-Efrat argues that "in most of the narratives it is possible to discern different parts or blocks, which are somewhat similar to acts in a play. The

3    Bar-Efrat, S., *Narrative Art in the Bible*, p. 93.
4    Gunn, D. and Fewell, D., *Narrative Art in the Hebrew Bible*, p. 102.

acts are sometimes delimited by the location of the incidents, and sometimes by the time at which they occur."[5] Thus, in Ruth, the reader can identify a series of scenes, delineated both by chronological sequence and by shifts in place. There is an overall circularity in the text since the story begins and ends in Bethlehem, with a 'full household'. In between, the action moves out from Bethlehem to Moab and back and from fullness to emptiness and back to fullness. Within this over-arching structure a number of particular scenes structure events, from Elimelech's decision to leave Bethlehem to the final scene of rejoicing by Bethlehem's inhabitants. Among these, several scenes stand out as having greater significance: the three women on the road, the field, the threshing floor, the gate. In each of these situations major contributions to meaning are made through the use of dialogue between characters central to events.

The scene on the way to Judah shows the intimacy of the link between two women, expressed through their conversation and Ruth's refusal to leave Naomi. As Orpah turns back while Naomi and Ruth press on, the next stage of the story is initiated. The harvest field then becomes the focus for the women's activity, or rather, for Ruth's activity. She produces enough grain for both women to survive through the summer while developing closer links with the household of Boaz. The field is a public space of danger to a young unattended woman yet is also the source of life. The reader wonders what the encounters of Ruth and Boaz there will bring about in the long term. The threshing floor meeting of the two emerges from this context. It, too, is a public space, even though Boaz sleeps in a 'private corner'. Once again risk and danger await both Ruth and Boaz but the overnight encounter of these two characters leads on to the Gate where there will be a further resolution of Ruth and Naomi's status in the Bethlehem community. The dialogue of this scene makes much of legalities connected with redeeming land and with marrying a female linked with the property. The scene ends with Boaz and Ruth settled into marriage – a marriage, which brings the final resolution of events in the scene, which expresses the verbal responses of the neighbours to the latest event, namely the birth of a son to the couple.

The combination of dialogue and movement in time and place bind the scenes together to form an overall message in which the hand of God is detected. This is both for pain, in Naomi's self-identification as a 'bitter' woman, and for pleasure, in Ruth's generous support of her mother-in-law and in the fruitfulness of her marriage to Boaz. This establishes a cosmic

---

5  Bar-Efrat, S., *Narrative Art in the Bible*, p. 102.

dimension to the story. God is not an active character within events. Nor is the text concerned with anything but the ordinary sequence of events in human lives, and the interplay of one person's actions with regard to the fortunes of other persons. Yet, when the story is read to the end, the nature of divine action emerges from the sequence of human events, and a close connection can be made between everyday life experience and the shadowing presence of divine intervention in the world.

The main focus of the tale, however, remains at the level of community. It is through the interaction of characters in a social group that the plot moves along and the final fortune, good or bad, of individual persons is decided. The fate of the group takes precedence over individual figures; thus, at the last scene, the child born to Ruth can be laid on Naomi's lap and Naomi is blessed, as a mother, by the crowd. As Ruth is acclaimed as more valuable to her mother-in-law than seven sons, the text expresses the social and personal worth of Ruth as one who has brought security and fulfilment to other members of her society.

## Family, Community and Moral Vision

The nature of that society, in Ruth, is primarily that of the family or household. It is a household, which sets out for Moab, whose survival is threatened by deaths in chapter one, whose return to good fortune and whose guarantee of posterity, is recorded in chapters two to four. It has already been pointed out, in earlier chapters, that the household was the foundational social unit in the ancient world.[6] The book of Ruth mirrors this daily social reality thus ensuring the attention of a readership whose own lives were tied into the fortunes of their several families. Waldemar Janzen argues that the familial perspective is the basis of Old Testament moral vision.[7]

Janzen goes on to create what he calls the 'familial model story'. He says that "we will search for Israel's inner image of a loyal family member, of a dedicated worshipper, of a wise manager of daily life".[8] To achieve this end he employs lines of thought drawn from the book of Ruth. Ruth and Boaz are viewed as central to the paradigmatic message of this text: "Their exemplary behaviour is related to the presentation of a family that

---

6   See chapters two to four, where the social-scientific background to the use of household
    models is dealt with in relation to moral personhood.
7   Janzen, W., *Old Testament Ethics*.
8   Janzen, W., *Old Testament Ethics*, p. 20.

might otherwise have become extinct."[9]  In supporting the poor and the widowed, Boaz acts in line with the Isrælite identity set out in law codes such as are found in Leviticus chapter nineteen and Deuteronomy chapter twenty-four: "Boaz and Ruth preserve a line that has behind it the story of Rachel and Leah . . . and their descendants."[10]  Jantzen argues that "unknown to the participants . . . it is also the family line that will bring forth David, Isræl's greatest king".[11]  In this vision, Janzen suggests, the household of Elimelech becomes a type of Isræl itself, viewed as an extended network of households: "one can hardly overlook the connection . . . to the story of a people who were strangers in a foreign land (Egypt) but received an inheritance through the grace of Yahweh".[12]

Proper response to family responsibilities brings with it blessings both in human practical terms of food and descendants and in broader terms of support and protection by a patron deity who is the family's benefactor. Thus the cosmic level of meaning is found through the community level in which individual persons each contribute something to the total message of the story.  In the familial model of moral order, then, there is a weaving in of all three strands of cosmos, community and person, but the prime level of investigation of narrative is that of the identity of the community. Janzen's paradigm assumes a continuity of identity from the household society of the text to the household setting of the implied reader.  In terms of a socio-scientific reading methodology, this appears to be justified by the plot of a book such as that of Ruth.

### Narrative Issues: Group Identity

Reading Ruth as a totality raises questions as to the precise nature of the book's contribution to teaching about social identity.  Here commentators make a number of parallel points with regard to the continuance, for example, of Isræl as a society and to the role of the woman in promoting the interests of a patriarchal group.  The positive benefits of the woman's actions turns a Tragedy into a Comedy since all ends in peace and happiness.  A central quality owned by the actors in the drama is that of *hesed* (loyalty, loving kindness) and it is this quality, manifested in the actions of several characters, which leads to a happy ending.  Ruth's *hesed*

9   Janzen, W., *Old Testament Ethics*, p. 33.
10  Chapter 4[11-12].
11  Janzen, W., *Old Testament Ethics*, p. 33.
12  Janzen, W., *Old Testament Ethics*, p. 35.

in serving Naomi elicits Boaz's generous protection of Ruth in his field and the broader protection of his role as redeemer (*goel*). Between them the characters display necessary attitudes among kinspeople.

Ruth's role in ensuring the continuity of Elimelech's clan can be read as a microcosm of the preservation of the wider Israel. Rabbinic texts such as that of Rabbi Moshe Alshich's commentary on Ruth suggest that Ruth's contribution to meaning in the book is her role as 'convert to Judaism'.[13] She is the outsider whose conversion brings lustre to Jewish tradition. Her origin as a Moabitess makes her the descendant of Lot's daughters and her union with Boaz marks the integration of Moab with Israel, which itself is a reward for the way in which the daughters of Lot ensured their family's continuance.[14] Ruth passes from unclean (Gentile) to clean (Jewish) status in the story. Each scene prepares for, and then effects, that change. Thus, Ruth and Naomi's arrival at the time of the barley harvest marks a three month period of purification.[15] Her washing before going to the threshing floor marks a need to make herself clean from idolatry: an idolatry she had already rejected by choosing Naomi's god on the journey to Bethelehem.[16] The climax of the story represents Ruth's final welcome into Israel/Judah with her marriage to Boaz whom the Zohar, for instance, regards as a reincarnation of Judah.[17]

The purpose of this conversion is the building up of the social group. In such a reading of Ruth the focus is on the Genealogy, which is found in the last section of the work, where Ruth is directly linked with women whose roles as mothers led to the start of Israel, namely Rachel and Leah. In this reading method Ruth, in choosing Naomi, does not choose an individual woman but a whole society and its deity. Ruth's status as a woman of loyal support for 'Israel' makes her into a reward for Boaz, who earns her through his generosity; far from being an unexpected burden she becomes a gift from God. Nor is this an easy role for Ruth to play; she has to abandon the known and risk danger in an unfamiliar society. For Brenner, "Ruth leaves family, home, religion and culture in order to accompany Naomi into a strange land and an alien cultural milieu".[18] Ruth's venture into the unknown, her prioritising of a relationship by marriage, is rewarded by

13  Alshich, M., Trans. Shakar, R., *The Book of Ruth – A Harvest of Majesty*, Jerusalem, Feldheim, 1991.
14  Alshich, M., *The Book of Ruth*, p. 230.
15  Alshich, M., *The Book of Ruth*, p. 129.
16  Alshich, M., *The Book of Ruth*, pp. 249 f.
17  Alshich, M., *The Book of Ruth*, pp. 345 f.
18  Brenner, A., *The Israelite Woman*, p. 119.

reciprocal kindness and a generous support from the patron deity of her in-laws.

It may be the case that this narrative of a foreign convert owes much to the time in which it was produced. There is no real indication of author and date within the book but a major suggestion has been that the work meets the interests of a Judahite audience in the sixth/fifth century BCE. The books of Ezra and Nehemiah reflect some tension about lines of descent and imply that, in the Persian Judahite province, 'foreign' wives were to be set aside, especially by priests functioning in the Jerusalem temple. This demand for divorce of established couples seems to have encountered opposition and Ruth may represent the interests of a section of society who saw the benefits of having a wife from an outside group.[19] Thus the narrative functions as social teaching, meeting the contemporary need for a moral vision of the significance of, and boundaries of, the regional culture, by the manner in which its plot structure shows the actual integration of a foreigner in the heart of Israel.

The society of ancient Judah, as portrayed in Ruth, was a patriarchal one.[20] That is public authority in society was vested in adult males and it is men's interests which dominate in the ordering of social structures and in the cultural values created by the group. The start of the story highlights this reality since it is Elimelech, as head of household, who takes the lead in the migration to Moab. Moreover, in the last scenes, at the Gate, it is the men who conduct the business of ransoming land and settling the future of the women. It is possible to read Ruth as a text, which functions to support that patriarchal structure of community, by the manner in which its plot unfolds. As Greenstein notes, "thinking politically, one may appeal to

---

19 The question of the dating of Ruth is fraught with difficulty. Two main dates are suggested; that of the Davidic period, which is in line with the setting of the book by the internal dating of the period of the Judges; and that of the Exile, in which case there is a deliberate archaising on the part of the writer. The relevant issues here are dealt with in detail in Sasson's work. See Sasson, J., *Ruth*, Sheffield, Sheffield Academic Press, 1995, pp. 240-252.

20 The subject of patriarchy and its effect on social images of men and women and on the imaging of the deity has been dealt with at length by modern scholarship. It is argued that this form of social organisation was in existence for many centuries in the ancient world and is the setting for the biblical material. See, for instance, Laffey, A., *Wives, Harlots and Concubines*, London, SPCK, 1988. Traces of the social patterns of this system can be detected in the Judah portrayed by the text of Ruth and this will probably have overlapped with the actual historical Judah of the pre-monarchical period, of which, however, little is known from archæology. See here Perdue, L., Blenkinsopp, J., Collins, J. and Meyers, C., *Families in Ancient Israel*, Louisville, Westminster John Knox, 1997.

Ruth for confirmation of a male dominant social system – after all, it is in an all-male forum that personal fates are decided".[21]

Reading the book from this perspective requires the reader to set the narrative of the women's actions within the patriarchal frame in which female interests are subordinated to those of men.  The centre of the plot structure, here, would be the continuity of the *beth-ab* (father's house).  Elimelech's sons should have carried on the ancestral line but though married they are childless.  Naomi's outburst in the road to Judah scene fits this social pattern since women have no role in such a society without male support/issue.  Naomi sees herself as empty, without social value, and with little self-worth.   She names herself 'bitter' because the deprivation of husband and sons comes as a bitter destiny from God who is in charge of all.  Ruth's 'clinging' to Naomi, a phrase, which is employed in Genesis chapter two for a marriage between husband and wife, enables the two women to set about completing the family line.  Ruth's willingness to risk gleaning in the field, where she could so easily be assaulted by a man since she has no male protector of her own, leads to her being described as a woman of strength (*issah hayil*) by Boaz.

It is this display of strength and courage, in her care for her mother-in-law, which recommend her to Boaz as a woman worthy of notice; thus the plot can roll on.  Contact with Boaz leads on to Naomi's planning and Ruth's arrival at the threshing floor.  The details of that scene are not fleshed out in terms of the intimate relations between Ruth and Boaz, but it is clear that Ruth here acts the part of a seductress, attracting Boaz to her side.  Thus Boaz finally acknowledges his role as kinsman and in the Gate scene takes up the kinsman's function of ransoming land.[22]  He combines this with the role of husband.  It appears that the text is here drawing on the law of levirate marriage – that if a man dies without issue his brother shall marry his widow and raise up a child to ensure the survival of the dead man's name.  This law is at the heart of the plot structure of the story of Tamar and Judah in Genesis.  Tamar is cheated of her levirate marriage and uses seduction of her father-in-law to restore her family rights and produce a child for her dead husband.  This is a move accepted by the narrator in Genesis as profitable because of its value for the family and Ruth may be presented in a similar light here.

---

21  Greenstein, E., *Reading Strategies and the Story of Ruth*, in Bach, A. (ed.), *Women in the Hebrew Bible*, London, Routledge,1999, p. 223.

22  There appears to be, behind the text here, a legal requirements for the nearest kinsman to redeem branches of the extended family group from debt slavery and parallel situations. With regard to Ruth see Sasson, J., *Ruth*, pp. 228-230.

However, the matter is not simple because Ruth does not in fact produce a son for Mahlon, in the story, but for Boaz. Obed is described as Boaz's son. Also the child is given to Naomi to nurse as its 'mother' but there is no mention of a memorial for Elimelech here. The stress on continuing a man's line is somewhat blurred here – a fact which has led to much scholarly debate as to the goal of the plot structure of Ruth at this point. Jack Sasson, for instance argues against levirate marriage as a shaper of plot,[23] whereas Rabbi Alshich argues that it is a matter of setting up a levirate arrangement.[24] Michæl Goulder explains the confusion by arguing that the plot sequence in Ruth acts as a commentary on, or exegesis of, some laws in Deuteronomy.[25] Whatever the position taken on this topic it is still the case that Ruth's actions contribute to the continuance of the Father's House and result in the future birth of a great king. Harold Fisch argues that the book of Ruth centres on "the opposition of family continuity/discontinuity".[26] Greenstein concludes that "the tension is restored through the female protagonist's taking matters into her own hands".[27]

Whereas the Old Testament tends to frown on women's use of their sexual powers and to regard these as dangerously subversive to proper family and social order, in a few narratives the position is reversed. The woman acts as a seductress but that is acceptable behaviour – Ruth and Tamar are examples here. The reason for the acceptance is because the use of sexual power does not serve to empower the woman herself, but, within the plot sequence, is harnessed to the overall needs of the patriarchal group. Brenner remarks that Ruth sets out to fill in the need for husband and children.[28] The plot deals with the success of her venture in which she chooses a victim with an eye to his social standing. However, Naomi, a respectable older woman, is the matchmaker here and her aim is to repair the breach in the social fabric of her husband's house caused by the deaths of her sons. Ruth and Naomi know, according to Brenner, "that if their plan fails society may reject, and even persecute, them for their attempt to ensure an orderly functioning of that same society through the production

23  Sasson, J., *Ruth*, p. 135.
24  Alshich, M., *Ruth, A Harvest of Majesty*, p. 279.
25  Goulder, M., *Ruth: A Homily on Deuteronomy 22-25?*, in McKay, H. and Clines, D. (eds), *Of Prophets' Visions and the Wisdom of Sages*, Sheffield, Sheffield Academic Press, 1993.
26  Greenstein, E., *Reading Strategies and the Story of Ruth*, p. 220.
27  Greenstein, E., *Reading Strategies and the Story of Ruth*, p. 220.
28  Brenner, A., *The Isrælite Woman*, p. 119.

of suitable heirs.    This kind of motivation and the extreme actions it requires is approved of, even admired."[29]

It may be that this patriarchal perspective on Ruth should be seen not just as a viewpoint in operation generally in ancient Judah but, more specifically, in relation to the dating of the book.    For the second line of thought on dating, as opposed to post-exilic inclusion of foreigners, is that the text is Davidic propaganda.    In this approach Ruth comes from an earlier period and serves to bolster David's claims to kingship in Israel.    The critical element here is the genealogy at the end of the book.    The argument would be that the rest of the narrative serves to explain the meaning of that genealogy with respect to David's role as king of all-Israel.    Through the names in the list David can trace his descent back to Abraham, founding father of Israel.    Ruth's role in this is that she signifies the inclusion of Ammon and Moab in Israel; David can rightly claim authority over these societies, argues Greenstein: "David, in his person, therefore, incorporates the various peoples he governs.    Their blood runs in his veins.    He is the one person who can legitimately reign over them all."[30]    The structure of events in the story of Ruth not only mirrors the needs of a patriarchal society it also serves the interests of one particular male leader whose political aims are enhanced by having Ruth the Moabitess in his baggage train.

Both 'foreign convert' and 'patriarchal woman' models of reading are connected to the theme of *hesed*, a term which expresses the quality of loyalty to contractual relationships.    The agreement made between God and Israel at Mount Sinai, for instance, involves loyalty to divine will on Israel's part, and loving protection on God's part, in providing food for his chosen community and in fighting their wars.    The term can be seen at work, in Ruth, in the narrower social setting of family life.    Ruth acts with *hesed* in chapter one by clinging to Naomi, and this is noted by Boaz in chapter three, when he speaks of her former kindness.[31]    In chapter three, also, Boaz praises Ruth for her kindness, now, to him in not preferring a younger man as husband.    Some scholars, such as B.M. Vellas, have suggested that this portrayal of family loyalty (or *hesed*) is a key element in the plot structure of Ruth.    The stress is on the appropriate responses of loyalty between members of a kinship group, each showing a generous response to another's needs.

---

29  Brenner, A., *The Israelite Woman*, p. 108.
30  Greenstein, E., *Reading Strategies and the Story of Ruth*, p. 216.
31  Chapter 3 [10].

However, the loyalty of God lies behind these family expressions of *Hesed*. Boaz blesses Ruth, in the field scene, because of her kindness to Naomi and prays that God will deal well with her since she has sought protection in the land where he rules as local deity. The use of the phrase "the Lord, the God of Israel under whose wings you have come to take refuge" in Ruth chapter two (verse twelve) is reflected in the threshing floor scene where Ruth asks Boaz to stretch out the "wings of his skirt" over her. Thus Boaz himself becomes the medium by which God's *hesed* reaches Ruth and then Naomi. When Boaz acts as Redeemer in the gate scene he performs an act of loving kindness inspired by the deity. In this reading of the plot, despite the hard message of the opening events, the strings of action are pulled by a benevolent deity who watches over a family to preserve it. As Gow suggests "there is an interweaving of prayer and providence, of the divine activity with human agency. So the divine will is accomplished in, and together with, God's people."[32]

All these readings of plot and meaning, illustrated above, are positive readings; they enhance the moral vision of the reader and offer paradigms for behaviour in which the social role of the individual, in contributing to the healthy state of the kinship group, is paramount. Individual interests are subsumed to the good of the whole group. Acts of *hesed* are not without long-term consequences, for the balancing quality with kindness is redemption. It is because of Ruth's loyalty to Naomi and of the two women's interaction that salvation in the form of food and offspring becomes available. They are redeemed from the social evils of widowhood and barrenness. Thus, despite the tragic opening, with its progress from fullness to emptiness, from life to famine and death, emptiness is not the final mood of the story of Ruth. The final message is fullness – in food and in children. The story can be defined, then, as a comedy.[33]

## Reading the Story of Ruth

The reading strategies outlined above arise from reading the text as a whole, which entails reading synchronically, at one go, with pauses for reflection on terms or meaning patterns which link individual sections of text together. Although the plot is formed of individual scenes these build up a coherent, developing story. The major scenes of the book – the journey to Judah, the field, the threshing floor and the gate – contain a great

---

32  Gow, M., *The Book of Ruth*, Apollos, 1994, p. 116.
33  Gow, M., *The Book of Ruth*, p. 112.

deal of dialogue and it is through those dialogues that the plot is developed.
Ellen van Wolde's commentary, *Ruth and Naomi*, offers the reader a tool
for reflecting on these major scenes.[34]  Van Wolde focuses on the major
public episodes in the book and offers the reader, in each case, a variety of
responses to the events in the story on the part of different characters.  In
this manner she seeks to illustrate the complexity of individual responses to
situations and the interplay of variant individual understandings of the
importance of a series of events.  At the same time she inserts an extra level
of meaning by writing monologues for the characters at key points in the
story, thus providing an additional narratorial voice.  The meaning, which
is added by this literary device, has a specific content in that it deals with
the role of the foreigner in a community.  As the story of Ruth unrolls and
with van Wolde's commentary written in, the reader becomes more
attentive to the ramifications of insider/outsider relationships.  Overall van
Wolde's account argues for the positive effects of a foreigner's contribution
to a settled community.

The journey back to Judah is presented first through Naomi's
perspective as the complaining mother-in-law; her gaze is a hopeless one.
Van Wolde imagines a further speech on Naomi's lips here: "I wouldn't
wish my life on anyone . . . I married very young . . . we were happy, but
the times were against us . . . we went away, we had to . . . Suddenly, like a
sledgehammer, the hand of YHWH struck me . . . since then my hope has
vanished; I have no future."[35]

This response sits alongside that of Ruth.  Ruth does not 'sit down'
under destiny's hand.  She wants to act, to accompany Naomi even against
Naomi's wishes.  Her view is represented, by van Wolde, 'in her own
words': "I read and saw around me that some people make more of their
lives by having the courage to undertake something and to run risks."[36]
The juxtaposition of these two reactions to a difficult event offers the
reader a choice of interpretation of life's meaning.  Within a social network
there is no one response to events – different voices offer competing
analyses.  It is through community that richness and plurality of meaning
can be found.  In this case the combination of Naomi's hopelessness
leading to a return to Judah, and Ruth's enthusiasm for life enables the plot
of Ruth to move on into an uncharted future.

As the story progresses so the response of individuals shifts ground.
Naomi, for instance, comes to see the value of Ruth who is prepared to go

34  van Wolde, E., *Ruth and Naomi*, London, SCM Press, 1997.
35  van Wolde, E., *Ruth and Naomi*, pp. 15 f.
36  van Wolde, E., *Ruth and Naomi*, p. 23.

alone into the field for food for both women. Van Wolde writes, "I have to confess something. I thought that this woman...was just like these other foreigners. But I was wrong . . . She's a good exception."[37] As more characters enter the story the variety of response expands. Thus Boaz finds that the appearance of Ruth touches his own existence. He notices her, standing on her own. Van Wolde says "I thought 'What an attractive girl!'".[38] He makes sure that the young men do not molest her and gives her food from his own hand. Van Wolde imagines his thoughts: "Leave that child alone, I told them . . . yes I'm becoming a real old bore . . . I'm not her anxious father . . . a little later I ordered my servants . . . deliberately to let some barley drop for this woman. They couldn't believe their ears . . . the boss has gone crazy."[39]

But Ruth finds that the field experience challenges her choices and values made previously, in a different way, according to van Wolde: "Sometimes I feel one with the family and clan of Elimelech, and then again I think, What am I doing here? . . . it's as if the whole problem of intercultural relations was being fought out in me".[40] Thus the field scene is a part of the plot which acts symbolically in interpreting community values through persons' responses to it. The field itself is a community event – gleaners, reapers, household members all relate to one another in the act of harvesting, looking, working, sharing food and drink. For Boaz this is a place of security, which opens out to new understandings of the self through extending friendship to a stranger. For Ruth it is a place of danger and risk where all may be gained or lost. She needs secure protection: that of the boss would be best but it is only a temporary relief since the field is a seasonal site of community. Ruth needs a more permanent community network to belong to. Yet it is the field which is the entry point to this goal.

In the night Ruth comes to Boaz at the threshing floor. Although this is a public place Boaz sleeps in a private spot. The scene turns on the interaction of just two characters, Ruth and Boaz. This is the climactic scene for Ruth the Moabitess. She has come so far on her own initiative and now she is pushed along, by Naomi's planning, to risk all that she has gained in terms of a social reputation of worth. The scene on the threshing floor is make or break for Ruth and also for the plot line of the narrative. The progress of the tale to a successful completion whereby the interests of

37  van Wolde, E., *Ruth and Naomi*, p. 35.
38  van Wolde, E., *Ruth and Naomi*, p. 48.
39  van Wolde, E., *Ruth and Naomi*, p. 48.
40  van Wolde, E., *Ruth and Naomi*, p. 63.

the major characters are secured turns on events at this point.   Here, suggests van Wolde, Ruth is forcing Boaz to make a choice by her request: "Perhaps this is just what a foreigner does: confronts one with the other in all her or his nakedness and shows one that one has to make a choice."[41]   In the sequence of events it is, rather, Naomi who forces Boaz's hand.   Ruth 'remarks' in van Wolde's account that "I was well content . . . but Naomi had changed . . . she saw a new future dawning and devised a dangerous plan . . . and here I was going through the fields on tiptoe . . . There is no way except to go on the way."[42] Ruth's daring to risk all on one throw, on one action, is matched by Boaz's generous response, as van Wolde notes: "That someone dares to offer herself in that way, without any masks . . . without status and without being backed up by anyone else, has moved me deeply . . . I'm changed.   I too want to show other people my strength by daring to be weak."[43]

The scene at the threshing floor employs the most intimate of social relationships, that of two people intensely committed to one another, to offer a broader comment on the value of community.   This relationship of Ruth and Boaz balances that of Ruth and Naomi and overlaps with it.   The social fabric is constructed around close personal ties, which are themselves undergirded by legal bonds – the relationships caused by marriage – mother-in-law, daughter-in-law, wife, husband.   The union of two persons in such a relationship is not an insular affair but reaches out to engage other community members.   By the end of the book the inhabitants of Bethlehem, men and women, are brought into the picture, blessing and rejoicing at the creation of new and strong social ties within the local community.   The privacy of two people within the public space of the threshing floor is symbolic of the need in community for intimacy.   It hints at the need for a private level of community existence within family or household, as well as the busy-ness of the bustling harvest field or the solemn gathering of elders for the judgement of local affairs, at the gate.

At the other end of the story the gate represents a parallel symbol for community values.   Here, too, a public space operates as the setting for community relationships.   But this is a setting for men alone – a community of males decides the future of the women.   As the story line has moved on so has the understanding, which Boaz has concerning his life and its meaning.   The planning of Naomi and the courage of Ruth have led to the threshing floor and to Boaz's commitment to Ruth.   Van Wolde writes,

41   van Wolde, E., *Ruth and Naomi*, p. 78.
42   van Wolde, E., *Ruth and Naomi*, pp. 80 f.
43   van Wolde, E., *Ruth and Naomi*, p. 90.

"Boaz is a man who is strong but at the same time subtle in his actions in the gate. He remains within the limits of the law, but also manoeuvres skilfully."[44] Boaz intends to marry Ruth but the unnamed kinsman has the nearer claim to act as ransomer of Naomi's claim to land which belonged to Elimelech. Boaz leads the kinsman on to claim his role as Redeemer only to confront him with the need to take Ruth along with the land. This would not be profitable at all and so the kinsman retires from the scene. Boaz's schemes mean that the final scene will be that of the marriage of Ruth and Boaz, a happy ending after all! Van Wolde comments, "The book is very like a game of Stratego. Three eminent strategists are competing in the field of life."[45] Ruth is the most enterprising and responsive character in meeting life's challenges with positive enthusiasm for moving into unfamiliar, but eventually rewarding, relationships. Naomi, too, gradually develops more resilience, in response to Ruth's own daring. Boaz is the stable, enduring strong man of life, secure in his own position and wealth. But he, too, meets a challenge, enters into a new relationship and engages in strategy to secure that relationship. The plot of Ruth thus interacts with the development of the characters. Each movement of the plot allows the characters to engage with and learn from each other, thus bringing about action to move the story on again.

At the end of the book the plans of all three characters come together to create a single social reality, that of marriage and birth. Boaz 'comments', according to van Wolde, "Ruth has shown me how boundless love is for Naomi . . . I've come to look through Ruth's eyes . . . as if our God is dependent on human frontiers! . . . Ruth is different . . . through her, the song of loneliness has fallen silent for ever in me".[46] The neighbours in Bethelehem add to that meaning. Naomi is once again full and can rejoice,[47] and Ruth is given her full value as a member of the social network, worth more to her mother-in-law than seven sons.[48] It is through the intermingling of character and plot that the story provides its message for the reader about a vision of community.

44  van Wolde, E., *Ruth and Naomi*, p. 98.
45  van Wolde, E., *Ruth and Naomi*, pp. 99 f.
46  van Wolde, E., *Ruth and Naomi*, pp. 105 f.
47  Ruth 4 [14-15].
48  Ruth 4 [16-17].

**Wider Issues: Community as Cosmos**

Community interests in the book of Ruth produce a common set of values but these are constituted, at the level of individual scenes in the narrative plot, of differing opinions and contrasting voices: Naomi as despair and Ruth as hope, for instance, in chapter one. It is possible to go a stage further here and to view community as a world, which has its own system of values. In this reading, community serves to offer the reader a cosmos to belong to. Women readers of Ruth have noted that this story offers women a world of their own where women's values can be assessed and explored. In the Old Testament, where so many stories are about men, here is a tale whose lead figure is a woman in relationship with women. This world of women may be set inside a male framework but nevertheless it can be explored in its own right.

Phyllis Trible, for instance, includes an account of Ruth in her book *God and the Rhetoric of Sexuality*. She points out that Naomi and Ruth struggle for survival in a patriarchal environment; bearing their own burdens they work out, together, a way to stay alive. In the story of their endeavours, symbolically, it is the women who live and become full persons, whereas men die and are non-persons.[49] Thus Naomi, Orpah and Ruth all have names and voices in the text but Elimelech, Mahlon and Chilion die without voice and the nearer kinsman is left nameless. When men join themselves to women, as Boaz does in field, threshing floor and gate, they promise life and they achieve life through a woman's aid.[50] Mieke Bal notes, in relation to Hugo's poem on Boaz, that in this version Boaz faces his impotence and childlessness. By using that perspective Hugo "changes the story of Boaz's generosity into that of Ruth's generosity, and he changes the very meaning of the concept: while Boaz gave what he possessed, Ruth gives what she *is*".[51] Thus, for Trible, the book is "a comedy in which the brave and bold decisions of women embody and bring to pass the blessings of God".[52] At the heart of this drama "one female has chosen another female in a world where life depends on men".[53] This harmony among females marks out a distinct pattern of living and a distinct value-system, according to Brenner: "Naomi

49  Trible, P., *God and the Rhetoric of Sexuality*, London SCM Press, 1978, p.168.
50  Trible, P., *God and the Rhetoric of Sexuality*, p. 178.
51  Bal, M., *Heroism and Proper Names, or the Fruits of Analogy*, in Brenner, A. (ed.), *A Feminist Companion to Ruth*, Sheffield, Sheffield Academic Press, 1993, p. 46.
52  Trible, P., *God and the Rhetoric of Sexuality*, p. 195.
53  Trible, P., *God and the Rhetoric of Sexuality*, p. 173.

and Ruth function harmoniously as a team. Whatever the internal shifts in the balance and power may be, they are in the struggle for survival together and they co-operate."[54]

Cheryl J. Exum raises the question of how far this harmony among women goes.[55] Working from a painting in an art gallery in Liverpool, which shows Naomi and Ruth in what appears to be an intimate embrace, she raises the question of gendered relationships. Such a posture would indicate to many viewers rather the partnership of Ruth and Boaz than that of Ruth and Naomi. Yet the painting is faithful to the plot of the narrative, where Ruth clings or cleaves to Naomi since this is the term for marriage in Genesis chapter two and so can be presumed to imply an intense friendship between the two women. Exum's investigation takes the harmony between two women to the further level of a social world where women supply emotional support for one another. Exum refers to modern American writers who use the relationship between Naomi and Ruth as a model for same sex female relations. In *Fried Green Tomatoes at the Whistle Stop Café*, "when Ruth decides to leave her abusive marriage, the text of Ruth 1[16-20], the biblical Ruth's stirring oath of loyalty to another woman, is the sole content of the letter her modern namesake sends to Idgie to declare her love".[56]

Whether either Naomi or Ruth love one another is not dealt with in the biblical text but the parallel relationships – Ruth and Naomi, Ruth and Boaz – allow for a blurring of modern clearcut assumptions concerning gender and role boundaries. In the book of Ruth, Ruth is husband and son to Naomi as well as daughter-in-law, wife to Boaz and mother to Obed, while Naomi is mother to Obed as well as mother-in-law to Ruth. Boaz aligns himself with the women as an honorary female when he seeks to fulfil their designs in the scene at the gate, thus subverting the redeemer system in connection with Ruth's future and the unnamed kinsman. Exum argues that "by destabilising our gender categories", "the book of Ruth, like Calderon's painting with which I began, invites readers to collapse the gender distinctions with which they themselves operate".[57]

In this way the 'cosmic' view of a social world, as an entity with clear-cut boundaries, is challenged by the level of community interests in the text. Jon Berquist raises parallel issues in *Role Dedifferentiation in the*

---

54 Brenner, A., *Ruth and Naomi*, in Brenner, A. (ed.) *A Feminist Companion to Ruth*, p. 83.
55 Exum, J.C., *Plotted, Shot and Painted*.
56 Exum, J.C., *Plotted, Shot and Painted*, p. 142.
57 Exum, J.C., *Plotted, Shot and Painted*, p. 174.

*Book of Ruth*.[58] He uses as a reading tool the concept of role blurring "the undoing of prior patterns and role definitions, resulting in a condition of less structure".[59] In Ruth this process can be perceived in the changes that occur following the famine crisis. Naomi is left totally bereft of a social role, she is a subject of role death, as a childless widow. Ruth responds to the crisis by picking up and interchanging roles. She is daughter-in-law but adds the male role of 'cleaving' as husband and, since Naomi accepts her loyalty, Naomi now has a son in Ruth also. But the future needs to be secured so Ruth adds the social roles of gleaner and seducer, with Naomi as matchmaker. These are all temporary roles but social stability is finally restored by Boaz's voluntary decision to act as Ruth's husband. Berquist argues: "Boaz the husband creates a long-term relationship between Boaz and the women that grants them society's greatest guarantee of economic and social security."[60]

In all these processes gender roles are continually deconstructed and differently applied. Berquist notes that "the deconstruction of gender empowers and enables, eventually resulting in the solution of the story's original problem".[61] This account of the shifting of social roles offers an image of the survival of the family and indicates the particular means by which it is effected. People have to step outside their normal social roles and function beyond the usual social boundaries if society is itself to survive. Once the breach in social order has been repaired those same people can once again take up mainstream social roles for their ordinary place in community.

All these readings have, variously, tended to view the text of Ruth as reflecting positive aspects of community. Kindness, generosity, loyalty, courage are key social qualities manifested by persons in the story. But, most recently, the shadow side of this tale has been examined. Van Wolde points out, in her projection concerning Naomi's thoughts in chapter one, that it is for Naomi's benefit that the daughters-in-law, the foreigners, be sent back so as not to embarrass Naomi when she returns to her homeland.[62] Silber remarks of this same section of the narrative that "Naomi is not presented as acting out of love for Ruth".[63] For Bonnie

---

58  Berquist, J., *Role Dedifferentiation in the Book of Ruth*, in Exum, J.C. (ed.), *The Historical Books*, Sheffield, Sheffield Academic Press, 1997.

59  Berquist, J., *Role Dedifferentiation in the Book of Ruth*, p. 84.

60  Berquist, J., *Role Dedifferentiation in the Book of Ruth*, p. 93.

61  Berquist, J., *Role Dedifferentiation in the Book of Ruth*, p. 95.

62  van Wolde, E., *Ruth and Naomi*, p. 16.

63  Silber, U., *Ruth and Naomi: Two Biblical Figures Revived among Rural Women in Germany*, in Brenner, A. (ed.), *Ruth and Esther*, p. 47.

Honig, writing in *Ruth, the Model Emigree*, Ruth is always a foreigner, sacrificed to the interests of the host culture.[64] Naomi can be re-integrated into Bethlehem society, Boaz is after all her relative, but "Ruth's fate is different because Bethlehem positions her and Naomi asymetrically in relation to their losses . . . Ruth's loss of Orpah-Moab cannot even be articulated as such. Ruth's mourning of Orpah is forbidden for the sake of a regime's stability and identity."[65]

This is a post-colonialist reading in which the interests of Moab as a minority culture within the text can be expressed. The model immigrant serves the interests of the host community and is then forgotten. In the last chapter it is Naomi whose fullness is hymned and Ruth's role is as servant to Naomi's need. Honig claims that "the Israelites need Ruth's foreignness to shore up their identity as a Chosen People; but that identity is also deeply threatened by her foreignness".[66] This viewpoint is in contrast with the interpretation that it is a cosmos of women's sisterhood, across national boundaries, which can be found in Ruth. In that approach, as Carol Meyers argues, the interaction of women's networks is vital to the life of agricultural, rural society: "The tendency to relate 'formal' with 'important' and 'informal' with 'unimportant' does not do justice to the dynamics of informal alliances; and it occludes the way women's networks perform essential social and even economic tasks."[67]

More negatively, Ruth and Naomi operate in a multi-cultural world where women's relationships mirror the tensions and the inequalities of social standing among the members of society as a whole. Laura Donaldson comments on these women, in the setting of the assimilation of conquered cultures in the Americas. From the view of Moab/native American Indians she asks "is there no hope in the book of Ruth? Is it nothing but a tale of conversion/assimilation and the inevitable vanishing of the Indigene in the literary and social text?"[68] Hope is found in an odd place, if the text of Ruth is read from a more traditional, Europe-centred view. Whereas the text discards Orpah who is not able to move across frontiers into an alien culture and endorses Ruth who is prepared to make

---

64  Honig, B., *Ruth the Model Emigrée: Mourning and the Symbolic Politics of Immigration*, in Brenner, A. (ed.), *Ruth and Esther*.

65  Honig, B., *Ruth the Model Emigrée*, p. 73.

66  Honig, B., *Ruth the Model Emigrée*, p. 74.

67  Meyers, C., *Women of the Neighbourhood (Ruth 4¹⁷): Informal Networks in Ancient Israel*, in Brenner, A. (ed.), *Ruth and Esther*, p. 117.

68  Donaldson, L., *The Sign of Orpah: Reading Ruth through Native Eyes*, in Brenner, A. (ed.) *Ruth and Esther*.

the change, now hope is found in Orpah. She is the one with the courage to resist the lure of the master-culture, who holds by her own foreign ways, who returns to the *beth-immah* (her mother's house). Donaldson states: "To Cherokee women, for example, Orpah connotes hope rather than perversity, because she is the one who does not reject her traditions or her sacred ancestors . . . Orpah chooses the house of her clan and spiritual mother over the desire of another culture."[69]

## Cosmos, Community and Person

Once more all three levels of cosmos, community and person work together. The identity of Ruth, Orpah, Naomi, and Boaz, as persons, turns on their social roles, their contributions to society and so on community values. The complex inter-relationships of these characters, worked out through events in the plot, produce different attitudes to the place of persons in community and shows that community is a rich and subtle reality, constructed of many small pieces. These pieces, or social functions, can and do, shift when events press down on society, in a social crisis such as a famine, for example. In turn the shifting of roles can produce challenges to accepted 'cosmic' or 'world' views. New social patterns challenge the fixity of cosmic norms and require the reader to think deeply about the particular moral vision which she or he holds.

In Ruth, God is found in, and through, the shifting dynamics of human society. If God is behind and within these shifting networks then the question can be raised as to what sort of deity presides over events. Is this the secure deity of the clan/kinship network, 'Our God'? Or is it the public, political deity of the male-dominated culture? Or of the colonial master-culture? Or the quiet, behind-the-scenes, yet socially effective deity of women's sisterhoods? Or does the cosmic level here embrace all of these approaches and include other interpretations yet to be explored by the future, as yet unthought of, commentaries on the book of Ruth? Is there room for the interpretations and the commentaries, which will emerge from the reading of the text by persons in a new and different social system, for the interpretations of those who perceive some points of contact between their culture's approach to the content and significance of community and the pattern of social relationships imaged within the plot of this narrative?

---

69 Donaldson, L., *The Sign of Orpah*, p. 141.

# Chapter Six

# The Story of Joseph

The book of Ruth shows how an individual's behaviour relates to a community's existence. Ruth, although a foreigner, helps build the Davidic line of descent and so endorses the value of Israelite culture. The story of Joseph which begins in Genesis chapter thirty-seven is that of another individual whose career benefits the wider social group of his own kin and validates its religious and social values. Like Esther, Joseph rises to great power at a foreign court and exemplifies good relations between the social worlds of two separate nations – in this case, Egypt and Israel. In both works, also, the emphasis is on the hero's salvation of his or her own people from annihilation, in this case from famine and starvation.

In Joseph's story also, as with Ruth and Esther, God takes a back seat as a character and does not directly drive the sequence of events. At the end of the narrative the reader may look back and detect that the God of Israel has presided over affairs, that the 'hand of God' has intervened in human life, but God himself is not someone who has major speeches or obvious actions to perform. One example of this is the phenomenon of dreams in the story. In the ancient world context, dreams were thought to have an origin in the sphere of deities and spirits so it could be argued that the God of Israel organises events by sending dreams to key figures, such as Pharaoh, and then providing a ready made interpreter in Joseph.[1]

A further point of contact between Joseph and narratives discussed in earlier chapters is that of literary genre. Joseph is another instance where potential tragedy has an up-turn, which transforms it into comedy. There are several disastrous plot lines in the story. The rivalry between siblings at the start of the narrative threatens Joseph with death and leaves his father in grief for twenty-two years. Joseph's brush with Potiphar's wife again threatens Joseph with potential death and lands him in prison. The outbreak of famine threatens Jacob's household with death. Yet, in each of

---

1 Although dreams could be messages sent from a number of deities, usually a particular dream came from the patron deity of the recipient. In this case, however, Joseph's speech to Pharaoh underlines the fact that the dream comes not from the gods of Egypt but from the God of Israel, indicating that deity's control of affairs across the whole region. For more information on the social value of dreaming in the Ancient Near East see: Cryer, F., *Divination in Ancient Israel and its Near-Eastern Environment*, Sheffield, Sheffield Academic Press, 1994, Husser, J.-M., *Dreams and Dream Narratives in the Biblical World*, Sheffield, Sheffield Academic Press, 1999.

these mini-plots comedy prevails. Jacob's grief will turn to joy when Joseph turns out to be alive. From prison Joseph arrives at the heart of royal power by interpreting Pharaoh's dream and the famine is the cause of the reunion between Joseph and his brothers. In the wider plot line of Torah, Joseph provides the means by which Isræl will grow into a nation, finding safety for the time being in a foreign land.

## The Story of Joseph

Joseph's story can be described as a small section of a larger story, the narrative cycle of Jacob. The story of Jacob has gone from his birth and will extend to his death. Joseph in Egypt is an excursus to this narrative flow and, indeed, Joseph's story returns the reader to Jacob for the last few chapters of Genesis. If the story of Joseph is read individually then the question arises as to whether there is one story here or several different ones. Commentators have regularly noted the unity of the narrative, its progression from an initial problem through growing tension to a resolution and ending.[2] But there are traces of seams in this story. A major example of this is the scene in which Joseph is sold to traders. In one version the brothers sell Joseph to traders and, in another, one set of traders pulls him out of the cistern and sells him to a further commercial group. It appears that there were at least two versions of this scene in the plot available to the writer who wove them together.[3]

At the same time the unity of the story leaves gaps and silences with regard to the motivations of characters and to why certain events happen as they do, leaving the final level of meaning to be decided by the reader. As Gabriel Josopovici has pointed out, that leads to different and even opposing meanings of the role of Joseph – as virtuous and merciful, with regard to his brothers and Mrs Potiphar, or as smug, flirting with sexuality,

2  This approach implies that the story of Joseph be read as an independent story and not simply as the last scene in the story of Jacob. The narrative is too developed and balanced within itself to be the work of rough editing: see Westermann, C., *Genesis: A Practical Commentary*, Grand Rapids, Eerdmans, 1987, pp. 256-258.

3  It is clear from the story that two versions of Joseph's sale as a slave exist in the text. In one account the brothers sell Joseph to the traders and, in the other, one set of traders sells Joseph to the others without the brothers' knowledge. In the first version the brothers know that Joseph is not dead, while, in the second, they do not know what has happened to him, he has simply vanished. At a later stage in the story, the scene in Potiphar's house is well enough developed to represent an independent story, which has been embedded in the final narrative by its writer.

and bearing a grudge.[4]   These variant readings of the textual message clearly impact on the moral vision of person and community encountered in this narrative.  To give two examples of variant perspective on the story, it is possible to look to the comments by Moberly and Josopovici.  For Moberly Joseph is an exemplar of worthiness and piety, a model family member.[5]  But Josopovici raises the question as to whether Joseph does not in fact remain, throughout the story, complacent and self-centred.[6]  In a complex mixture of these opposing views it may be argued that the stress falls on the public face of Joseph's career in this story, where he is indeed the source of salvation for his people.  There is less need for his inner life to be thoroughly virtuous and disinterested in this line of approach since what matters is the effect of external actions on the workings of society.

## Meaning and Narration

In the last chapter the reader's attention was drawn to the manner in which the development of plot, a series of inter-connected scenes, gives rise to moral perspectives on human activity.  The scenes themselves develop meaning in the narrative by revealing what happens when several characters inter-act both in action and in speech.  What occurs is a complex series of events, which presents the characters with important decisions regarding their own behaviour.  The manner in which the narrator of the plot tells the story of these events shapes the reader's understanding of the value to be attached to human behaviour and its social effects.

The issue of fraternal rivalry, for instance, has been dealt with in earlier sections of Genesis, as in the Cain and Abel scene, but so far no solution to the problem of social rivalry has been produced.  White comments that "in the Joseph narrative the problem of rival brothers is placed on centre stage and explored in depth.  One reason for this may be the unprecedented critical problem posed by sibling rivalry to the transmission of the promise which must take place here at the end of the patriarchal history."[7]  Since Joseph and his brothers together inherit promises made originally to only

4   Josopovici, G., *The Book of God*, Yale University Press, 1988, throws doubt on the role of
    Joseph as an ideal hero in connection with his responses to his brothers in Genesis chapter
    45. See esp. chapter four.
5   Moberly, R., *Genesis 12-50*, Sheffield, Sheffield Academic Press, 1992, p. 33.
6   Josopovici, G., *The Book of God*, p. 84.
7   White, H., *Narration and Discourse in the Book of Genesis*, Cambridge, Cambridge
    University Press, 1991, pp.238 f.

one brother, in each generation the socio-moral question arises as to the precise manner in which such a process could occur. Jacob's favouring of Joseph then marks the opening of a story, which can deliberately explore social matters relating to the foundations of the community of Israel as one people before its God.

The fact that this matter is socially highly charged and difficult to resolve is highlighted by the final scene between Joseph and his brothers in Genesis chapter fifty. They finally dialogue with him as brothers to one of their number but their talk is all about distrust among siblings and fear of attack. A social boundary is made within which the brothers can feel secure by the calling on the name of the father for protection of sibling rights. Joseph's rejection of any revenge for past hurts may settle this fear of social fragmentation for the time being but the shadow remains since it is has been necessary to invoke the dead father at all.

Within the boundaries of the father's house the story has explored these social issues of moral perspective by interweaving scenes set within completely different households: that of the foreign official; that of the prison in a foreign land; that of a royal court at the heart of a nation. Within these settings, a tension can be found in the narrative. In some places, the narrator offers the view that events have a deep and positive value, as when it appears that God is with Joseph in Egypt and is moving his life along purposefully, and, in some places, offers no comment on events from a cosmic viewpoint. These last scenes are places where the human beings in the text, and the readers, must fend for themselves in putting meaning into life's affairs, as in the initial scenes of the story.

The narrator leaves gaps and silences which the reader must endeavour to fill in order to clinch the meaning of the text.[8] In Genesis chapter forty-two, for instance, Jacob fears to send Benjamin to Egypt with his older brothers – why? Is it due to fear of the external dangers of distant travel, the attacks of animals and thieves, the residue of the loss of Joseph, or, is there a hint that Jacob does not trust his older sons, even if only for their not taking sufficient care of a brother? The reader feels the echo of twenty-two years before in present events. In a second instance, when the brothers arrive in Egypt, Joseph, watching them bow down, remembers the dreams of his youth and is sad. Immediately he tells them: "You are spies!" – why? Is it because he sees a need to jolt them into facing their own past or is it because he seeks revenge for his own hurts? Joseph's insistent

8   Brenner, A. and van Heuten, J., *Madame Potiphar through a Culture Trip, or, Whose Side Are You On?*, in Exum, J. C. and Moore, S. (eds), *Biblical Studies: Cultural Studies*, Sheffield, Sheffield Academic Press, 1998.

questioning of his brothers has multiple layers of meaning.[9] For the brothers it remains mysterious since this is the act of a stranger, a man of power whose whims one does not understand, or query too much! The reader is empowered by the knowledge that the brothers lack, that Joseph wants to know about his own family. But why? Is it simple curiosity or is Joseph afraid that the brothers will have killed off Benjamin as well as attacking himself?[10]

These gaps and silences in the scenes relating to Joseph and his brothers open up, for the reader, the possibility of examining deep issues concerning family matters. The reader shares Joseph's own perspective as he overhears his brothers debate their past actions; the role of Joseph and that of narrator come together temporarily. The reader is thus invited to stand in Joseph's shoes and to take up an opinion on the appropriate response to be made by one brother to his siblings. More than one response could be put forward here and these allow for variant social and moral approaches to the basic issues of how a household of father and sons can operate internally.

Embedded in this over-arching narrative regarding Joseph is a story, which, in turn, raises social issues regarding household affairs. In the story of Joseph in Potiphar's house it is not a question of father and brothers but of one adult male in another man's house. The scenes between Joseph and Mrs Potiphar explore the social issues created by this kind of community living. What is the appropriate behaviour for a person who exists in this social niche? The story, here too, leaves gaps and silences which balance against the explicit and obvious. Mrs Potiphar is explicit in her speech to Joseph and Joseph's response, too, may appear to be clear-cut in terms of direct speech. But there are ambiguities in the story. Why, for example, did Joseph go into an empty house given his knowledge of the woman's desires and her sexual harassment of him? Could it be that he secretly entertained the idea of assenting to a relationship only to flee away at the last moment, when he realised the enormous social consequences of such a liaison?

The story of Joseph's actions in this scene is told twice, once by the narrator and once by Mrs Potiphar. The two tellings end by confronting the reader with opposing interpretations of the roles of Mrs Potiphar and

---

9   Genesis 43 [7].

10  One major suggestion about the context of Joseph's behaviour here is that it is connected with the appearance of only ten brothers and his fear that Benjamin has also been disposed of by them. See Sternberg, M., *The Poetics of Biblical Narrative*, Bloomington, Indiana University Press, 1985, pp. 289 f.

Joseph, a device which highlights the ambiguity of social actions in themselves. Going into a room, handling clothing, are actions capable of sending more than one social message and of being given more than one rating in terms of their effects on a community of people.


## Reading the Story

By reading the story of Joseph as a whole, the reader arrives at an understanding of the flow of the plot, building up meaning by the succession of scenes and the interplay of characters therein. It is from within this synchronic act of reading that the different levels of moral vision within the narrative emerge. In a text which is structured around repetitions of motifs such as clothing and dreams but which leaves many connections between events to the reader's imagination; divergent interpretations of human behaviour are likely. By examining two separate readings of the story made by recent commentaries the reader can discover the variety of possible meanings.

Robert Alter, in his commentary on the book of Genesis, establishes the base line of the story in Joseph's bad relationships with members of his household of origin. He notes Joseph's insalubrious profile as a tattle-tale against his brothers and one who is "self-absorbed, blithely assuming everyone will be fascinated by the details of his dream".[11] It is largely Joseph's own anti-social behaviour which leads to action against him. His isolation is emphasised by the ornamented coat, which Jacob gives him, since this gift makes the gap in esteem among the brothers so obvious. Thus Joseph presents a profile of a not very pleasant young man and offers a negative moral vision of impending social disunity.

Joseph's lack of depth and sensitivity produces hatred and fear among his brothers, inducing their act of fratricidal crime in plotting to kill him. Here the family as a supportive community falls apart, with the result that the inner moral strength of the unit is sapped. Joseph's supposed death, the brothers' crime, festers at the heart of family life for the next twenty-two years. Dramatic irony in the story line, the gap between Joseph dead and Joseph a member of Egyptian society, underlines the shadows on community and person and forms a backdrop to Jacob's intense grief. Alter comments that "all this language of mourning and grieving suggests a certain extravagance, perhaps something histrionic . . . at the very moment

---

11  Alter, R., *Genesis*, pp. 208 f.

Jacob is bewailing his purportedly dead son, Joseph is sold into the household of a high Egyptian official".[12]

The house of Potiphar offers one kind of entry to a 'foreign world' but prison proves to be a safer social context. Prison also reminds the reader of the earlier incarceration of Joseph by his brothers. Joseph calls prison a pit:[13] Alter notes that "twice he has been put into a pit for what he must feel is no good reason".[14] It is a moot point whether Joseph learns social prudence and gains moral vision of his role in society while in these two incarcerations. Although it is possible to apply to him the words of an Old Testament psalm as the one who is cast down to the depths, acknowledges his suffering and turns to God as the boundary marker of order in existence and source of hope for a renewal of life.[15]

Thus Joseph languishes until eventually the cup bearer recalls his power to interpret dreams. Alter remarks on the significance of the term 'remembering' at this stage in the plot. The cup-bearer 'remembers' Joseph, thus paving the way for his release and aggrandisement. When the brothers come to Egypt for food, Joseph recognises (remembers) them, thus creating a narrative link with Jacob's recognition of Joseph's bloodstained garment years before. As Alter notes, "when he sees [his brothers] again after more than twenty years of separation, this same crucial verb of memory, *zakhar*, will be invoked for him".[16] This leads Joseph to an elaborate testing of his brothers which causes them to own their own dark memories and their past deadly actions. In this manner the festering family sores will finally be healed.

For the brothers *do not* remember Joseph; they fail to recognise him, thus opening the way for a play on the theme of memory and its contents. Alter writes: "There is surely an element of sweet triumph for Joseph in seeing his grandiose dreams fulfilled so precisely, though it would be darkened by his recollection of what the report of his dream led the brothers to do."[17] Joseph's harshness to his brothers thus carries ambiguous

---

12 Alter, R., *Genesis*, p. 215.
13 Genesis 40 [15].
14 Alter, R. *Genesis*, p. 232.
15 It is possible to interpret Joseph's feelings in the prison as picking up on his feelings in the first pit, which the reader discovers from the brothers' speeches and which were full of pain and fear. This mood is echoed in the lamenting psalms of the Old Testament while Joseph's ultimate trust in God as the redeemer of dangerous situations also finds expression in the book of Psalms. Moberly here attaches Psalm 19 [21] to Joseph's attitude while in prison (Moberly, R., *Genesis 12-50*, p. 34).
16 Alter, R., *Genesis*, p. 233.
17 Alter, R., *Genesis*, p. 246.

tones – is he taking his revenge for his own sufferings?  Or is he using harsh measures to jolt his brothers into recalling their sorry past so that unfinished family business can be sorted out once and for all?  Either interpretation is possible for, according to Alter, "it is only now, not in the original report, that we learn that Joseph pleaded with them when they cast him into the pit, a remarkable instance of withheld narrative exposition".[18]

As the story turns back to its beginning, Jacob's grief for Benjamin mirrors his extreme sorrow over Joseph.  There is, for Alter, "an ironic disparity between Jacob's sense of a world of predictable dangers, threatening his beloved son, and Joseph's providential manipulation of events, unguessed by his father and brothers".[19]  For, in the long run, mercy and forgiveness dominate over grudge and painful memory.  The weeping of Jacob is balanced by the weeping of Joseph as he overhears his brothers' debate on their own careers and the flaws of their past behaviour.  Tears now become healing, as Joseph finally declares himself to his family and seeks reunion with them.

Whereas Alter's commentary focuses on Hebrew language and its narrative power, Westermann's commentary has as its goal the highlighting of broader social and cultural issues.[20]  He begins by noting that the story of Joseph, like other patriarchal stories, is about family and kin and, as Joseph is the last in the patriarchal cycle, the story "represents the transition from family history to national history".[21]  Thus a story of sibling rivalry reflects larger social questions relating to the pattern of power in a state or kingdom, according to Westermann.  "How is it that a man can lord it over his brothers?"[22]  As a literary family opens up to contact with the outside world, this is mirrored in the two locales of the story, home and royal court in a foreign kingdom.

While the gift of the coat to Joseph is a turning point in family life because it makes a special treatment of a sibling a matter of the public domain, dreams are a second source of rivalry and Westermann sees this motif as relating to the future of Israel.  Joseph does not just divine his social future, his dreams work to point forwards to the 'national condition'

---

18  Alter, R., *Genesis*, p. 247.
19  Alter, R., *Genesis*, p. 251.
20  Westermann, C., *Joseph: Studies of the Joseph Stories in Genesis*, Edinburgh, T&T Clark, 1996.
21  Westermann, C., *Joseph: Studies of the Joseph Stories in Genesis*, p. ix.
22  Westermann, C., *Joseph: Studies of the Joseph Stories in Genesis*, p. ix.

to come.[23] Hence the tension between the terms brother and lord. Brother here indicates a social relationship among men of a given family, not an emotional link. "On the one hand this membership carries with it the right to a protected place at home and in the family. On the other hand, it also implies the obligation to stand up for the family if the need arises."[24] Thus rivalry is an acceptable part of a scene in which brotherhood is a legal and social bond but there are boundaries to sibling envy beyond which hurt is done to the society at large. Joseph's story explores these boundaries. Reuben's and Judah's part in the brothers' debates concerning the fate of their young sibling explore the functions proper to elder brothers with regard to family responsibility. Judah later atones for his guilt here by taking the lead in supporting family solidarity before the foreign official, when he tells the tale of their family problems to the unrecognised Joseph.

As the story moves to Egypt, Westermann notes that "in the world of this story, important processes and changes are . . . to be read . . . in the open displays that come about in the common face-to-face displays between one person and his fellow".[25] Thus Mrs Potiphar's desire is told not through her inner emotions but through her blunt statements to Joseph in the public sphere. It is in this same public world that Joseph rejects her, since she is the property of his master, one who has favoured him, practically, by giving him the freedom of the house. Here Joseph honours the common male social bond of honour among 'equals'.

Joseph finally enters fully into the alien society, becomes an integral part of a foreign culture and its leadership. Joseph acquires an Egyptian name and an Egyptian wife,[26] but, domestically, he remains an Israelite, as

---

23 The Commentary on Genesis made by Westermann and his study of Joseph both emphasise the duality of the text, dealing both with family and national business. This mixture is to be read against the backdrop of the manner in which the Hebrew Scriptures came into being. The story of Joseph would have been written in the post-exilic world, which already knew that Israel had been a nation. From this perspective the story functions to explain the development of the ancestral past and would have made sense to a reading community which were living long after the events dealt with in this story.

24 Westermann, C., *Joseph: Studies of the Joseph Stories in Genesis*, p. 12.

25 Westermann, C., *Joseph: Studies of the Joseph Stories in Genesis*, p. 23.

26 When Joseph is given an Egyptian name this signifies, in the cultural world of the Old Testament, a real shift in his inner identity, since names carry the true inner value of a person. Joseph here moves culture and becomes capable of dwelling in a foreign culture not as a resident alien but as a full social member. If this text was created in the post-exilic world of the Jewish diaspora this element indicates the possibility of his remaining Jewish whilst also being integrated into a host culture politically and economically. Within the text the motif serves to underline Joseph's place at the heart of the Egyptian court.

evidenced by the names given to his children.[27] Ultimately these two strands, Joseph as son of Jacob and Joseph as vizier in the Egyptian state, come together as the famine bites and Jacob's other sons come looking for food. In all the following scenes a great paradox is at work. Those who are brothers and equals in a family context, moved by glimpses of a great court, bow before their own sibling, unwittingly, while Joseph maintains publicly the social distance proper to a great official and yet, in his own private space, grieves over his family of origin. For the brothers it is this experience of being powerless before the powerful state, which leads to a re-appraisal of their own family relationships and the burden of sin/guilt, which they carry. Westermann notes that "they find a meaning in their anxiety, a meaning that they can also relate to that anxiety, and that is the fear of death. They once plunged their own brother into this fear; now the same pitilessness that they once showed him is crushing them."[28]

This is the crux, the beginning of resolution of the plot. From this change in the brothers' attitudes, overheard by Joseph, comes a newly sorted family. The holding of a meal to welcome the brothers on their second journey to Egypt reflects the recreation of a family. For Westermann, "the fracture and healing of a society, which is the point of the Joseph narrative, receives a particularly strong and clear expression in this little scene . . . [Joseph's] emotion points more clearly than could any words to that which is the main point – the wholeness of a society and what that means for those who belong to it".[29] In this way a family of semi-nomadic pastoralists is re-united while, at the same time, the separate social worlds of migratory households and settled farmers and urban dwellers are brought together. Joseph has bridged the social worlds of family and state and now enables a pastoral household to live within a settled, ordered, social system.

## Community and Person

These two readings highlight different aspects of the story. Alter illustrates the complexity of the narrative in itself, while Westermann dwells on its social messages. A comparison of the two styles, however, reveals common elements in the area of a moral vision of the relationship between

27  Westermann, C., *Joseph: Studies of the Joseph Stories in Genesis*, pp. 58 f.; also Alter, R., *Genesis*, p. 242.
28  Westermann, C., *Joseph: Studies of the Joseph Stories in Genesis*, p. 68.
29  Westermann, C., *Joseph: Studies of the Joseph Stories in Genesis*, p. 79.

community and person. The two are, for instance, forever intertwined. Joseph may live hundreds of miles from his own community, may have entered a second community, and many years may have passed, but his life is intimately linked with that of his kinship group. Joseph's success is completed when he is re-united with his kin. Their destiny, likewise, is dependent on the brother whom fortune has cast out of the father's house. Neither Joseph nor his father and brothers can be healed as persons until the ancient rupture of the family unit has been overcome. Moreover it is in these areas that the cosmic dimension must be located since God does not appear directly in the story. Family order can be said to mirror the cosmic order, which is made plain by the balanced operation of a narrative that moves between the rupture and repair of family harmony.

## Plot and Houses

It is now possible to look more closely at some of the major scenes, which mark the movement of the plot in order to explore these issues of community and person with regard to the moral vision of family existence. From the readings of the story presented above it can be seen that critical scenes, which shape the narrative, take place in a house or household. This scene-setting mirrors the social issues with which the text is concerned, for what are examined are the complexities of behaviour patterns among members of different household units or communities. It is, therefore, pertinent to examine these key scenes in relation to the varieties of perspective, which they can offer on social, moral vision and ethical behaviour. To that end the following sites will be investigated:

> The father's house.
> Outside the father's house.
> In Potiphar's house.
> House of prison: house of Pharaoh.
> The house of Joseph.

## The Father's House

The role of the father's house is to set out a stable foundation from which matters of family loyalty can be explored. The major issue to be explored by the story line is clearly the complexities of social behaviour among a father and his sons.  Here the reader is dealing not with a modern nuclear family but with a large household composed of one male and his several wives and their offspring.  The male head of house holds together a range of human beings, on equal terms, since all are equally dependent on the one male for the establishment of social order in their community.  However, within this ordered social world there is room for jostling by sibling rivals for their father's notice.  In Genesis chapter thirty-seven this unease among brothers is heightened by the behaviour of the father and the young son.  It is not surprising that Jacob would be especially attached to a son born in his old age, evidence for a line surviving beyond the procreator's death.  But the matter becomes problematic when Jacob takes practical steps to elevate Joseph above his brothers.  Claus Westermann notes that "the storyteller's perspective of Jacob's favoritism is utterly free of criticism".  He adds: "Instead, the fault should be located in the fact that Jacob's special love for Joseph is openly proclaimed in the form of [a] gift."[30]

The gift is a special garment, of whose nature scholars are not certain though it is agreed that it denotes high social status because it is worn by a princess in the second book of Samuel, chapter thirteen.[31]  In this manner Jacob has changed the social relationships of his sons; Joseph, it seems, is to be given power and authority over his brothers.  Here it is important to note the value attached to dress in the ancient world, as indicating a person's social and political role in a community.  In Joseph's story, dress issues come up, significantly, several times.  His superior dress, now acquired, will be stripped from him when his brothers relegate him to the pit.  Clothed again, in Egypt, Joseph is once more stripped of clothes and status in the flight from Mrs Potiphar.  Ultimately he puts on the royal ceremonial robes, which mirror his role as second-in-command to Pharaoh.  According to Matthews: "Clothing and other forms of personal adornment have an important function in every human community . . . in the Joseph narrative, clothing or the lack of it provides one of several structural elements.  An *inclusio* is formed by the two investiture ceremonies (when Jacob gives Joseph his robe and when the Pharaoh vests him in robes of office)."[32]

30  Westermann, C., *Joseph: Studies of the Joseph Stories in Genesis*, p. 5.
31  The style of the garment has been much discussed.  Did it have long sleeves, was it made of vertical stripes as an Egyptian painting of Canaanites might suggest?  It becomes a royal dress through the Tamar link.  Cf. Alter, R., *Genesis*, p. 209, and Matthews, V., *The Anthropology of Clothing in the Joseph Narrative* in Rogerson, J. (ed.), *The Pentateuch*, Sheffield, Sheffield Academic Press, 1996.
32  Matthews, V., *The Anthropology of Clothing*, p. 355.

As a result of the gift, the text is full of socially fragmenting terms – hate and jealousy. The brothers cannot offer a sign of peace to their sibling. Moral matters, here, are made up of a community's social network and they involve realistic questions of social power and the access to it of a younger generation. In the household the father controls all; to 'get on in life' a son must have a share in that power through the bond between father and son. Many sons may be the source of major social problems since only one can inherit the head of household role.

## Outside the Father's House

While all the sons are under the same roof their behaviour is held in check by the presence of the patriarch. But when they come together in the out-of-doors the rage and frustration can emerge and spill over into violence. In Genesis chapter thirty-nine the action moves outside. The geographical distance created here allows for a social distance, which makes it possible for the brothers to act on their own authority. From a distance they identify their hated rival, the master of dreams, wearing his badge of office. What they see is not their blood brother but the improper social pretensions of a younger son and it is these that they attack.

Their response, nonetheless, focuses on a brother's life and so everyday sibling rivalry spills over into fraternal crime. In plotting to kill Joseph the brothers threaten the order of household society whereby all are ultimately members of a single kinship with the duty of maintaining the life and security of fellow members.[33] The enormity of the crime is evidenced by the reactions of Reuben and Judah, both of whom try to lessen the crime from direct death – to imprisonment (Reuben) and to slavery (Judah).

Now the real cost of sibling rivalry must be born. The actions of the brothers mark all the actors in the drama. Joseph faces death and then a life of slavery far from his home. Jacob faces a life of enduring sorrow, permanently short of his son. The brothers cannot even own their action for what it was and so find remorse and forgiveness. They and their father are now sewn into a life of deceit. The social order is twisted from its

---

33 Clearly many of the Old Testament narratives and legal codes relates to family matters. Ruth explores the role of the *goel*, the kinsman who should legally take care of land and property issues for the widowed. The law of Levirate marriage forms the setting for Genesis chapter 38. The Abraham cycle shows not only the tensions between kinsmen over land use but also the responsibility for saving a relative from slavery and death, in Genesis chapter fourteen.

proper shape and cannot be restored. Yet this is an event, which could easily occur in a large household. White points out that the narrator has set out all these complexities of social action without creating obvious heroes or villains: "The actions of each [side] are both understandable and reprehensible so nuanced is this brief description of the 'generations' of Jacob. The effect of this form of narration is not to evoke the identification of the reader with one party against another, but to convey a fundamental instability stemming from communicative alienation and unbalanced, obsessive passions."[34]

## In Potiphar's House

The narrator moves next to the career of Joseph, who is established "in a role which he is to play consistently", says White. Here Joseph acts "as the solitary hermeneut, who exists between alienated realms of discourse and social positions, such as between Potiphar and his wife . . . between the royal court of Egypt and Semitic tribal life . . . between the role of tribal patriarch and that of national king".[35] His solitary career will in the end provide a means for bringing his two homes, that of Jacob and that of Egypt, into social dialogue with one another. Although Joseph is a solitary Semite in a foreign culture he is not unaided. For the narrator informs the reader that YHWH, the God of Israel, is with Joseph, aiding him and blessing all those who look favourably on him. This is the first explicit reference to the cosmic level of affairs; its introduction may imply, for the reader, that some over-arching plan is at work and that the household strife recently witnessed is not just a murky human muddle.

If Joseph is helped by a male deity, he is hindered by a human woman. The narrator states that Joseph was beautiful, but this description is not introduced for its own sake. Rather, it provides the context for the following statement, that Mrs Potiphar cast her eyes on him. Westermann remarks that "in the Old Testament beauty is always more of a process than a static quality. Human beauty is always seen primarily as something which becomes significant in relationships between people."[36] In this scene it is the social value of Joseph's beauty, which is a key item since it provokes Mrs Potiphar into an anti-social action. From the perspective of the male narrative voice this position places Joseph in jeopardy. He is in

---

34  White, H., *Narration and Discourse in the Book of Genesis*, p. 242.
35  White, H., *Narration and Discourse in the Book of Genesis*, p. 240.
36  Westermann, C., *Joseph: Studies of the Joseph Stories in Genesis*, p. 24.

danger of creating social chaos here, just as his earlier actions brought trouble to another household. However, the surface level of the text underlines Joseph's integrity. He refers to social honour and shame in a household context and refuses to lie with his master's wife. When the story climaxes it is because the woman lays hands on Joseph and not the other way round, thus turning the woman into a force for chaos and Joseph into a champion of proper social behaviour and true moral vision.

In response to this textual explanation of the social roles of male and female within the household, Alice Bach points out that the narrator places responsibility for social disorder on the female rather than on the male.[37] The woman is consistently undervalued as a human person here. She is never given her own name but identified only as X's wife, a code endorsed by Joseph's attitude to her as his master's wife. Bach argues that the woman deserves to be named and thus given a personal identity.[38] Then the feminist reader can begin to search for signs of this character both in Genesis chapter thirty-nine and in later literature such as Rabbinic Midrash and the Joseph Sura of the Qu'ran. In seeking to understand more about Mrs Potiphar, Bach argues, the reader "risks being assigned to the ranks of the disloyal and the unfaithful. The story of Mut-em-enet reflects the fate of such a woman. The narrator underscores the uncertainty of her position through the tepid response of her husband . . . in my view the universal story and its expansions reflect a desire to enclose women's uncertainty in an image of woman as only the specular reflection of man."[39]

## House of Prison: House of Pharaoh

But Joseph has found favour with the God of Israel and so danger is a form of safety.[40] Joseph has upheld the male social code and is now freed from hassle and, indeed, exalted to a place of authority in the prison. The prison is a bridge in the text transferring Joseph from one Egyptian household to another, greater one. The link here is clearly that of dreaming. The cosmic level of meaning comes into play here since Joseph does not learn the skill of dream interpretation from a human teacher, as the wise men of Egypt do,

37 Bach, A. (ed.), *Women in the Hebrew Bible*, London, Routledge, 1998.
38 Bach points to the need to name an anonymous woman and takes her term from the name given by Thomas Mann in his account of the story. See Bach, A., *Women in the Hebrew Bible*, Chapter three.
39 Bach, A. (ed.), *Women in the Hebrew Bible*, p. 126.
40 Alter, R., *Genesis*, p. 228.

but has it given to him, interiorly, by his God. Joseph can save Pharaoh and the Egyptians, together with his father's house, because of this cosmic intervention in personal and community affairs.

Joseph's ability to act decisively in public affairs is highlighted, in the text, by Pharaoh's seeming diffidence. Unable to understand his dream he seeks an interpreter; having been given a clear warning of the possible destruction of his people he then asks what to do and finally appoints the one who has made the running in this scene, namely Joseph, as his other self. It is possible to view Pharaoh here as the epitome of a good monarch, one who cares for his people and knows a sensible and gifted counsellor when he meets one. Westermann remarks that "a king must be provident for his people and his land; their woe or welfare depend in a great degree on his foresight, decisions and deeds".[41]

## The House of Joseph

For Joseph himself the link with Pharaoh enables the fulfilment of those shadowy foretellings of greatness in his early dreams. Now indeed he is master and all must bow down before him.[42] Joseph takes on the part of wise ruler, wise in the sense of practical administrative skills, preparing people to weather an extended period of crop failure and famine. In this role Joseph becomes a householder himself, acquiring wife and children.

On the surface this series of events connecting the house of Joseph to that of Jacob reconciles all the communities referred to in the narrative: father and son, brother and brothers, shepherds and farmers, patriarch and king. But is the theme of social harmony fully endorsed? A great deal turns on the person of Joseph here. Does Joseph experience inner peace with regard to the past? Eric Lowenthal argues positively that Joseph's false social notions were dispelled in the pit: "From then on he grows in humility and humanity, constancy and diffidence, charity and wisdom."[43] Gabriel Josopovici, however, doubts this style of reading: "Genesis forty-five suggests that Joseph has not really learned anything at all. He is still the hero of his own psycho-drama. He still has in mind those early dreams."[44]

41  Westermann, C., *Joseph: Studies of the Joseph Stories in Genesis*, pp. 46 f.
42  Genesis 41 [43].
43  Lowenthal, E., *The Joseph Narrative in Genesis*, New York, KTAV, 1973, p. 31.
44  Lowenthal, E., *The Joseph Narrative in Genesis*, p. 85.

Although Joseph weeps over his brothers' conversation, is that because of a deep sympathy for the effects on them of their social crime, or because he feels for his own hurts at their hands? It could be that Joseph now owns his social responsibility for healing the inner sorrows of his kin. Lowenthal argues that "it dawns on him in fear and trembling that it is up to him to cause his brothers . . . to repent of their sins",[45] something which is achieved when Judah speaks of Joseph's 'death' and Jacob's grief. In this context sin and forgiveness as social concepts are explored through the members of one household. Here, states Lowenthal, "it is perceived that guilt, punishment and forgiveness have their authentic reality only in relation with the real history of a person and a people . . . it is recognised that in the hidden relation of guilt, punishment and forgiveness there is a power of historical bonding".[46]

Equally possible is the reading that some social ills carry permanent scars and that Joseph takes compensation in the sufferings of his brothers for all that they did to him, stopping short at taking life itself. The crux is what is going on in Joseph's mind, and that is hidden both from the brothers and from the reader. As White says, "the dynamic for the reader changes . . . to uncertainty regarding Joseph's motives and purposes".[47] Only after the father's death is it quite clear that Joseph regards his brothers and himself as socially bound to one another in a manner which forbids any other harm being done to those who are so related. The ultimate effect of Joseph's actions, therefore, is to bring about the healing of social fragmentation in the household, and the acknowledgement of unity as a superior value to the forces of social disintegration. Sternberg sums up the scene as follows: "That the sons of the hated wife should have come to terms with the father's attachment to Rachel . . . and her children is enough to promise an end to hostilities and a fresh start . . . but that Judah should adduce the father's favoritism as the ground for self-sacrifice is such an irrefutable proof of filial devotion that it breaks down Joseph's defences . . . one anguished cry about the patriarch draws out another, 'I am Joseph. Is my father still alive?'"[48]

45  Lowenthal, E., *The Joseph Narrative in Genesis*, p. 67.
46  Westermann, E., *Joseph: Studies of the Joseph Stories in Genesis*, p. 87.
47  White, H., *Narration and Discourse in the Book of Genesis*, p. 259.
48  Sternberg, M., *The Poetics of Biblical Narrative*, p. 308.

## Sexuality and the Common Good

Although the scenes concerning Joseph and Mrs Potiphar are a sub-unit in the main Joseph story they have attracted a good deal of attention from readers, ancient and modern.[49] One issue, which clearly emerges from the text as a matter for communal interest, is that of the social role of sexuality. For a modern reader sexual activity may be seen as the prerogative of an individual human being and only secondarily as contributing to wider social systems. This focus on the individual can cause commentators to address mainly Joseph's personal integrity in the scene with Mrs Potiphar but this may be to misread the interest of the narrator.[50] As Westermann remarks, "the conventional commentary on this episode . . . separates the instant of temptation out of the totality of what happened, and creates the fiction that the focus of events consisted simply in the encounter of man and woman".[51]

Westerman argues that sexual activity cannot validly be separated from other kinds of human activity. In this story Joseph's acceptance of Mrs Potiphar's demand would have caused social offence and a fragmentation of the household unit as a social system: "Propriety in sexual matters depends on the strength of non-sexual relationships."[52] Thus the text does not discuss sexual behaviour for its own sake but rather as part of an overall picture of human society whereby a person accommodates him/herself to the social structures of the community.

It is reasonable to reflect here on a person's sense of duty. Joseph refuses Mrs Potiphar because it is his social duty to do so; whether he desires, emotionally, to do so or not does not enter into the debate. Ancient re-tellings of Joseph's story underline this style of moral vision, according to Brenner and van Heuten: "In Jewish and Christian texts of the Roman period, Joseph is a model figure for self-control and self-restraint."[53] Such restraint makes Joseph an ideal person for the community to imitate: "He is used as one of the proofs for Israel's obedience to God and his Torah commandments."[54] In the Testament of the Twelve Patriarchs, a non-

---

49  Brenner, A. and van Heuten, J., *Madame Potiphar through a Culture Trip*, p. 207.
50  Westermann, C., *Joseph: Studies of the Joseph Stories in Genesis*, p. 25.
51  Westermann, C., *Joseph: Studies of the Joseph Stories in Genesis*, p. 26.
52  Westermann, C., *Joseph: Studies of the Joseph Stories in Genesis*, p. 27.
53  Brenner, A. and van Heuten, J., *Madame Potiphar through a Culture Trip*, p. 208; Brenner, A, and van Heuten, J., *Madame Potiphar through a Culture Trip*, pp. 209 f.
54  The Testament of the Twelve Patriarchs may be viewed as either a Jewish text adapted by Christians or as a Christian text with a Jewish foundation, since the work has been preserved by Christian communities. Hollander, H., *Joseph as an Ethical Model in the*

canonical Jewish work, Joseph recalls, at the end of his life, the many trials of his earlier years.[55]  Mrs Potiphar, here portrayed as a beautiful and attractive woman, presents the greatest of these tests.  Joseph's resistance thus becomes 'heroic' and marks him as a man of moral vision suitable for moral leadership.

Some less positive interpretations of the encounter between Joseph and Mrs Potiphar also turn on the issue of sexuality, but here Joseph partially succumbs to desire.  This unchastity, however, is analysed with regard to its social impact.  In Rabbinic texts such as the Midrash Ha-Gadol, Joseph is held to be partly responsible for the threat to social order.  The Midrash expanded the silences in the text of Genesis to point to Joseph's lack of social maturity.  Kugel discusses the fact that "Joseph's guilt was a theme dear to the hearts of the Rabbis who held it as an article of faith that punishment comes about as the result of sin . . . if the story of Joseph presents its hero as thrown into jail on false pretenses then this ordeal must nontheless come about as the result of misdeeds on his part".[56]  The Babylonian Talmud[57] makes the community aspect of this even more evident since Joseph is about to enter into sexual relations with Mrs Potiphar when he has a vision of his father who reminds him of his true cultural principles.[58]  Whether Joseph totally withstands Mrs Potiphar's seduction as a 'foreign woman' or not the issue is the same, namely Joseph as role-model for readers of the text.  As he turns from sexual and social identity with Egypt he does so because he has a part to play for Israel, under the guidance of his deity.  Even his successful career at the Egyptian court is passing glory (*doxa*) compared with his true social and moral identity as a humble servant of the real Lord, the God of his fathers.[59]

Ultimately, all Jewish versions of the story make Joseph into a man true to his kin and culture, despite all threats to this loyalty.  Thus he provides a model of not 'marrying out', a key cultural theme of Jewish family life.  It

*Testament of the Twelve Patriarchs*, Leiden, Brill, 1981, takes the second view while Brenner and van Heuten stress the Jewish nature of the work Brenner, A. and van Heuten, J., *Madame Potiphar through a Culture Trip*, p. 213.

55 Kugel, J., *In Potiphar's House: The Interpretive Life of Biblical Texts*, Massachusetts, Harvard University Press, 1990; Kugel, J., *In Potiphar's House*, pp. 94 ff.
56 Kugel, J., *In Potiphar's House*, pp. 94 ff.
57 Sotah 36b.
58 Hollander, H., *Joseph as an Ethical Model in the Testament of the Twelve Patriarchs*, p. 43.
59 Hollander, H., *The Portrayal of Joseph in Hellenistic Jewish and Early Christian Literature*, in Stone, M. and Bergren, T. (eds), *Biblical Figures outside the Bible*, Harrisburg, Trinity Press International, 1998, p. 250.

is noteworthy, then, that later in the narrative Joseph does indeed marry an Egyptian woman. The expansions of the plot of Genesis offer a social perspective on this anomaly. Joseph and Aseneth was probably written in Egypt, around 100 BC to 100 AD.[60] In the first part of this work the marriage between Joseph and the foreigner is examined in a manner, which claims Aseneth as an 'insider', thus protecting her husband's cultural reputation. Aseneth herself repudiates Joseph as an alien, but, on seeing him, falls in love. Now it is Joseph's turn to reject a union with a cultural alien. He prays to God for the lady and there follows a dramatic scene of Aseneth's remorse for her idolatry and her conversion to Judaism. Thus Joseph is again vindicated as a model of true piety and respect for ancestral values, above matters of marriage and sexuality.[61]

In all these readings of the story of Joseph, the focus for sexual activity is social reality. They are intended to lead the reader to regard sexuality as a social matter first and a personal interest as secondary. Only in Islamic interpretations was a different focus made concerning the person to person aspect of the Potiphar episode. In these versions Joseph and Zuleika (Mrs Potiphar) are both young and beautiful and drawn together by true love. But here, too, a moral vision emerges: not a community model but one, which attaches these two persons to the cosmic level. Brenner and van Heuten point out that "in Sufi mysticism the story of Madame Potiphar and Joseph has come to symbolise a love relationship between the human and the divine. The story has become a religious symbol."[62]

Thus, Joseph, his brothers and father, Mrs Potiphar and the royal court officials and Pharaoh are caught up in a cycle of events whose meaning is only finally revealed in the last stages of the story. The reader is encouraged to read events both as short-term affairs and with regard to their long-term consequences. This is a method of reading, which leads the reader to the understanding that the deeper interpretation of daily living is a matter for ongoing reflection and debate as each sequence of living unrolls and can be viewed after the event.

---

60 Hollander, H., *The Portrayal of Joseph*, p. 251.
61 Brenner, A. and van Heuten, J., *Madame Potiphar through a Culture Trip*, p. 218.
62 The regular presentation of kings in the Ancient Near East as Shepherds makes a further symbolic link with the world of agriculture. In Jeremiah and Ezekiel, for instance, there are references to the kings of Judah as bad rulers who have failed to protect their kingdoms (Cf. For instance, Jeremiah chapter twenty-three). Egyptian iconography shows the Pharaoh carrying a crook as a sign of the royal role of protector of the land and its people; this role is carried out by Joseph in his function as second-in-command to the king.

# Chapter Seven

# The Story of Jonah

The book of Jonah is part of the prophetic section of the Old Testament. A book named for a prophet would usually contain the written oracles of that person, but the oracles of Jonah amount only to five words in the whole book – the prophetic sentence he utters as he walks through Nineveh in chapter three.[1] Yet, in other ways, the text fits into the category of prophecy. It opens, as do other such books, with the word of the Lord coming to a chosen messenger concerning a message of doom, which must be delivered. Here, however, the doom is not addressed to Judah or Israel but to a foreign city, the great city of the Assyrians, Nineveh. Even so this move is not without precedent; in each of the three major books of prophecy there is a section of material called by scholars, Oracles against the Nations.[2] Also, Nineveh was, historically, the enemy of Judah and YHWH could be going to destroy it, as indeed it was destroyed by the Babylonian take-over of the Assyrian Empire.[3] Yet the Oracles against the Nations are 'curse' texts spoken versus an enemy rather than oracles spoken to the opponent, offering the chance of dialogue and change of behaviour.

So the book of Jonah as such is a literary puzzle in the Old Testament. It is even difficult to be sure of the background of Jonah himself though commentators usually make a link with the second book of Kings, where a

1 Although there are many references to prophetic utterance in Jonah, these are largely descriptive of Jonah's task (in chapter one) or reflective of its consequences (in chapters three and four). Unlike other prophetic books, where the material is largely that of actual oracles delivered by the prophet, this book is mostly composed of the story of the prophet rather than his words.

2 Each of the major works of prophecy (Isaiah, Jeremiah, Ezekiel) has this collection of material, with nearly the same content in each case. This close literary dependency indicates a common origin for these texts but there is no extant *Vorlage* known to scholars. These Oracles attack the neighbours of Judah/Israel and would presumably have been spoken within the geographical boundaries of the home community in order to affect the destinies of the nations named from a long distance away. In Jonah there is a clear shift since the prophet takes the message into Ninevite territory thus inviting an historical response from the inhabitants.

3 The Assyrian Empire finally collapsed circa 612 BCE with the fall of Nineveh. For a short, clear account of the background here see Salters, R., *Jonah and Lamentations*, Sheffield, Sheffield Academic Press, 1994, chapter six.

Jonah Son of Amittai prophesied in Jeroboam II's reign.[4] However, there is no clear proof that these two characters are connected, that is that the character in the second book of Kings represents a historical person who is the same man as the Jonah who is a prophet of the Lord in the book of Jonah. Indeed, there are aspects of Jonah's story which point to fiction rather than biography: such as the presence of the fish, the lack of any name for the ruler of Nineveh and the unhistorical size attributed to that city. The story of Jonah can therefore be treated as a Wisdom Story, intended to instruct the reader about knowledge about human affairs. It can also be viewed as a fantasy tale, a story floating free in its own right, to be measured only with regard to its own frame and contents. For, unlike other books of named prophets, the work is mainly a narrative prose account of the prophet's career and not a collection of individual poetic oracles.

## The Story of Jonah

The English version of Jonah usually contains four chapters, each of which relates a separate scene. It would be possible to re-order these chapters as a story in two parts, namely chapters one to two and chapters three to four. This suggests that there are two movements to the story, each beginning with the theme of a divine calling. The elements of each of these two parts can then be viewed as balancing one another. Thus the community of sailors and that of Ninevites are two parallel Gentile groups; the fish and the plant are two parallel aspects of the natural world.

Although these elements are now integrated into a single narrative there are some doubts as to whether they were all part of a single tale originally. The psalm in chapter two has particularly raised questions about textual integrity. There appears to be an incongruity that Jonah praises God for salvation when he is still in the belly of the fish. Moreover there are close linguistic parallels between this song and other songs in the Book of Psalms, as has been indicated by Katherine Dell and James Limburg, for instance.[5] There is also an awkwardness at the start of chapter four where Jonah waits to see what will happen to Nineveh even though the preceding

---

4    Cf. II Kings 14 [23-27]; See here Salters, R., *Jonah*; and Dell, K., *Re-inventing the Wheel: The Shaping of the Book of Jonah*, in Barton, J. and Reimer, D. (eds), *After the Exile*, Mercer University Press, 1996, p. 65.

5    Dell, K., *Re-inventing the Wheel*, refers to the many psalm connections with the text of chapter two. Limburg, J., *Jonah*, London, SCM, 1993, refers to the particular link between Jonah chapter two and psalm thirty.

verses have indicated that he knows that nothing will happen to the city. Despite these problems Jonathan Magonet has argued strongly that the book should be read as a literary whole – a view echoed by Jack Sasson.[6]

If the story is read synchronically then the dynamics of the narrative can be examined. Meir Sternberg, for example, has dwelt on the narrative tension caused by the gaps in the story.[7] The reader wants to know why Jonah flees in the first scene and so reads on and on, for the answer only comes in the last scenes of the book. Even when the gap is filled, this raises further questions, which remain unanswered and leave the reader to complete the story him/herself. Among these are: why was Jonah so upset that God is a compassionate being? Is it because Jonah has been put through such troubles by the plot sequence? Or is it because of wider social issues connected with Nineveh standing for 'them' against 'us'? The uncertainty at the start of the narrative is balanced by the uncertainty of the ending. The plot stops dead without a scene, which definitively reconciles the deity and his prophet. The message of the book is open-ended, therefore, and each reader can close the story line as she or he wishes.

Already there is some relevant material, here, for a discussion of the links between cosmos, community and person. Cosmos and person are the two most prominent areas dealt with in the text, as witnessed by the contest between the human person, Jonah, and the cosmic force, the Lord of Israel. But the matter debated by this contest is in fact one of community. What is God's approach to community, for instance? Does God view Judah/Israel as the only truly valid community because of its knowledge of Himself? Does that mean that there is no authentic existence for another community, such at that of Nineveh? Does Jonah share the divine viewpoint, either of judgement or of compassion?

## The Genre of Jonah

It might be suggested that the literary style of Jonah is that of historical record, but, as was noted above, there are significant problems in the text in this regard. Against the doubts it can be argued that there appears to have

---

6  Magonet, J., *Form and Meaning: Studies in Literary Techniques in the Book of Jonah*, Sheffield, Sheffield Academic Press, 1983. This work represents a major breakthrough in the use of literary criticism as a tool for reading a biblical book. See also Sasson, J., *Jonah*, New York, Doubleday, 1990, p. 19 f.

7  Sternberg, M., *The Poetics of Biblical Narrative*, Bloomington, Indiana University Press, 1985, p. 318 f.

been a historical prophet called Jonah (in the second book of Kings) and that places such as Joppa and Nineveh were real towns. Joppa would have been a port in the eighth century BCE and Nineveh was the city of the Assyrian ruler. On the whole, however, commentators opt for the view that the book is not an historical biography.[8]

If Jonah is not historical record what sort of work is it? It could be described as a fable, that is an account of symbolic events; this viewpoint is reinforced by God's speaking to the fish, which swallows Jonah, and the involvement of animals in the acts of repentance in chapter three. It could be an allegory of Isræl's experience as a society, as Salters remarks: "Jonah represents Isræl, the three days and nights in the fish symbolise the exile, his disobedience the sin of Isræl."[9] It could be a wisdom story told to put across particular instruction. Jonah himself is certainly 'taught a lesson' about answering God's call in the first part of the book, but no one obvious didactic message comes through clearly in the text, as is evidenced by the variety of interpretations which will be referred to in more detail later.

Generally it seems accurate to classify the work as a narrative, thus making a link between it and the books of Ruth and Esther, as well as the story of Joseph.[10] That is, the work is written as a story with a beginning, middle and end; it has a visible plot. Limburg argues with regard to the plot, that the sequence of the story is held together by a series of questions, fourteen in all, which are asked in the course of the tale. It is this use of questions, which not only holds the narrative together, but also gives it direction. Thus, in the first part of the story all of the questions are directed at Jonah.[11] This use of questioning focuses the reader's attention on Jonah himself and on his intentions, just as the questions asked of God by Jonah and of Jonah by his God, in chapter four, highlight the contrasting perspectives of the book on the role of mercy and compassion in human society.

As well as questions there is a great deal of direct discourse in the text – a literary device which enlivens a story by making it possible for the reader or story-teller to take the role of the various characters in the story.[12] R. F. Person has studied the role of discourse in Jonah, coming to the conclusion

---

8   Cf., for instance, Lacocque, A. and Lacocque, P.-E., *Jonah: A psycho-Religious Approach*, University of South Carolina Press, 1990, p. 8.
9   Salters, R., *Jonah and Lamentations*, p. 44.
10  Salters, R., *Jonah and Lamentations*, p. 44.
11  Limburg, J., *Jonah*, p. 25.
12  Limburg, J., *Jonah*, p. 26.

that dialogue controls the entire narrative.[13]   In this regard the book opens with a major dialogue.  God speaks to Jonah and he 'replies' to God by immediately fleeing away.   From this opening dialogue the narrative expands in a widening circle of speech-pairs, returning at the end to a final series of speech and response pairs between Jonah and God.  As the narrative breaks off, the conversation is still in process and could continue further.

Person links these devices to an over-arching literary style of Satire. This literary genre can be found in the selection and arrangement of material, in the narrator's voice and in the narrator's attitude to his material. The overall effect is to make Jonah himself ridiculous and overbearing in his concern to hang on to his own attitudes to community values. Thus by the omission of speech, such as the silence of the text with regard to Jonah's reply to God in chapter one, the way is opened up for Jonah to appear to be 'over the top' in his responses to God in chapters one and three.[14]   Jonah emerges as a stubborn and wayward human being, who stands apart both from God and from the human community whether on board ship or in the great city.

Here Jonah is a parody of the usual prophet of Israel/Judah, who stands with the deity in opposition to his own people, as in the portrayal of the prophet Jeremiah.  The complexity of his character is built up through his dialogue with the deity and the shift from narration to direct speech throughout the book of Jonah highlights the dramatic development of the relationship while calling attention to different points of view.[15]   This reading of the text combines attention to details of individual scenes with establishment of an overall literary perspective on the book, in this instance, satire.

## Two Interpretive Readings of Jonah

Phyllis Trible reads from the viewpoint of rhetorical criticism, looking at the Art of Composition and at the Art of Persuasion.[16]   Trible discusses the symmetry of the text, balancing chapters one and two against three and four

---

13 Person, R., *In Conversation with Jonah: Conversation Analysis, Literary Criticism and the Book of Jonah*, Sheffield, Sheffield Academic Press, 1996, p. 47.
14 Person, R., *In Conversation with Jonah*, p. 153.
15 Craig, K., *A poetics of Jonah*, South Carolina, University of South Carolina Press, p. 65.
16 Trible, P., *Rhetorical Criticism – Context, Method and the Book of Jonah*, Minneapolis, Fortress, 1994.

and showing how parallel units are used in each half. This balance is endorsed by verbal parallels, such as the repetition of the call by God, at the beginning of chapters one and three. But the match between the two parts is not exact, leaving room for the reader to come to his/her own conclusions about the ultimate meaning of the book. Thus in the first part the impending disaster (storm) threatens both Jonah and the sailors, whereas in the second part it is Jonah himself who announces impending disaster to Nineveh.[17] The reader may wish to reflect then on Jonah's ultimate relationship to disasters, which threaten human communities.

From the start of the story the reader is aligned with God's view on affairs since the voice of the narrator is aligned with the divine perspective, reporting God's speech directly but Jonah's only indirectly, thus making the human character distant and diminished.[18] The meaning that emerges here is that God is angry and must be obeyed in the matter of the judgement of evil. Jonah, it appears, cannot agree with that approach to human community. Only at the end of the book does it become apparent that Jonah had correctly gauged God as merciful, and that it was this fact which caused Jonah to default. The reader's sympathies are constantly alerted to God, sailors and citizens as against the prophet himself. There may be an opening for social contact when Jonah makes a confession of faith in a non-cultic setting to non-Yahwistic sailors, in chapter one.[19] But it is easier to find sympathy with the sailors than with Jonah, for they proceed from faith in God to faith in the specific Lord of Israel, whereas the prophet appears to be largely untouched by the progress of events, passively accepting social responsibility for events. The scene with the sailors is balanced by that with the Ninevites, who likewise come across to the reader as a sympathetic community.[20] For they also move to belief – even faster than the sailors– and act appropriately for that belief in their society. Once again the prophet comes off worse, being presented as preferring a community's death than its release from sinful attitudes.

These scenes of ship and city are separated by the psalm from the inside of the fish. This psalm appears to be at odds with the progression of the story, since, for instance, Jonah gives thanks for salvation while still in danger. On a further level narrative and psalm describe different characters. The psalmist thanks YHWH while Jonah defies YHWH to the

17  Trible, P., *Rhetorical Criticism*, p. 117.
18  Trible, P., *Rhetorical Criticism*, p. 130.
19  Trible, P., *Rhetorical Criticism*, p. 141.
20  Trible, P., *Rhetorical Criticism*, p. 190.

end.[21] Yet there is some continuity here in the mood of the prophet. Trible argues that in both the fish scene and in that of the city the prophet is mostly concerned with how life events impinge on himself. "In the belly of the fish he manipulates a testimony of thanksgiving to boast about himself: in the city of Nineveh he manipulates a theology of repentance to justify himself."[22] At neither stage does he truly relate to the actual human group whose affairs form the context for what is happening to him.

The book details a contest between deity and messenger as to the meaning of social existence and, in chapter four, the climax is reached. A balance is offered between the opposing moral visions involved in the contest with thirty nine verses given to God and to prophet. This structure allows each person to place before the reader a view on the meaning for human society of the events in Nineveh. The audience of readers must choose between these alternative moral perspectives, since the narrator does not offer a resolution of the contest. As the text closes structurally it opens out rhetorically, drawing the public assembly of its readership into the ongoing life of the text.[23]

In this context two communities are profiled – that of the ship and that of the city. What is the reader to make of Gentiles? Are they idolaters and evildoers? But that paradigm is challenged since, when the storm strikes, the sailors are more attentive to the divine causation of events than the prophet and also are anxious not to destroy Jonah unnecessarily. When faced with the absolute need to throw Jonah out of the community they accept this behaviour as required by the God whose storm it is. The same flexibility of mind and action can be found in the city. Nineveh is evil by repute but its inhabitants manage to make a positive response to the prophetic message, which has reached them. On both occasions there is a contrast between Jonah's indolence or rigid judgement as an example of poor responses to cosmic level activity and the keen enthusiasm of the human cohorts to search for the true meaning of events. This contrast implicitly offers the reader a moral vision of appropriate community behaviour when faced with cosmic intervention.

Whereas Trible highlights the artistry of the text in structural terms, William Whedbee looks to Jonah as the product of a comic vision.[24] Whedbee is aware that the story of Jonah has its serious aspects, but argues

---

21 Trible, P., *Rhetorical Criticism*, p. 160.
22 Trible, P., *Rhetorical Criticism*, p. 200.
23 Trible, P., *Rhetorical Criticism*, p. 225.
24 Whedbee, W., *The Bible and the Comic Vision*, Cambridge, Cambridge University Press, 1998. Whedbee entitiles his commentary on Jonah, Jonah as Joke.

that its seriousness can be combined with laughter. For him, an over-emphasis on the didactic nature of the work "illustrates once more a superficial awareness of the range and depth of the comic vision which can profoundly engage topics that are 'deadly serious' as well as 'very funny'".[25] Whedbee argues that an examination of the structuring of the plot leads the commentator to regard this work of comic vision as a literary expression of 'The Joke' because an originally simple plot moves into strange twists and turns.[26] Thus, whereas most prophetic stories move from the word of the Lord, 'Go to X and preach Y' to the actual preaching of that word as the completion of the messenger role of the prophet, there is, in Jonah, an immediate negation; Jonah goes West instead of East.[27] But the disobedience of this first movement in the narrative is balanced by obedience in the second movement and, paradoxically, disobedience and obedience both lead to acts of deliverance grounded in divine mercy.[28] Both the sailors and Jonah are freed from pain in the first part – as celebrated in the psalm in chapter two. This is a detour which ends in a fish but the detour is itself part of the plot sequence, adding depth to the meaning of the second part of the story. Whedbee comments that "what illuminates the basic plot is the image of detour in its double sense of deviation and delay, that is, a spatial sense of being deflected from the most direct route, as well as a temporal sense of losing time, of deferred fulfilment".[29]

There is irony in the way in which Jonah sleeps during the storm of which he himself is the cause. In this scene the sailors are shown to be pious and generous in a manner which highlights, satirically, the inadequacies of Jonah's response to cosmic events.[30] The comedy is continued in the fish motif. There exist a number of ancient near-eastern stories of combats between heroes and sea-monsters with which Jonah can be compared. But Jonah does not battle with the fish like the heroes of old.[31] Whedbee argues that "In Jonah's case the manner of ingestion and

---

25  Whedbee, W., *The Bible and Comic Vision*, p. 193.
26  Whedbee, W., *The Bible and Comic Vision*, p. 194.
27  Whedbee, W., *The Bible and Comic Vision*, p. 194.
28  Whedbee, W., *The Bible and Comic Vision*, p. 195.
29  Whedbee, W., *The Bible and Comic Vision*, p. 194.
30  Whedbee, W., *The Bible and Comic Vision*, p. 196.
31  For an account of the mythological motifs used here and their role as archetypal symbols see Lacocque, A., *Jonah*, chapter three. For its relevance to Jonah chpater two see Sasson, J., *Jonah*. For its background in antiquity see eg. Wolff, H., *Obadiah and Jonah*, Minneapolis, Augsburg, 1976.

especially regurgitation finds a ridiculous portrayal that can best be called comic."[32]

The comic mood found in the fish scene is at work in the second part of the story in the rapid conversion of Nineveh, where the reference to the animals appears to underline the comic mood of the work, as Whedbee notes. "The prescribed domestic animals dutifully decked out in sackcloth join their human owners and cry out mightily to God."[33] The Ninevites are then delivered from punishment, in a "wonderful reversal of fortune, presenting another example of deliverance in this comedy of multiple deliverance".[34] Jonah's refusal to accept this eventuality leaves him tied to his own egocentricity. For Whedbee, "the narrator creates a caricature of a prophet, whose parody of famous prophetic words and images intensifies the satirical effect".[35] Jonah being angry – at God, at Nineveh, at the loss of the plant – offers a comment on the paradoxical nature of a person's response to cosmic and community affairs.

God asks whether Jonah is right to be angry – at events, which may have shattered his own sense of control over events and challenged the correctness of his moral vision about the link between actions and their due consequences. Jonah remains sure that his perspectives are appropriate; he shows little sign of changing his attitudes, preferring rather to die! Not that he is choosing death for its own sake, but because that option signals an ultimate challenge to a cosmos, which will not stay stable and predictable. Jonah will simply opt out of such a world. Yet his presence in ship and in city has led many others to opt in, to choose a proper cosmic vision which enables their community to survive – at least for the present.[36] Here is an ultimate moral irony – that a person can offer true vision to a community while himself or herself being locked into a destructive self-identity and into views which could indeed lead to the destruction of those who have shared social relations with him or her.

---

32 Whedbee, W., *The Bible and Comic Vision*, p. 201.
33 Whedbee, W., *The Bible and Comic Vision*, p .205.
34 Whedbee, W., *The Bible and Comic Vision*, p. 207.
35 Whedbee, W., *The Bible and Comic Vision*, p. 211.
36 This is to take as the context the dating of the book as a post-exilic text, since the reader would then know that Nineveh had actually been destroyed after the events of Jonah. That is assuming the events of Jonah are associated with tthe prophet mentioned in 2 Kings. For a short account of the city of Nineveh see Limburg, J., *Jonah*, pp. 39-40 and the bibliography included in the notes to these pages.

## Key Interpretive Scenes

These two readings of the whole narrative have demonstrated that the text contains relevant ideas for the construction of models of community. This community dimension is revealed through the struggle between two main characters, God and his prophet, whose dialogue creates the text. Both societies in Jonah's narrative are at the mercy of this contest. Yet, though community is subordinate at one level to cosmos and person, community comes off well in the end. They are 'pawns in the game' but not treated as soulless objects, discardable, an effect heightened by the role allocated to domestic animals in Nineveh.[37]

These events of struggle for true moral vision, that is true understanding of the world and its affairs, between a God and a human being, are expressed in a few key scenes which are initiated by God's word and which find their climax also in divine purpose. In between the direct encounters of God and Jonah the narrative travels through ship, storm and fish: then through city, plant and worm. Thus the key scenes of the story draw human societies and the world of nature together in a union where weather, seas, creatures and plants are all part of the ultimate society of the cosmos, the created environment.

## God and his Prophet

The first scene of Jonah offers foundational material for the understanding of the entire book. God and Jonah are introduced not in their own right but in relationship to the city of Nineveh and God. The God who appears here is YHWH, the specific deity of Israel who sends messages via his prophets, a paradigm recognisable to the reader from other prophetic material in the Old Testament. The sequence wherein God calls *but* Jonah flees sets the tone for the whole story which will engage in a long debate between two characters as to the fate of communities of other persons.

Human society is dealt with here in relation to God's universal power. There are two poles to community, Israel and Nineveh, which sum up human society as that which is close to God and that which is sinful, with the corollary that Israel and Nineveh are thus enemies of each other. God is the one who determines the value of human society and is a figure who

---

37 Commentators differ in their opinions as to whether the references to the animals are part of everyday culture or a form of satire. See Limburg, J., *Jonah*, pp. 82-3 for a neutral account, Sasson, J., *Jonah*, pp. 254-8 for the view that this is normal cultural usage, Whedbee, W., *The Bible and Comic Vision*, pp. 205-6, for an account of its satirical possibilities.

insists on justice being carried out in human affairs, who attacks evil civilisations. As Limburg argues, "it is clear that for the author of Jonah, the Lord is more than a local or tribal god. The worldwide, ecumenical focus of the book is evident from the first sentence".[38] But Jonah refuses to accept this perspective, expressing his mental reservations about the divine approach to community by his physical act. At this stage it appears that "Jonah is too tender-hearted to carry a message of doom to a great city. He obviously protests against a wrathful God."[39] As Sternberg points out, here the reader is led to form an opinion of God and Jonah by supplying a gap in the narrative, namely what Jonah replied to God's call.[40]

## The Storm and the Ship

Thus battle is joined between Jonah and God and the divine response is not long in coming. God *hurls* a storm at the ship. The anger of God turns against the rebellious prophet in a move which means that Jonah's disobedience has an immediate effect on one particular community, that of the ship. The language of the text draws in even the ship itself, for the term 'threatened to [break up]' attributes a conscious selfhood to the very timbers, just as the sailors 'break up' with fear.[41] As a practical response they *hurl* the cargo into the sea to lighten the vessel. Clearly the term *hurl* and its associations of violence are central to the message here. Limburg describes the chiastic structure of this sequence, where *hurl* is a key term at the start of the action, re-appears in the sailors' behaviour and in Jonah's speech of instruction to the crew, and finally closes the scene when the sailors *hurl* the prophet overboard, whereupon the storm miraculously ceases.[42] Thus the life of this sea-faring community is conditioned by acts of violence mirroring the violence of the cosmos itself.

In the midst of this violence Jonah goes to the depths of the ship and falls asleep. Unlike the sailors he does not cry out to his God to save them. But the community, in the person of the sea captain, engages him in action. Ironically the captain uses the same verb as God had done. 'Arise', he says, 'and call'. Jonah, the individual, now faces interrogation by the group, for the lot falls on him. The community, acknowledging the cosmic

---

38 Limburg, J., *Jonah*, p. 46.
39 Sternberg, M., *The Poetics of Biblical Narrative*, p. 318.
40 Sternberg, M., *The Poetics of Biblical Narrative*, p. 318.
41 Limburg, J., *Jonah*, p. 49.
42 Limburg, J., *Jonah*, p. 48.

origins of the trouble, seek by the traditional means of divination to ascertain the cosmic meaning of events.[43]   Jonah becomes the mouthpiece of that cosmic force: "I am a Hebrew, and fear the Lord, the God of heaven, who made the sea and the dry land."[44]      Thus Jonah's religious understanding brings the community towards a solution to its destiny. Once again a linguistic parallel emphasises the close link between cosmos and community.   We are told that the sailors fear the storm, similarly Jonah, the text says, fears the Lord.  Fear makes a link between nature and human understanding.

Violence and fear dominate community affairs on the surface.  But there is a paradox here.  For the community (of Gentiles) act in an honourable and appropriate manner as opposed to Jonah who brought trouble on them but abandoned them to the consequences until forced to own his part in affairs.  Even when the sailors realise that Jonah is a 'curse' on them they attempt to row him ashore rather than be guilty of his 'innocent blood'. Finally the sailors abandon Jonah to his fate.  Outsider as he has been, so he finishes, on the outside of the community, at the mercy of the cosmos itself.

In all this the Hebrew word *ra* forms a linking chain.  This Hebrew term carries various meanings in English – evil, unhappy, troublesome, for instance.  This variation in meaning is significant in Jonah chapter one. God declares against the moral evil of Nineveh.  The sailors cast lots to discover the source of the natural evil, the storm, which has come on them. The repeated use of the same word joins these plot sequences together but they relate to more than one level of meaning so: "Evil is no longer static but dynamic, constantly changing as does the relationship between characters in the book."[45]   In the ship community it is Jonah who is the focus for evil.  His response to the Lord's declaration against evil has brought evil on his fellow community members.  The community must purge itself, by the ritual act of 'sacrifice' for the guilt it bears through one of its number.

**The Fish**

This context of evil carries further layers as the scene shifts.  The seas themselves, the great deeps, represent chaotic power in Genesis chapter one, and this theme of watery chaos is found in various texts throughout the

---

43  Limburg, J., *Jonah*, pp. 51 f.
44  Jonah, chapter one, 9.
45  Magonet, J., *Form and Meaning*, p.25.

Old Testament.[46] The personification of the chaotic sea into threatening sea-monsters is to be found, for instance, in Job chapters forty and forty-one. But it is significant that God delights in Leviathan in that passage, for it is God himself who, in Jonah, calls up the sea-creature to swallow Jonah and then to vomit him up again. In this sense the fish is a kind of sea-taxi, taking Jonah from ship to shore. But this is not simply a friendly dolphin. When Jonah falls into the sea and enters the fish he engages with chaos and comes to the Pit or Sheol, the realm of the dead.

Jonah is face to face with the forces of the cosmos when he enters the fish. The image or archetype of a hero battling a monster can be found in myths and legends from earliest civilisation.[47] As the work by Lacocque and Lacocque points out, "what is striking about most hero myths is the gruesome and frightening dimensions of their ordeals".[48] By contrast Jonah is at ease in the stomach of the fish, displaying no desire to fight the creature, to cut his way out of the stomach or to chew up the monster's flesh. Instead Jonah prays to God. Though the pain of his recent experiences is echoed in verses three to five, and his present existence in the land of death is recognised in verse six, the overall tone of this song is hopeful.

This is because God, according to the psalm, has already answered the prophet's need and so God is to be praised for saving Jonah. Jonah puts his trust in the cosmic power of God here and thus experiences the fish not as a threatening, uncontrollable cosmic evil but as a place of refuge in which he has access to the divine presence. Thus the fish stomach is a type of sacred space and Jonah links himself with the community of the faithful, those who go to God's Temple to offer sacrifice and to pay vows. Just as the community of sailors promised vows and offerings to the Lord of Israel for their deliverance so, too, Jonah makes promises of votive offerings. In the belly of the fish, then, Jonah acknowledges his position as part of the human community and as a human being under the control of cosmic powers. It is this shift which makes the next scene logical, for God starts

---

46 There is a long tradition in Syro-Palestinian religions of the sea representing chaos, a role found also in Babylonian texts such as the Enuma Elis. For a study of the theme of God's struggle with the sea see Day, J., *Gods Conflict with the Dragon and the Sea*, Cambridge, Cambridge University Press, 1985.

47 Lacocque, A. and Lacocque, P.-E., *Jonah: A psycho-Religious Approach*, p. 53.

48 Lacocque, A. and Lacocque, P.-E., *Jonah: A psycho-Religious Approach*, p. 53.

the story again.  He calls on Jonah *a second time*, to prophesy against Nineveh and this time Jonah obeys.  As Lacocque and Lacocque argue, "the prophet discovers his 'higher morality' and is 'wondrously reborn'. The acknowledgement of his 'higher self' helps him to go to Nineveh".[49]


## The Great City

Limburg points out: "Now the spotlight is on Nineveh, a second Gentile community, parallel to the ship and its crew."[50]  Jonah engages directly in their life, preaching the message: yet forty days and Nineveh will be overthrown.  The Ninevites believe in God, and lament and fast as a sign against Jonah's cursing speech.  Limburg comments on the speed of the conversion here: "Given just a glimpse of the reality of the true God . . . the citizens of Nineveh immediately believe."[51] A second Gentile community has here found religious truth through the presence of God's prophet.  As in the ship the headman takes control on behalf of the community so here the king hears the news and takes charge of affairs, in this case, of repentance. For God may change his mind and avert the violence.

    The reputation of the Assyrians was that they were a people of violence and brutality, but in this scene they stand as a model for positive community behaviour, in response to cosmic decree.  Limburg suggests that "the author of Jonah . . . is shaping the Assyrian king according to the model of Israelite piety", thus indicating the provocative nature of the text.[52] For foreigners operate as a paradigm for the values of the insider-community, and readers may remember, from reading other works of prophecy in the Old Testament, that the home community was not so prompt to obey prophetic words of warning.[53]  Once again Jonah's presence has caused dismay but this troubling of people has positive results in that it promotes proper conduct of human affairs and, in particular, the emergence of true religious understanding.  In the face of this change of heart God also changes.  The angry God of chapter one becomes a forgiving God who decides against violence.


49  Lacocque, A. and Lacocque, P.-E., *Jonah: A psycho-Religious Approach*, p. 51.
50  Limburg, J., *Jonah*, p. 77.
51  Limburg, J., *Jonah*, p. 80.
52  Limburg, J., *Jonah*, p. 83.
53  Magonet, J., *Form and Meaning*, pp. 91 f.

## The Plant and the Worm

Presuming that Jonah fled originally because he did not want to preach doom the reader may now expect the prophet to be pleased and the story to end happily for all. Here comes a surprise reversal. Jonah stands aloof from the city, acting as its judge. Now it is not God who has righteous anger, but Jonah. Jonah is extremely angry; he experiences the reprieve as evil, especially as personal evil for him. That evil which began as the moral evil of the city and moved to the natural evil of the storm here shifts again into the personal pain of one man. Now, at the end, the reader discovers Jonah's original response to God, back in chapter one. Jonah fled precisely because God is compassionate and ready to change his mind about punishing. As Meir Sternberg points out it is not only Jonah who is shaken up but also, and less expectedly, the reader: "This series of informational thunderbolts shatters the entire model of the narrative world and worldview, so that the reader cannot find it easy to get his bearings. Hardly has he recovered from the surprise of God's repentance, contrary to all expectations about the future, when he discovers his readings of the past turned upside down."[54]

Once more Jonah rebels against his God, revealing himself in a poor light as opposed to the Ninevites in their ready response to the deity. What is more Jonah shows himself to be egotistically self-centred in this stand; he would prefer to see other humans die and, indeed, die himself, rather than concede his moral vision that inherently flawed human communities should be destroyed. In the final scene Jonah watches over the city, still hoping to live through its destruction.

It is cosmic forces, which again mediate God to human existence. The plant and the worm, like the sea monster, have mythological echoes within Ancient Near-Eastern literature, as in the *Gilgamesh Epic* where a plant, sought as life giving, is destroyed by a serpent and so lost to the hero with all its benefits.[55] In Jonah, chapter four, the plant stands for the city, but unlike the city, it is destroyed. Ironically, Jonah can feel sorrow for the plant though not for the city which, in divine eyes, is more important. It seems that Jonah's anger comes as a result of his own discomfiture. In the case of the city this is caused by his belief that he has come across publicly as a 'false prophet'. Sasson believes that Jonah is the "victim of a particularly human illusion, that his own imagination and responses cannot be different from God's; Jonah is turning tables on God, forcing him to

54 Sternberg, M., *The Poetics of Biblical Narrative*, p. 319.
55 Lacocque, A. and Lacocque, P.-E., *Jonah: A psycho-Religious Approach*, p. 155.

acknowledge that the dignity of one individual is as precious as the salvation of a whole city".[56]

God now responds to the challenge of Jonah's self-centred anger. According to Sasson the deity uses nature as a means of teaching the prophet that justice and mercy "are not necessarily synonymous in God's lexicon and that no issue can be framed solely in terms of a prophet's personal satisfaction".[57] And there the story ends, with the contest between God and Jonah still unresolved. To the end Jonah is a person who 'rocks the boat' in a group, while thereby bringing about a greater understanding of morality in a cosmic setting, leading the community to peace and safety. He himself, however, is driven by passions to emotional upheavals and clings self-centredly to his sense of his own destiny as a person at odds with the cosmos.[58] Thus God, Jonah and the Gentile communities are sewn together in this book but the relationship is not harmonious since all three levels, cosmos, community and person, pull against one another. Of the three it is community which emerges most positively, finding ground for unity with cosmic power, while person illustrates an inability to change and to develop as a result of being in contact with world and society.

## Wider Issues in the Story of Jonah

Since Nineveh, as a city within the story world of Jonah, stands in conjunction with the historical Assyrian capital, and the passage from the second book of Kings is often viewed by commentators as offering an historical origin for the character, Jonah, it is possible to put this tale back into Judahite history. Assuming that the text is edited (or written) in the post-exilic period raises questions about its message for those citizens in the Judahite province of a great empire concerning their identity in such a world empire, and their attitude to their Gentile neighbours. Here issues of particularity and universalism are significant as well as the knock-on effect of viewing a national deity as the God of the entire cosmos. Since Jonah is accessible, as a piece of literature, to readers across many centuries and from divergent cultures it is also important to ask what meanings, cultural and social, have emerged from the existence of Jonah as a text open to any interested reader. Here, too, matters concerning a narrow understanding of

---

56 Sasson, J., *Jonah*, p. 297.
57 Sasson, J., *Jonah*, p. 316.
58 Sasson, J., *Jonah*, pp. 348 f.

community membership, or the right place to insert social boundaries, have arisen.

## Community of Israel: Community of Nineveh

Jonathan Magonet raises the question as to whether Jonah is set out as a type of the self-contained 'nationalist' or 'particularist', who cannot make community with anyone who is a stranger.[59] The literary relationship between Jonah and the pagan communities of the book is one way of studying issues of boundary crossing. Jonah, it seems, is less likely to cross boundaries between 'us' and 'them' than his own deity who offers oracles of warning judgement against Judah and Nineveh alike, but also respects human freedom to change behaviour patterns, wherever such freedom is found. Yet, it is through Jonah that salvation comes to the outsider, allowing them also to find a way through to true religious understanding.

Whedbee's comments on the nature of Jonah as joke highlight this narrative tension between the insider prophet and the outsider social groups: "The good and generous sailors provide a strongly satiric contrast with the foolish Jonah, who alone knows the will of God even though disobedient."[60] The outsiders show a better religious instinct than the insider. But paradoxically, they need the insider viewpoint to draw that instinct to its true moral vision. It may be that the figure of Jonah is a parody of the 'inclusivist' community, which cannot see any good in the 'outsider'. Whedbee argues for a clear contrast here between Moses and Jonah as models for Judahite attitudes: "Whereas Moses makes positive use of Yahweh's attributes . . . Jonah construes the same categories negatively . . . to undercut God's compassion for a foreign people."[61] God, in playing an elaborate theological joke on Jonah in chapter four, forces the Judahite, through that joke, to move from self-centred concern to an inclusive embrace of the alien 'other'.[62]

As Salters points out, the purpose of the book would then be to announce a message of universalism, namely that the salvation offered to Israel is now extended to Gentiles.[63] Jonah is a dramatic playing through of the theological shift involved in this move from particularist to inclusive

---

59 Magonet, J., *Form and Meaning*, p. 181.
60 Whedbee, W., *The Bible and Comic Vision*, p. 200.
61 Whedbee, W., *The Bible and Comic Vision*, p. 211.
62 Whedbee, W., *The Bible and Comic Vision*, p. 217.
63 Salters, R., *Jonah and Lamentations*, p. 53.

attitudes to human community, based on a shifting moral understanding of cosmic vision. But going for all out universalism may be too simple a reading. As David Gunn and Donna Fewell argue, "is it so clear that Jonah's frustration at God's change of mind is totally unwarranted? . . . a good question, especially when we reflect on that repentance scene . . . it is ludicrous! The overnight conversion of the whole of evil Nineveh – including the animals?"[64]

The reader may agree with Jonah that such repentance is only skin-deep and will prove ephemeral. But Jonah still has to learn a further lesson here. Gunn and Fewell point out that "God's *hesed* displaced his desire for order, re-directing the plot that was set in train by his instinct for justice".[65] In this topsy-turvy world of shifting social and community values a thought has to be spared for the complex issues of moral vision facing the Judahite, and for the bewildering complexity of God's cosmic level of vision.

## The Human Community

As well as discussing particularist issues in the book of Jonah it is possible to argue that the text deals with the subject of community at large – the wide community of all human nations. Integral to this is the issue of theodicy, of God's justice. Divine compassion is set against divine justice. This may link up with the second book of Kings, since there God acted with compassion rather than justice.[66] In Jonah, chapter four, God makes a firm plea to Jonah to accept that compassion is as important as justice and can over-ride strict legalism. It is this divine perspective on community, which the prophet refuses to accept as proper moral vision. The moral issue under debate then turns into the question: "Are God's compassionate ways just?", as Dell states.[67]

The answer to that lies in the nature of the power which controls the cosmos. Can human beings hold the deity to cosmic rules as they have understood them? If God is creator of all then he "owns" all and can choose freely how to deal with each community. Katherine Dell believes that both Jonah and Job are books which deal with matters of cosmic justice, in that the debate between God and Jonah resembles the debate

---

64  Gunn, D. and Fewell, D., *Narrative Art in the Hebrew Bible*, Oxford, Oxford University *Press*, p. 140.
65  Gunn, D. and Fewell, D., *Narrative Art in the Hebrew Bible*, p. 140.
66  Cf. II Kings 14 [25]; Dell, K., *Re-inventing the Wheel*, p. 96.
67  Dell, K., *Reinventing the Wheel*, p. 96.

between Job and his friends on the problem of retributive justice.[68] In this case the two books would be parallel ways of dealing with post-exilic social problems which develop from an increased emphasis on monotheism and the role of YHWH as controller of the destiny of even those communities which act as Judah's oppressors. Thus foreign oppression is used by God to discipline his own, sinful community.[69] There is a corresponding issue of personal integrity for Job and Jonah as they explore the incongruity between beliefs they had held and the reality of experience.[70]

Lacocque and Lacocque focus on this personal dimension. In part two of their work they examine the psycho-theological aspects of Jonah as person vis-à-vis community. In the plot sequence Jonah can be described as trying to find his identity in himself alone, in isolation. But the story continually challenges this attitude to the links between person, community and cosmos. The intimate nature of the link between the individual and the group is reflected onboard ship – where one person can endanger the whole community.[71] The anxiety of the sailors as they throw Jonah overboard likewise reflects the bond between groups and individual. For he is a substitute for them, his imminent death replaces their death, since he functions as a projection of the social group. In a similar fashion Jonah acts as a catalyst on religious beliefs. He is at odds with the ship community and with each social group which he encounters but, paradoxically, wherever he goes everyone converts. Thus Jonah learns that personal growth cannot be achieved without a person being born into the world of community. What matters is what the community expects of the person and not what the person him/herself expects of life.[72] The temptations to run away from social responsibilities and growth can be described as the 'Jonah complex' since the story of Jonah typifies this psycho-social nature of human development.[73]

---

68 Dell, K., *Reinventing the Wheel*, p. 99.
69 This is the usual prophetic view. Thus in the first book of Isaiah, chapter one, there will be war and battle because of the rebellion of the people against their God. In Jeremiah chapter 1 the vision of a pot boiling over from the north links with the description of the prophet as an embattled city or fortress. In Second Isaiah Cyrus of Persia is specifically labelled the leader chosen by God to rule over his people and to bring them peace.
70 Dell, K., *Reinventing the Wheel*, p. 99.
71 Lacocque, A. and Lacocque, P.-E., *Jonah: A psycho-Religious Approach*, p. 86.
72 Lacocque, A. and Lacocque, P.-E., *Jonah: A psycho-Religious Approach*, p. 178.
73 Lacocque, A. and Lacocque, P.-E., *Jonah: A psycho-Religious Approach*, p. 197.

## Nature, God, and Human Society

In the book of Jonah it is noticeable that these matters of person and community are dealt with through the mediation of nature. As Magonet remarks, the reader is struck by the magical stage effects of great fish, magic plant, destructive worm and harsh wind.[74] Yet these devices are not there purely for dramatic effect; rather they lead the reader into a consideration of complex issues concerning the role of God in the cosmos. The storm typifies the timeless power of nature, but in Jonah it is not a random force, but one directed to the specific purpose of preventing the prophet's journey to the west. Likewise the fish acts as the partner of the storm in the entreprise of returning Jonah to his task. The plant and the worm are similarly joined in the activity of changing Jonah's moral perceptions, though here one attacks the other.

But the reasons which the deity has in using these natural elements are not always fully declared by the narrator. Trible argues that alongside the dominant testimony of faithful sovereignty and sovereign fidelity runs the counter testimony of ambiguity, unreliability and negativity.[75] God is known to Israel through his word expressed by the prophets and initially the storm functions to confirm that justice is a key concern in the cosmos. Words of entreaty cannot manipulate or coerce this deity, as the storm scene proves.[76] However, whereas the storm and the fish work to display God's freedom to seek justice the natural symbols in part two of the story prove divine freedom to seek mercy. At the heart of this movement in meaning is the theme of divine repentance, present in Jonah through the vocabulary of *nacham* (pity) and *shub* (turn, turn again).[77]

Surely the cosmos has a dignity and worth of its own? Yet God uses nature indiscriminately to deal with human affairs, summoning up cosmic energies and dismissing them, allowing plants to grow only to be attacked. As Trible states, "to bring Jonah around, YHWH spares nothing in the entire cosmos. This depiction of God is as chilling as it is comforting."[78] The word 'chilling' alerts the reader to the fact that nature's rights are not inviolate. A further paradox in the book of Jonah thus emerges from the influence exerted by the cosmic level on person and community. For

---

74  Magonet, J., *Form and Meaning*, p. 181.
75  Trible, P., *Divine Incongruities in the Book of Jonah*, in Linafelt, T. and Beal, T. (eds), *God in the Fray*, Minneapolis, Fortress,1996, p. 198.
76  Trible, P., *Divine Incongruities in the Book of Jonah*, p. 200.
77  Trible, P., *Divine Incongruities in the Book of Jonah*, p. 204.
78  Trible, P., *Divine Incongruities in the Book of Jonah*, p. 206.

Cooper, "Jonah's strange encounter with God brings about deconstruction and re-mystification of the superficially simple tale of Nineveh's repentance and salvation".[79] A key issue here is that of the reliability of God.[80] There are clear indications that he is not consistent but this may be a source of hope for the Ninevites even if it is a cause of despair for Jonah.[81] Alternatively, to put it in terms of the natural world, of hope for the animals in the great city but of distress to the plant growing outside.

In this matter Jonah and God both show signs of inconsistency of behaviour, being affected by personal considerations. As with nations, so with cosmos. God alone controls all created existences and so may choose each one's fate. God the warrior is not only the source of the defeat of watery chaos he is himself its shaper, making use of chaos for his own creative ends.[82] Before the military might of the cosmic creator all must give way and yet, paradoxically, that might is controlled by movements of compassion, which stem the tide of destruction. Yet why should the animals do better than the plant? Is it not that each belongs to a human community and that seals their fate since as God deals with the humans so he allots the same destiny to creatures? In this case, then, the plant suffers in order that Jonah himself may grow. Jonah laments the death of the plant but does his moral vision thereby deepen?

## Jonah and the Home Community

Since the book of Jonah exists in a collection of Jewish/Hebrew texts its message must be examined in terms of that home community.[83] Jonathan Magonet takes up a reading of the book from within Jewish tradition. Specifically he relates to the traditional reading of Jonah on the Day of Atonement. The preparatory acknowledgement of sin and repentance in the liturgy of atonement is gathered up in the theme of repentance in Jonah.[84]

---

79  Cooper, A., *In Praise of Divine Caprice: The Significance of the Book of Jonah* in Davies, P. and Clines, D. (eds) *Among the Prophets: Language, Image and Structure in the Prophetic Writings*, Sheffield, Sheffield Academic Press, 1993, p. 153.

80  Cooper, A., *In Praise of Divine Caprice*, p. 154.

81  Cooper, A., *In Praise of Divine Caprice*, p. 154.

82  Wilt, T., *Jonah: A battle of Shifting Alliances* in *Among the Prophets*, p. 168.

83  That is, this book forms part of a Judahite book collection from the sixth to the second centuries BC. Even without an exact date for the work it is clear that it is produced from within a Judahite perspective.

84  Magonet, J., *The Subversive Bible*, London, London, SCM Press, 1997, p. 76.

Magonet views the effect of reading the text as subversive,[85] in that "the Book of Jonah has a very uncompromising attitude towards all sorts of pietistic acts which may become substitutes for the real requirements of God".[86]

The fact that Gentile cities repent in the presence of Jonah marks the need for the home community to be even more aware of its own dependency on its deity and his compassion. If these foreigners can find humble acknowledgement of their sins how much more should Israel do so and how much greater the scandal if they do not?[87] Yet, even if Jonah himself cannot bow to God's ways his 'spiritual' descendants can find a positive reply. For Jonah sits within Tanach and his uncertain loyalty to God can be balanced against the models of other characters, such as the Patriarchs, whose loyalty to God can be re-deployed within contemporary Judaism.[88]

If Magonet's commentary on the public use of Jonah by the Jewish community serves partially to restore the prophet to value in the reader's eyes, Serge Frolov goes further in his positive evaluation of the prophet's stance. He concludes "all this convinces me that it is possible to read the book of Jonah as a story of the sacrifice of its main protagonist".[89] Jonah was faithful to his beliefs – and the Ninevites *were* evildoers. Why should not the prophet stand by his integrity? The heart of this question is whether great evil should be forgiven and whether morality includes gratuitous self-sacrifice. Frolov remarks "as a former Soviet national, I know too well that whenever sacrifice of an individual for the sake of a collective . . . becomes permissable, oppression and terror ensue".[90] "And, as a Jew born after World War II, I refuse to believe that the genocide of my brethren was the only way to make Europe repent and renounce the abomination of anti-semitism."[91] If Jonah refuses to engage in cosmic games with God and stands by his experience of human community should his response, "yes, I do right" not be a true moral vision?

Whereas Frolov utilises Jonah as a model for fellow Jews in the twentieth century, J. Ackerman relates this community dimension to Jews of the past, specifically to post-exilic Judahitism. The focus in that

85  Magonet, J., *The Subversive Bible*, p. 78.
86  Magonet, J., *The Subversive Bible*, p. 78.
87  Magonet, J., *The Subversive Bible*, p. 79.
88  Magonet, J., *The Subversive Bible*, p. 84.
89  Frolov, S., *Returning the Ticket: God and his Prophet in the Book of Jonah* in *Journal for the Study of the Old Testament*, Volume No. 99/86 (1999), p. 97.
90  Frolov, S., *Returning the Ticket*, p. 104.
91  Frolov, S., *Returning the Ticket*, p. 104.

community was the Temple (Mount Zion).[92] This view may be reflected in the temple references in the psalm in Jonah chapter two. But post-exilic Judaism did not find it easy to identify with this assurance of God-with-them, a concern mirrored in the many temple-related images in Jonah. Ackerman argues: "Of the many protective shelters in the Jonah story (Tarshish, ship's hold, fish's belly, Temple, booth) three have allusive connections to Mount Zion."[93] But these function satirically in the story, since the Temple is equated with a fish's stomach, and the plant is attacked by a worm. Ackerman points out that "the prophet who in chapter four, verse three, would rather die than live in a capricious, immoral universe now asks for death rather than live in a world without divinely-provided shelter".[94]

The community focus for this uncertainty may be the continued existence of Nineveh. The continuance of Nineveh is balanced against the Judæan community's very difficult time re-establishing itself in Jerusalem after the Exile.[95] It is not surprising then that Jonah continues to sit on his windy hillside waiting and waiting to see if perhaps Nineveh will receive its own share of pain and sorrow. It is a very hard vision, which will make a moral good of invasion and deportation and colonisation. And this is the more extraordinary while the invaders, deporters and colonisers remain free to flourish, and to justify their own social vision of their valid mastery over a number of small communities, whose own culture is thus threatened.

Thus the story of Jonah is at once laughable and deadly serious. It is easy to stay on the surface of the tale and to be caught up in the pantomime quality of the scene-shifting and special effects. But this narrative does not avoid the complexity of the moral matters it deals with. Jonah himself can equally be viewed as an arrogant, self-opinionated man who finds it difficult to listen to the perspectives of other characters and as a dignified man who stands by the integrity of his human experience, becoming justifiably angry with a deity who cannot stand by his own judgement. A human community can, at the same time, be a home for evil and full of

---

92 This refers to the restored temple, whose rebuilding is associated with the names of Ezra and Nehemiah in the Old Testament. Although not a national sanctuary since Judah was a province of the Persian and, later, hellenistic empires, the Temple retained the role of civil and religious focus, operating within the framework of theocracy, a state ruled directly by the deity. See Berquist, J., *Judaism in Persia's Shadow*, Minneapolis, Fortress, 1995.

93 Ackerman, J., *Jonah*, in Alter, R. and Kermode, F. (eds), *The Literary Guide to the Bible*, London, Harper Collins, 1997, p. 241.

94 Ackerman, J., *Jonah*, p. 241.

95 Ackerman, J., *Jonah*, p. 242.

innocent citizens who do not know their right hand from their left. Ultimately these complex issues reach out to find solutions in the cosmos itself; but the interplay of natural forces brings the reader back once again to the human scene of person and community as the site in which moral vision has to be realised and communicated.


## Morality and Plot: A Summary

Whereas Section A has looked at individual characters in stories and drew out the many-sided aspects of an individual person's behaviour, Section B has focused on the plot sequences of three narratives. Studying plot has entailed an examination of each character in relation to others in the story and an exploration of how scene builds on scene to convey meaning. As with Section A it has been possible to trace a variety of potential meanings for the term moral vision in relation to the story.

### The Stories of Ruth, Joseph and Jonah

Both Ruth and the story of Joseph are set in the context of home and family, dealing with the building up or re-building of the kinship unit. Thus Ruth maintains the family of her husband after the death of the bread-winners and, by her marriage, ensures its continuity in the future. Joseph is both the source of family breakdown and the means by which family fractures can be healed and father and sons restored to their original kinship relations. Jonah deals with the 'wider family' of God and his 'sons': more especially, with the question of whether human beings who are not Judahites are indeed part of God's family with the deity as a caring father. Thus Ruth and Joseph deal with actual human families and Jonah with a kind of fictive kinship in which God acts as head of a household or community.

This family or kinship interest is discussed through the historical dimension. All three stories are set against particular time frames in the history of biblical Isræl and the issues explored through the plot are appropriate to that time context. Thus Ruth is set in the time of Judges, in a village community; Joseph in the time of the patriarchs and their semi-nomadic lifestyle, which takes a clan group in travels across a whole region; and Jonah in the time after the rise of Assyria, when Nineveh, the city of the great king, could be identified as a symbol of foreign oppression. In addition the stories use the passage of time as an essential plot device.

Both Ruth and Joseph balance an immediate judgement on the state of a family – Naomi's grief at her losses, Jacob's grief at his loss – against the fortunes of that kinship group in the long run, where grief is mellowed by the eventual survival of the family unit. Thus moral vision may require a long period of development and reflection before judgement can be passed on the significance of life's events. Jonah, too, is time-bound though less time passes within the story than in the other two narratives.

## Cosmos, Community and Person

This section has highlighted the theme of community via the plot line of a narrative. Clearly this area of investigation lies parallel to that of character and person; the study of any one narrative as a whole would require cross-referencing between these levels of literary analysis. But here the focus has been on person in relation to group. Ruth and Joseph deal mainly with community and person dimensions; the cosmos is subordinate in these stories though the deity has some part to play. Jonah, by contrast, while focusing on person and community does so directly through the cosmic, since one of the key actors in the story is God himself.

These stories raise important matters for debate with regard to community values. The person, for instance, acquires value only through his or her contribution to the well being of their communities. Ruth makes a contribution to her new family while Joseph's social value is bound up with his old family. Jonah is inextricably linked to Gentile community and cannot avoid his destiny as a catalyst for conversion. A key issue, which is debated through the medium of these stories, is the tension between the insider and the outsider, and the difficulties associated with crossing social boundaries.

Ruth is a foreigner. As such, is she exploited by her new community? Is she fully valued by it or is she tolerated because she helps out? Perhaps Orpah has the better vision in holding by her own kin? The scene between Joseph and Mrs Potiphar examines the difficulties attending a young man who is making his way as an outsider in a new community. Joseph's success at court implies that it is possible for an outsider to get inside a society while retaining his own cultural norms, as with the character Esther, in Section A. Jonah is very obviously at a crossroads between group boundaries, boundaries, which are sharply defined and well policed. Nineveh is not only an outsider community but also one at war with that of Judah, and yet the call is for the prophet to preach to, and not at, this city. Which means that it has to be counted as 'inside' since the God of Judah reigns over its affairs and allots its fate of survival. Here the question of boundary keeping and boundary crossing bites deep since Judah suffered at the hands of its God while Nineveh apparently escapes. In this moral vision of community and theodicy all groups are equal in sin but offered hope through repentance. What constitutes an insider group, from the cosmic viewpoint, is the community, which accepts both parts of this statement and acts accordingly.

# PART III:
# MORALITY, TIME, AND PLACE

# Chapter Eight

# Morality and World Order in Genesis Chapters One to Eleven

This chapter opens the third section of the present volume, that which deals with moral vision from the perspective primarily of cosmos and which finds its narrative base in the study of time and place setting. In particular the chapter will explore the connection between morality and world order in relation to the narrative of primæval history in the Torah, that of the first eleven chapters of Genesis. Thus, whereas section A looked to the delineation of characters in stories as its major reading tool and section B to plot sequence, this section will examine the narrative uses of time sequence and place setting in establishing meaning in a story. By means of character and plot, sections A and B explored the moral frames of person and community; this section will move to the third moral frame outlined in chapter one, namely that of the cosmos. This dimension of existence will deal, in particular, with the role of the divine and the supernatural in expressing moral attitudes constructed by human beings living in social groups.

In order to fulfil these aims the chapter will examine Genesis chapters one to eleven which, at one level, provide an example of a single narrative, while being capable of being broken down into several separate stories each with its own narrative structure. Genesis chapters one to eleven are typically described by commentators as the primal history, since they deal with events at the very start of creation and cease at the point when the focus moves from nations to one nation and its founding members.[1] Although they describe the origin of the world and of the human species at large, the text is in continuum with the later stories about the fathers and mothers of Israel, and so forms the basis for an Israelite cultural perspective. It is not to be regarded as the same genre as a systematic philosophical treatise on the state of the world and on the nature of human existence. Although the issues examined are eternal – such as the origins of the universe and the role of humans in world order – the material is edited into Torah as the first stage in the historical development of Israel and it is the

---

1   See here, for example, Westermann, C., *Genesis: A Practical Commentary*, Grand Rapids, Eerdmans, 1987, for a basic account of the use of this term with relation to Genesis One to Eleven.

same deity who appears in the beginning and in later stages of Isrælite affairs.[2]

## Basic Issues in Genesis Chapters One to Eleven

The stories in Genesis chapters one to eleven balance between these two aspects, an interest in the whole of humanity and a concern for the particular society of biblical Isræl, insofar as they answer questions such as 'where does the world come from?' and 'what are the boundaries of human existence?'. These narratives deal with humankind as a totality and the answers provided are open to reception by any readers whatever their social origin or time-setting. But in the flow of the Torah, these stories are the focus for the specific understanding of God, nature and human relationships among Isræl, which in the long run, was held by the ruling groups in Judah in the sixth to the fourth centuries BCE.[3]

Turning from the broader perspective of Pentateuchal themes to the particular content of Genesis chapters one to eleven, it should be noted that a major function of this material is to establish order, order in the cosmos and in the community. The world is set in place in chapter one in a manner which conveys a basic optimism about world stability, the succession of days and night, of seasons and of time. This stability allows life to emerge and to flourish. The human species is one form of created life among others and is regarded both as aligned with the natural environment and as intimately linked to the nature of the deity who formed it. The order of the world is stable but yet fragile. Chapters three to six explore the nature of this fragile balance between God, world and human community and offer some explanations for the collapse of order and the breaking of harmonious relationships between God and humans, between humans and humans, between humans and nature.

---

2   This is not to argue that the characterisation of God is stable across the entire Old Testament, but the name YHWH is the key term for God as the deity of Isræl, in this literature. For a discussion of the framework created in the narrative of Genesis chapters one to eleven by the writer(s) using that name for the deity see for instance, Hiebert, T., *The Yahwist's Landscape*, Oxford, Oxford University Press, 1996.

3   The matter of the dating of Old Testament works is one of considerable debate, with no agreed conclusions among scholars. The date taken here is the later date, that by which any earlier traditions, which may have existed were being edited by a post-exilic Judahite elite.

## Law and Order

In the context of law and order themes, Genesis chapters one to eleven can be viewed as a more directly legal or ethical narrative than the other narratives examined in this book. It can be noted that the text refers to laws, which were made by God, as with the use of trees in the garden, or with regard to God's own future response to the cosmos, after the Flood. Given the existence of some form of legal framework to existence it is then possible to discuss the nature of human behaviour as ethical, fitting into that framework, or unethical, transgressing its boundaries. Terms relating to violence, corruption and degeneration are to be found in chapters three, four, and six, for instance.[4] As J. Rogerson notes, "there is an important link between creation as order and human moral behaviour, such that the latter can affect the former. If creation is order, that order must include ordered human relationships; and if God only guaranteed the stability of the physical universe, but was unconcerned about inter-human relationships, then the creation would be fundamentally immoral."[5]

Yet, as pointed out in chapter one above, it is not helpful for a reader of Old Testament material to separate out legal texts from other aspects of the literature in which they are embedded. Rather narrative is to be read as a whole and examined via the tools of narrative criticism so that the moral perspectives contained in it may be more fully explored. Nanette Stahl offers the viewpoint that the ambiguity of narrative context must be allowed to colour the reader's interpretation of actual legal material, which is so embedded: "I am convinced that the biblical mixture of genres and voices is the manifestation of a series of underlying tensions, a way to allow for the expression of a complex, even contradictory, ideology."[6]

Stahl argues that this phenomenon is more obvious in liminal areas of narrative, such as the Creation or the Flood scenes in Genesis chapters one to eleven: "All liminal moments . . . share some defining characteristics: they are concerned with transition, and function as focal points of the biblical vision of the often tenuous, always dynamic relationship between God and his elect."[7] In such liminal moments the tensions in the text

---

4 See for instance, in Genesis chapter three references to cursing, in Genesis chapter four 'sin' crouches at Cain's door and in Genesis chapter six the whole earth is corrupted by human violence.
5 Rogerson, J., *Genesis*, Sheffield, Sheffield Academic Press, 1991.
6 Stahl, N., *Law and Liminality in the Bible*, Sheffield, Sheffield Academic Press, 1995, p. 12.
7 Stahl, N., *Law and Liminality*, p. 13.

emerge, as in the post Flood scene where God sets out his laws for Noah in the new creation. There is an echo of the original law of chapters one and two in the food regulations, for instance. However, the terms have changed. These new laws acknowledge that law itself is fixed by what has happened in the story. God accepts human fallibility in a manner which tends to deconstruct the very idea of absolute boundaries and unchanging codes of behaviour.[8]

This is an interesting critique of the narrative since it incorporates the concept of fallibility and change in a positive manner, unlike the interpretation of Genesis one to six to be found in traditional Christian theology. St. Augustine, for instance, viewed God's decrees as absolutely fixed and human behaviour as negatively contravening these laws.[9] This establishes absolutely the concept of sin, original sin, which comes to define the human species in its relations with the deity and the cosmos. Although life continues, it has fallen from perfection into a flawed state which must be acknowledged as such and from which human beings should strive to move back into the originally intended state of obedience to divine decree.

In contrast to these solemn themes of sin, disobedience and punishment, themes, which tend to the tragic, William Whedbee argues that the narrative can be viewed as comic rather than tragic.[10] He suggests that the story is seen as a cosmic joke, created around puns and parodies.[11] Thus Adam is made from the *Adamah* (soil) and so the two are complementary. Yet Adam can only get on with his task of caring for the *Adamah* once expelled from the garden. Instead of tragic fall, loss serves rather to bring the reader's attention to everyday reality as the norm, through a comic mixture of pun and paradox: "The movement of the story shows how far it stands from a plot featuring a tragic fall. Such a trajectory represents a particular kind of Christian projection of Lucifer's fall from heaven . . . in contrast to the largely Christian version, in the Genesis rendition Adam and Eve do indeed suffer losses, but losses countered by significant gains."[12]

8   Stahl, N., *Law and Liminality*, p. 14.
9   See Augustine's comments on the book of Genesis which are incorporated in his Confessions, where he debates the meaning of the garden scene as a fall away from God, an event which he links with human desire, not just sexual desire, though that is part of the matter, but uncontrollable passions. He argues that these are inherent in human nature and represent the basis of sinful orientation in each new generation.
10  Whedbee, W., *The Bible and the Comic Vision*, Cambridge, Cambridge University Press, 1998.
11  Whedbee, W., *The Bible and Comic Vision*, p. 24.
12  Whedbee, W., *The Bible and Comic Vision*, pp. 27 f.

## Cosmos, Community and Person

In these ways the topics of cosmos, community and person begin to take on their own shape with regard to the primal history of the world. The key persons are few in number in the earlier stories of this material, before the Flood, but their actions impact decisively on the evaluations to be made of human conduct and the dynamics of human relationships. Since God is continuously a character in these stories and the whole cycle begins within the cosmic realm of chaos and divine creative energy, the cosmic level undergirds all evaluations of person and community, but can itself be subjected to critique. Did God have to experiment in order to arrive at the proper nature of human society?[13] Why did God put a forbidden tree in the garden and not prevent human error? Does God, then, exclude human beings from *his* garden because he is threatened by them or is jealous of them? These are all questions, which can be posed by the reader.

The concepts of time and place have a part to play in the development of moral meaning under the headings of cosmos, community and person since they are key contributors to the structuring of the story. "At the beginning" states the opening of Genesis, and it is in this setting of beginning that events unroll, each stage moving away from that distant start but still emerging from it through a process of generation rooted in the original first time. The material appears to have been specifically structured to reflect this time sequence. Fokkelman points to a series of begettings (*toledoth*) as time boundaries in the narrative.[14] The list of begettings serves to separate the generations of human characters from each other while also indicating the connections in which parent produces child, one generation as the source of the next. Unusually, in the second chapter of Genesis, this term is used for the begetting of heaven and earth, thus establishing a continuity in time from the very dawn of the first day to the development of the human species as it expands to fill the earth. These usages form a pattern with a third function of this term, that of introductory phrase and division marker for each major short narrative within the whole – stories such as that of Abraham and Jacob. Fokkelman argues that this time continuity dramatically connects the promise of fertility and blessing made by God in Genesis chapter one with the events that follow.[15] This promise also serves to link time with space. The promise can only be fulfilled in the context of

13 Cf. Genesis chapter two.
14 Fokkelman, J., *Genesis*, in Alter, R. and Kermode, F. (eds), *The Literary Guide to the Bible*, London, Harper Collins, 1997, pp. 41-43.
15 Fokkelman, J., *Genesis*, pp. 42 f.

an earth to be fruitful in.  Thus time and space are established, divided, ordered and sanctified, within the primal story.

In Genesis chapter one there is chaos and there is order; order produces 'place' since the separating of the elements brings about earth, sky and sea. Living beings can then emerge from within each created space: animals, birds and fish, each having its own niche in existence.  By the second chapter of Genesis, the theme of the garden further defines the concept of earth (*aretz*) and soil (*adamah*).  The Flood story threatens to remove place altogether as the waters of chaos are unleashed, yet a place of safety remains, in the Ark floating on the flood-tide.  After the re-emergence of dry land, earth again becomes a focus for moral vision, with the final tension, in chapter eleven, between City and Earth as possible places of human habitation.

## Time and Place in Narrative Criticism

These themes can be explored through the methodology of Narrative Criticism.  Gabriel Josopovici sets the tone for this line of interpretation in his account of how Genesis chapters one to eleven follows its own rhythmic patterns.[16]  He points to the grammatical ambiguity of the opening phrase of the text: in the beginning.  This may be an absolute reference to the first thing that ever happened or may be a relative reference to what happened when God began to create.  In this way the opening gambit of the narrative is not, in fact, a stable beginning, but allows the story to float free in time.  Josopovici notes the similarity to Proust's *A la recherche du temps perdu*, which opens with an ambiguous temporal reference thus enabling the writer to explore "time, memory, imagination and the mysteries of the body in a kind of limbo, neither past nor present, neither in this place nor in that, but in a space and time which can truly be the space and time of utterance".[17]

Thus the biblical writer starts in the middle of something which is linked to the next event by the word *and*, and this sequence of clauses joined only by *and* stretches out across the whole primæval narrative.  In the course of the series the chapter advances sometimes by repetition of a word or concept and sometimes by innovation, thus building a fabric of symmetry and disymmetry.[18]   Nor does the writer produce stability through

16  Josopovici, G., *The Book of God*, New Haven, Yale University Press, 1988.
17  Josopovici, G., *The Book of God*, p. 61.
18  Josopovici, G., *The Book of God*, p. 64.

characterisation; the story begins with God but no profile of this figure is given as a basis for the sequence of activities that follows. "The book begins with his presence, but it is not a presence which can be seized. Who and what this God is we can only learn as the relationships between him and Adam and him and Adam's descendants develop; as with the *Commedia* and Proust's *A la recherche du temps perdu*, his potential is only realised (in both meanings of the word) in the unfolding narrative."[19]

## Time and Narrative Meaning

As S. Bar-Efrat notes: "A narrative cannot exist without time, to which it has a twofold relationship: it unfolds within time, and time passes within it."[20] The reader encounters the text unfolding over a period of time spent in reading and the story being read has its own internal timeframe governing the narratival sequence of events. It is thus time which gives meaning to events, since narratival time may flow forwards and backwards, may start in the middle of events, may pass swiftly over sections of narrative sequence or may pause in an extended manner on one particular event in time. "Because the author can manage time with complete disregard for the laws governing physical time, events from the past or even the future are sometimes introduced into the narrative outside their chronological order."[21] It is by choice of sequential ordering of events that an author produces emphases and climaxes within the narrative and provides clues for the reader's understanding of the plot as a whole.

The details of this time usage are covered under terms such as anachrony, where events are introduced in a different time order from that of the normal sequence of events. This device may mean that a future event is anticipated by the narrator, or that a flashback occurs to an event already past. The span of these embedded time references may be short or long, as Mieke Bal points out.[22] Furthermore there may be time gaps in the narrative with periods of time skipped over or omitted altogether. It is this variable use of time, which helps to create focalisation in a story through the relationship of what is skipped over to the over-arching *fabula*.[23] By

---

19  Josopovici, G., *The Book of God*, p. 73.
20  Bar-Efrat, S., *Narrative Art in the Bible*, Sheffield, Sheffield Academic Press, 1997.
21  Bar-Efrat, S., *Narrative Art in the Bible*, p. 143.
22  Bal, M., *Narratology: Introduction to the Theory of Narrative*, Toronto, Toronto University Press, 1997.
23  Bal, M., *Narratology*, pp. 212 f.

emphasising certain events in time at the expense of others, the narrator leads the reader to a particular sense of the meaning to be attached to a succession of scenes in life. If plot is the core of a story by the manner in which it builds up a series of connected events, then time is the servant of plot. For a story's events are processes which presuppose change and development, thus making a succession in time or a chronological sequence central to the creation of meaning.[24]

## Time in Genesis Chapters One to Eleven

When applied to Genesis chapters one to eleven, these considerations of the literary function of time add to the reading tools by which the reader finds meaning in the text: in this case with regard to the value to be attached to the over-arching level of cosmos. For instance, an examination of the use of time sequence in these eleven chapters shows it moving at different speeds. The slow and regular movement of time in Genesis chapter one is separate from the swift passage of time in Genesis chapter two, where the creation of all the animals occurs in a single scene, and from the focusing on specific moments of time in Genesis chapter three, as in speaking of the cool of the day.

In the early part of Genesis, events are narrated in a chronological sequence where time is broken into individual components each of which carries equal weight.[25] Time is measured by days, and each day by morning and evening. A day is a unit of creation and all creation is summed up by a succession of time sequences each in chronological order and in logical order with regard to the events from the separation of the waters to the creation of the heavens, earth and seas. This use of time as part of the formal process of separation and ordering of creation itself is the means of imparting a particular moral vision, namely that the world is a stable and reliable environment with an authorised place for all that exists.

This creation-time overlaps with the use of time in the second stage of creation. Whereas the reader knows that creation is complete, including animals and humans, there is now a regression in time to a still incomplete period of existence. The earth exists as dry land but neither humans nor beasts yet live. Whereas, in Genesis chapter one, God announces the arrival of humankind through a moment of speech, here the appearance of humans is spun out in time and becomes the focus of the narrative. And, in

24 Bal, M., *Narratology*, p. 208.
25 Cf. Genesis $1^1 - 2^4$.

verses eighteen to twenty, there is a fast track through animal creation to arrive at verse twenty-one, where the appearance of *Issah* (woman) slows the narrative time down as it opens into a timeless statement of the relationship between *Ish* (man/ husband) and *Issah* (woman/wife).

This account of creation introduces the reader to the garden and there is no time gap between chapters as the next scene develops from the presence of humans and serpent in the garden. Nor is it clear how long the time sequence of the dialogue with the serpent was, though there is some indication of day sequence since God appears in the cool of the day. This may be the evening or the morning. In the first instance it would mean that the creatures interact in the normal period for business in the daytime and thus what occurs comes directly out of the ordinary life of the humans, though it then disrupts that normality. In the second interpretation the events would have occurred at night, a signal that the activity is itself flawed and deviant in the symbolic world of biblical texts.[26] The narrative pauses now for the focus of meaning is on the inevitable changes caused by the eating of the fruit.

The period of God's speech offers a prolepsis, a looking forward to what will happen in the future. This future will be the ordinary time of the human world, a world known to the original readers. What the narrative offers from the beginning, and then differentiates sharply from what happens next, is the distant past for the reader; what is shown as divine prophecy for the future is in fact a summary of what human beings actually experience. Thus the narrative functions to explain to an audience in the present how their condition has come about. It is prophetic by analepsis, by looking back to a primal time as a means of creating moral vision.

The opening of the next chapter with a genealogical reference marks the beginning of a new time period. Now man and woman begin the life of small farmers and the sequence of human procreation unrolls. This use of time moves the attention of the reader from the cosmos per se to the community of humans as a source of moral meaning. The story of Cain and Abel marks the opening of this new focus, with its emphasis on the relations between brothers. Yet, by its many linguistic echoes of chapter

---

26 Night, associated with darkness, is a time for negative events, within the Christian bible worldview. In Genesis chapter one darkness is on the face of the deep before God creates order and brings in light. This is taken up in the Gospel of John where light is of God and darkness indicates separation from God. Night is a time when human beings are susceptible to supernatural attack, as in Psalm ninety-one, verses five and six. Night as a time of negativity is indicated in Job chapter three where Job calls on those who return order to chaos to curse his day of birth and so return it to gloom and deep darkness.

three, it touches upon the cosmic origins of humankind, taking the reader back to the original events in time, even though this is at one remove now.[27] God still speaks to the humans and is the arbiter of human conduct. When a boundary has been broken God still offers protection to the transgressor, putting a mark on Cain as he provided clothing for Adam and Eve.

This story also shows signs of anachrony since there are, according to the broad narrative, only four people on the earth, but Cain talks of anyone who meets him killing him, implying the existence of much greater numbers of humans. This highlights a continued tension in the narrative of Genesis chapters one to eleven between the reference to foundational unrepeated time, and ongoing, changeable time, in human society. Human beings are mortal, but human existence operates within the ordered world created by the presence of the firmament – itself a symbol of the timeless control of the deity over the cosmos and all it affairs. Chapter five seems to put a line again under the time-span of origins, looking rather to human communal time, only for the narrative to be thrown back to the beginning with the decision of the deity to destroy creation in the Flood. Ordinary human time vanishes for a while, as community vanishes under the judgement from the cosmos. Only Noah's Ark remains, a time capsule waiting to be re-inserted into a world of human history. The use of time here both links and divides the scenes post Flood with the earlier events. The period of the Flood can be measured and so an end is fixed to this event; this measurement begins with the onset of rain in the old days and ends with the waters subsided in the new age of human community. The words of God at the end of chapter eight echo the divine speech at the end of creation in Genesis chapters one and two – peace, prosperity, fertility, are set forth again as goals in time. But this pattern is to be interrupted one final time with the Tower of Babel scene, where humans attempt to gather time together into one great human assembly, in the tower-city. The scattering of the nations across the earth endorses the perspective that the cosmic level of meaning for human activity is tied up with farming the earth, with an endless progression of mortal generations. The alternative view of society as itself a cosmos where human beings control their own destiny is thereby eroded.

---

27 Genesis chapter four echoes Genesis chapter three, rather than quoting it directly. There are clear parallels in the pairing of human actors in each scene, for instance, and in the fact that earth is cursed because of the actions of a man, in each case. See for instance, Van Wolde, E., *Stories of the Beginning*, London, SCM Press, 1996, for more details on these comparative elements.

## Time Begins

Time is, then, vital to meaning in Genesis chapters one to eleven from the beginning. According to van Wolde, a timeline whereby only God is present from the beginning puts human existence in its proper place. She argues that "Genesis chapter one seeks to present a fundamentally different approach: the starting point lies elsewhere than with human beings; the primacy lies outside us."[28] When God confronts the shadow over the great deep there is no before and after, no events to describe because there is no progression of time. Only with the creation do time and space come into being.[29] Van Wolde notes: "God did not exist so much before time, since without time there is nothing that can go 'before'; God is outside time."[30] Once God speaks then time starts to tick over and a progression of becomings can occur.

According to van Wolde, "Genesis chapter one is primarily focused on the heaven . . . the heavenly bodies are permanent and propagate themselves. They indicate order and time on the earth."[31] It is the contrast between these fixed bodies, and the movement of change over time, in the earth over which they preside, which produces moral boundaries of order in the universe. Human beings live within these boundaries because they were created after such boundaries came into being.

And behind all this is God's self. God's speech-acts come before all. God is a character but the narrator does not set out his characterisation in detail. There is a tension here whereby other characters are created by the words of God and the narrator can only let them move or speak after God's creation, and at the same time it is the narrator who introduces God as a character and allows him to speak.[32] Van Wolde points to this as a pre-modern approach to the cosmos: "The initiative in speaking and creating and the starting point lie with God, not with human beings."[33]

White concurs with van Wolde's viewpoint here: "The bold performative speech in Genesis chapter one through which the world is established clearly shows that the divine voice is not one among many voices in this world, but the single transcendent voice which is the source

---

28  Van Wolde, E., *Stories of the Beginning*, p. 32.
29  Van Wolde, E., *Stories of the Beginning*, p. 14.
30  Van Wolde, E., *Stories of the Beginning*, p. 15.
31  Van Wolde, E., *Stories of the Beginning*, p. 19.
32  Van Wolde, E., *Stories of the Beginning*, p. 23.
33  Van Wolde, E., *Stories of the Beginning*, p. 23.

of the world's order."[34] Though God shares speech with other characters, "the initial, pivotal biblical characters are presented by the narrator as creatures of the Word; they are personages [whose] . . . personal being in the narrative is . . . formed from the outset by the divine Word".[35] For White it is the occurrence of divine speech addressed outside itself, which initiates creation. Speech over time is thus the key to the narrative structures of Genesis chapters one to five.

## Motion and Rest

The development of creation over time is balanced by a definitive pause in time. On the seventh day God rested from all his work in creation. Van Wolde comments that "God also enjoys himself. He sees that everything that he has made is very good. And he takes a rest. He blesses and sanctifies the day on which he rests . . . there is a time for work and a time to stop working."[36] Resting makes no sense without its paired concept of the passage of time spent working, but working can itself then be defined by the boundaries of rest. Rest incorporates completion and the goal of positive identity for created life. Time thus includes not simply moments of time but that which is accomplished within those moments.

William Brown points out that the seventh day has its own epithet, 'holy', and is not shaped by the familiar events of the other days.[37] There is no speech-act, no evaluation of work done. Yet "day and deity share common ground . . . it is this day alone that God consecrates in order to rest . . . Creating temporal space for divine rest, the Sabbath day marks a scheduled indwelling of holiness, God's distinct domain."[38] Brown sees rest as a form of dwelling. God indwells the Sabbath so time itself becomes sanctified, a meeting point between deity and creation. Because this day is holy, holiness is possible to the other measurements of time and God can be found in the progression of events. Thus creation is achieved not by conflict, as in Mesopotamian accounts, for instance, but by co-

---

34 White, H., *Narration and Discourse in the Book of Genesis*, Cambridge, Cambridge University Press, p. 100.
35 White, H., *Narration and Discourse*, p. 102.
36 Van Wolde, E., *Stories of the Beginning*, p. 131.
37 Brown, W., *The Ethos of the Cosmos*, Grand Rapids, Eerdmans, 1999.
38 Brown, W., *The Ethos of the Cosmos*, p. 50.

ordination and enlistment.[39] Thus all time can progress to its ultimate, positive destiny. "Goodness and holiness, bounded and separate as they are, are also bound up in teleological correspondence, an integrity of temporal coherence."[40]

## Time and Chaos

Yet this positive movement is not the only moral vision in Genesis chapters one to eleven. Time leads to greater violence and conflict by chapter six. This in turn leads to God the creator becoming God the destroyer. The wording in chapter six balances chapter one – God saw and creation was very good/full of corruption. This opens out into a vision of time as endtime, when all returns to the primal ocean. Van Wolde lays out the parallels in the text, between the positive succession of sevens in Genesis chapter one and the negative pattern of these in the Flood Narrative.[41]

The difference in the role of time in these two accounts is that, in the second, God has put time into the hands of human beings in their generations and they have made of time not a thing of beauty but of bloodshed. Yet time itself is not destroyed. Even the Flood is measured in days, for instance. Thus the time of Noah is critical for the whole of life. Brown comments that "amid the swirling chaos and the breakdown of creation Noah is commanded to build. He is a constructionist in a world on the brink of deconstruction".[42] For God cannot go back entirely on what time has already set up: "God solemnly pledges that the boundaries set in place between earth and water shall prevail."[43] The rest of holiness is balanced by the pause of Flood, and yet this is not simply negation for Noah, whose name means rest, is destined to bring peace to humankind's relations with Creator and the natural order.

---

39 The Mesopotamian stories of the origins of the world and of humans are largely couched in the form of a battle between deities for supremacy, as in the war between Tiamat and Marduk. See Brown, W., *The Ethos of the Cosmos*, p. 50.

40 Brown, W., *The Ethos of the Cosmos*, p. 52.

41 Van Wolde, E., *Stories of the Beginning*, pp. 122 f.

42 Brown, W., *The Ethos of the Cosmos*, p. 54.

43 Brown, W., *The Ethos of the Cosmos*, p. 57.

### *Ur*time and Historical Time

The main moral vision of time in these early chapters of Genesis is thus the laying out of cosmos through the rule of God over time. Time is holy, but can also be endtime, with a judgement on humans and the world. All these messages about time and meaning (incorporating beginning, *Ur*, time and end time) preface an account of Israel, which begins with the historical time of Abraham, father of the nation. Before that time begins, linked to the origins by the device of genealogical lists there is a final pause in the narrative. The Tower of Babel scene involves a human attempt to stop time insofar as the inhabitants appear to aim at becoming a self-sufficient and timeless community whose order is self-determined. God's action in destroying the foundations of that communal unity by diversifying speech leads the human beings to dependency on the progression of events in time as they spread out, scattering across the face of the earth, each group to its own time-scale and destiny. In addition, this story is bounded by two genealogical lists, that of all kinds of dwellers in Genesis chapter ten and, in Genesis chapter eleven, the genealogies of Shem and Terah, the originators of one particular people.

By this device a move is made from *Ur* time to historical time, a significant shift occurs in the overall narrative of Torah. Van Wolde says "up till now the human being has been described in relation to the earth . . . here the social aspect of the human being is developed: a human being is a social being living in a people and a land, in a particular social group with its own language".[44] This is not the 'us' of all human beings gathered in one time and place but the 'us' of many peoples and nations, scattered in time and place. Yet, as one community becomes the special focus of the narrative, connections are still made with the world order set up in the early chapters of the book of Genesis. Brown, for instance, stresses the priestly linkage between the holiness of God's sabbath day and the holiness of Israel in its days. Symbolically the Ark of the Tabernacle is where God rests and this is a form of indwelling of his people, Israel.[45] Thus the social order of a

---

44  Van Wolde, E., *Stories of the Beginning*, p. 161.
45  See Brown, W., *The Ethos of the Cosmos*, pp. 73-91. Brown here makes use of the priestly writer's viewpoint on the tabernacle or ark of the Lord. In the wilderness this forms the heart of the Israelite encampment and signifies the presence of the deity with his people. When the nation pitches its tents, the tent of meeting is put up first and so God rests, with his people. This abiding accompaniment of the divine makes Israel both a chosen and a holy people.

human community is tightly linked to the world order established by its patronal deity.

## Place, Space and Narrative Meaning

Equally important as time sequence is the location of characters and events. This may involve long descriptive passages separating action and speech or it may be worked into a story through a character's visual perception of places moved through, such as walking in streets or in a park, for instance. By whatever means, the narrator creates a visual setting of the story in the mind of the reader who then applies this level of perception to the meaning of the narrative. Characters operate in a spatial frame, a structure discussed by M. Bal: "Spaces function in a story in different ways . . .[as] a frame, a place of action . . .[as] an object of presentation itself, for its own sake."[46] Space, as reflected in journey, may be the main focus for interpreting characters as, for instance, when "the hero of a fairy tale has to traverse a dark forest to prove his courage".[47]

Bal suggests that if spatial thinking is a general human tendency it is not surprising that spatial elements are important in narrative.[48] If the narrator gives little detail on the location of events the reader will tend to supply these, using his/her imagination to create the scene in their personal visual perspective. Based on this a writer can deliberately develop a point around location – countryside or city, for example: "The opposition between city and country can take on different meanings, sometimes as the sink of iniquity as opposed to idyllic innocence or as a possibility of magically acquiring riches in contrast to the labour of the farmers."[49]

Bar-Efrat argues that biblical narrative tends to be weak on place, giving very few depictions or descriptions of places or people, though journeys between different geographical sites are used to structure the narrative, in Abraham's case, for instance.[50] The lack of pauses created by long descriptions of place leads to the particular dynamism of biblical narrative whereby one action swiftly follows another, joined by the *and* (*waw* consecutive) referred to by Josopovici.[51] In Genesis chapters one to eleven,

---

46  Bal, M., *Narratology*, p. 136.
47  Bal, M., *Narratology*, p. 136.
48  Bal, M., *Narratology*, p. 215.
49  Bal, M., *Narratology*, p. 216.
50  Bar-Efrat, S., *Narrative Art of the Bible*, pp. 146 f.
51  Cf. Josopovici, G., *The Book of God*, especially pp. 61-73.

however, there are signs that space/places are significant aspects of the structure of the story and that they have a role in the creation of moral perspective.

In Genesis chapter one it is the creation of places, which is central to the emergence of living creatures. Only when sky, earth and sea are available as places, with boundaries to mark their existence, can living creatures come into being, each species belonging to its setting – birds of the air, fish of the sea and beasts of the land. Thus human beings owe their appearance not only to the overall divine purpose but, in local detail, to the provision of a stable place where they may dwell.

In chapter two this stable place is defined as earth, covered in rough vegetation. The link between creature and place is made more explicit now with the pun on the creature's generic title – an Adam from the *Adamah* (earth). Moreover the earth cannot achieve its full growth, until it is tended by the creature designed for it. But chapter two also introduces the garden, a place which is described in some detail, although its exact nature is mysterious. This garden is more than just a cultivated spot, it contains also the tree of the knowledge of good and evil as well as the tree of immortality. Moreover, although the man and the woman are its tenants, the garden is the place where God walks and talks to human beings face to face. The garden therefore is a mythological place, a sacred site where human existence opens to the divine. As such this place brings forth safety and happiness and danger and risk. Thus the garden is a place of moral significance. For it provides answers to questions of the proper boundaries of human life.

Garden and earth stand in tension with one another to the extent that humanity, designed to fulfil the earth, cannot do so until cast out of the garden. It is the earth, or rather the field, which becomes the centre for the dispute between Cain and God. The earth then becomes the setting for human conflict since Cain takes Abel into a field and there slays him. As in Genesis chapter three, the ground is cursed by God on account of a human being but this time the earth itself will not contain the transgressor who is condemned to be outcast not only from a garden but from all settled life on the earth. Cain perceives this as a huge disaster, which will deprive him also of access to God. Cain thus becomes a person of no-place, for he has broken the boundaries of communal stability.

Cain's sin is the first sin to defile the earth with blood but, by chapter six, the earth has been filled with bloodshed, and is a place corrupted by the impact of human habitation. It has become a forbidden area, which God will return fully to the chaotic nothingness which is beginning to define it.

While the waters swirl over the earth its role as a place for human self-definition is taken over by the Ark.  Like the garden, the Ark exists parallel to the earth and affords a place of safety.  Garden and Ark are symbols of the nurture of human existence within the cosmos but they are not the proper places for human beings to fulfil their true role in the cosmos.  That belongs to earth alone and the process of human development re-starts with Noah and his sons.

There is here a constant theme that earth and human beings go together, in mutual inter-dependence.  The moral function of the earth is highlighted by the existence, in the text of Genesis chapters one to eleven, of other places, which are good in themselves, but which do not lead human beings to their true identity.  The last scene in the primal history, the tower-city, is another such place.  In itself a symbol of human unity and of the scope of human powers of knowledge, it is presented by the narrator as not in keeping with the cosmic role of human beings.  The inherent powers of knowledge and physical skill are to be fully developed only when human beings scatter across the earth and cultivate it.  World order, then, requires that space be made in the cosmos for human beings, but space is no good if it is not in the proper place.

## Cosmos and Place Setting

The first audiences of this moral message about place and human society must have lived in Judah in antiquity.  Even allowing for a late date of writing, this means that the text would have made sense in the cultural setting of that society where agriculture would have been the main lifestyle.[52]  Theodore Hiebert, in his recent work *The Yahwist's Landscape*, has made an attempt to read Genesis through the spectacles of topography and land-usage.[53]  Because of geography, the climate of Judah is one of dry

---

52  If this material is dated to the monarchic or earlier period, that is, to the time, in biblical Isræl, when the land was first settled, it could be said to reflect the attitudes of that early stage of land settlement, with scattered farming communities. However, this early dating is much disputed (see for example, Davies, P., *In Search of Ancient Isræl*, Sheffield, Sheffield Academic Press, 1992). However, the topography of the region is such that agricultural patterns probably did not change massively and the occupation of the area of Judah by small farming groups would have been maintained in the Persian period of post-exilic Judah. See here the volume, Davies, P. (ed.), *Second Temple Studies*, Sheffield, Sheffield Academic Press.

53  Hiebert, T., *The Yahwist's Landscape*.

seasons dependent on electric storms coming from the coast to provide its water for irrigation, unlike Egypt and Mesopotamia where the existence of great rivers makes canal irrigation more useful. In this setting there are few great cities and the natural mode of habitation is in small farming communities. It is this reality which lies behind the moral perspectives of the Yahwistic material in Genesis chapters one to eleven.[54]

## Earth and Garden

There are three major terms for land in the early chapters of Genesis: *Aretz* (land), *Adamah* (soil), and *Gen* (garden). Taken together these terms shape the moral vision of the text with regard to place setting. The early reference to earth reflects the normal mode of land usage for highland farming, except for the reference to the source of water.[55] The idea of God causing water to come up to the land reflects rather the Egyptian or Mesopotamian mode of canal irrigation. However the proper source of water in Judah, by rain from the sky, is instituted in the text when human beings appear to cultivate the earth.[56]

But the Yahwist's story moves fast to a very different setting – the luxuriant Garden of Eden.[57] Hiebert notes that scholars have suggested previously that this image is taken from Mesopotamia with its great rivers, but he himself argues that the symbols for the garden come from nearer home, namely a Jordan valley oasis.[58] Thus a symbol of place is created where food comes easily and living is pleasant, without the unremitting toil needed for the production of arable crops on dry and difficult soil.

It is from the soil that a human being's survival and purpose stems. There is a unitary vision of the human being and the cosmos here. The worst that can happen is the soil's sterility – something foreshadowed in Genesis chapter three and fulfilled in Genesis chapter five. According to Hiebert, the scene of Cain and Abel mirrors this pattern of humanity understood through a place context. Thus Cain, dependent on the soil and

54  Hiebert bases his arguments on the traditional splitting of material in Genesis chapters one to eleven between different literary sources. He takes the material scholars have allotted to the Yahwist approach (so-called from its title for God, YHWH) and aims to show that this material has an over-arching unity which stems from its cultural context in Judahite society.

55  Cf. in Genesis 2 [4-5].

56  Hiebert, T., *The Yahwist's Landscape*, p. 35.

57  Hiebert, T., *The Yahwist's Landscape*, p. 51.

58  Hiebert, T., *The Yahwist's Landscape*, p. 55.

its crop is the real character here. Abel, named from the Hebrew *Hebel* (vapour, emptiness), has only a shadowy presence but yet his blood pollutes the soil and makes it unusable for Cain. Cain must now abandon a life tied to soil and, in the perspective of the writer, go outside the ordinary cosmos.[59] This linking of agricultural reality with moral vision is continued into the presentation of God himself as an agricultural figure. For Hiebert, "J's God, a strongly anthropomorphic figure, lives a very earthly life. He plants the Garden of Eden, walks in it, and talks to its residents whom he has fashioned from the ground."[60]

## Earth and Ark

The account of the Flood also fits into this earthbound perspective. Thus there is a unity to this primal history which, for Hiebert, climaxes and is completed in the Flood story.[61] Human life is now totally separated from its natural ally and source, the earth. Human beings can only survive at all because God provides a replacement 'earth' in the ship that floats over the waters. In the earlier stories of Adam and Cain, humanity showed itself to be self-reliant and independent of divine advice or warning. The effect of this is to move humans progressively further away from their cosmic role and thus from their happiness and safety. This trajectory is completed in the Flood where the earth disappears beneath the seas. Yet when the waters abate, the dry land is revealed and God promises never again to break the link between human existence and cosmic framework.

In place of Adam and Cain comes Noah, who builds the Ark which alone will provide refuge in the coming deluge. After Noah will come Abraham. For Hiebert these post-diluvian heroes counter-balance Adam, Eve, and Cain, and provide a dual image of humans in relation to cosmos, fruitful as opposed to unfruitful.[62] The key to all this drama is *adamah*, according to Hiebert: "In the anti-diluvian period, as a consequence of the behaviour of J's primeval citizens, it lies under the curse. The power of the curse reaches its climax in the catastrophe of the Flood and is resolved immediately afterward by God's decision to lift the curse . . . J never again refers to the curse on arable soil."[63]

---

59 Hiebert, T., *The Yahwist's Landscape*, p. 69.
60 Hiebert, T., *The Yahwist's Landscape*, p. 64.
61 Hiebert, T., *The Yahwist's Landscape*, pp. 80-82.
62 Hiebert, T., *The Yahwist's Landscape*, pp. 81 f.
63 Hiebert, T., *The Yahwist's Landscape*, p. 81.

## Nature and Religion

Hiebert's argument implies that to be a human being is to be a farmer within this worldview which represents, in the cultures of the ancient near-east, a "remote, small and marginal" landscape.[64]  The ideal sites for existence here are the natural everyday ones though with some hopes for better land and water provision.  So also the nature of the cosmos as figured through the person of the deity mirrors this farming society: "J's God shares many of the essential characteristics of the Ancient Near-Eastern storm god . . . just as rain is considered a manifestation of divine power, so is the germination of seeds in fertile soil."[65]  Human beings are defined as servants of the deity, worshipping him through altars such as those set up by Noah, and of the soil, which they need to care for.  In this approach the moral vision of the cosmos is very different from that of the Priestly writer of Genesis chapter one, who creates humans in the image of gods and gives them mastery over the world.[66]  Hiebert offers an extension of this earthy view of the Yahwist for modern readers: "The recovery of the Yahwist's modest view of the human place within the world from the very long shadow cast by the Priestly viewpoint in the history of scholarship and its modern environmental theology broadens our understanding of ancient Israelite thought."[67]

## The Heavens and the Earth

Hiebert here contrasts two parallel modes of creating a moral vision of human beings in a creation context.  William Brown describes this latter view as an irenic cosmogony in which God does not make a powerless and slavishly dependent world.[68]  But the focus then moves to the earth; what will human beings make of this peaceful start?  The answer is violence and bloodshed.  So, what will the heavens do next?  The answer, according to Brown, is that "the boundaries between earth and heaven are dismantled from above and below".[69]  However God seeks a new collaborative compact through Noah and his sons down to Abraham and Israel.  "As

---

64  Hiebert, T., *The Yahwist's Landscape*, p. 146.
65  Hiebert, T., *The Yahwist's Landscape*, p. 73.
66  Hiebert, T., *The Yahwist's Landscape*, p. 136.
67  Hiebert, T., *The Yahwist's Landscape*, p. 159.
68  Brown, W., *The Ethos of the Cosmos*, p. 147.
69  Brown, W., *The Ethos of the Cosmos*, p. 55.

humankind's propensity for predation and violence is checked in the institution of the blood prohibition, so also God's inclination to rectify measures through destructive intervention is categorically restricted."[70]

In this approach human beings are mirrors of the cosmos and the cosmos finds its identity through their activity within a context of heavenly control. This is a quite separate form of world order and moral vision from that of the Yahwist, set out above, but it too tends to establish firm links between human beings and their cosmic context. Luise Schotroff asks: "Do we live as images of God or do we live as masters? The creation leads us to this practical question."[71] For her the solution to this matter of the link between heaven and earth is the nature of the comic creator as a source for the powers of justice and a heart that can love.[72] This profile leads to a service model of morality and not to one of manipulation, engendering a need to examine the style of human use of the environment. She suggests that modern Christian readers of Genesis chapter one should make some contemporary moral decisions "against nuclear power plants or for a church policy of asylum, in which the church provides an inviolable sanctuary".[73]

## The Garden

A great deal of scholarly debate has focused on the description of the garden in the East, perceiving in this place-setting clues to timeless truths about human existence. One strand here is the issue of wisdom – the tree of the knowledge of good and evil. Eating from this tree brings Eve and Adam a new self-awareness. In becoming like gods, as the serpent promises, they learn to see themselves objectively. Carmichael suggests that this kind of knowledge is pessimistic, not unlike the tone of Ecclesiastes.[74] Although they can know about the future and about their destiny, "such enlightenment as is provided to them is not the buoyant kind of knowledge that is offered to the young men of the book of Proverbs".[75] A tension may occur, then, between acquiring wisdom, thus "threatening

---

70  Brown, W., *The Ethos of the Cosmos*, p. 60.
71  Schotroff, L., *The Creation Narrative: Genesis 1:1-2:4*, in Brenner, A. (ed.), *A Feminist Companion to Genesis*, Sheffield, Sheffield Academic Press, 1997.
72  Schotroff, L., *The Creation Narrative*, p. 34.
73  Schotroff, L., *The Creation Narrative*, p. 35.
74  Carmichael, C., *The Paradise Myth: Interpreting without Jewish and Christian Spectacles*, in Morris, P. and Sawyer, D. (eds), *A Walk in the Garden*, Sheffield, Sheffield Academic Press, 1992, p. 53.
75  Carmichael, C., *The Paradise Myth*, p. 51.

the distinction between gods and humankind",[76] and the stress on the limited life span of humans as a way of re-stating the boundary between humanity and God.[77]

By distinction Mara Donaldson argues that the message of Genesis chapter three is not a plain negative with regard to wisdom.[78] She suggests that the text operates as a fantasy tale in which limits are transgressed.[79] This viewpoint offers a moral paradigm in which the key issue of human existence is boundaries and their crossing. When Eve contemplates the fruit on offer and makes her choice, the narrative of her action can be classed as fantasy, because it deals with what Donaldson labels a border-crossing.[80] The focus here is on the challenging of the status quo which endorses the boundary, thus re-shaping the possible order of human affairs: "The religious dimension of fantasy, therefore, is not beyond, but within this moment of hesitation and its ability to interrupt, and thus subvert, our expectations about the world."[81]

Bechtel takes this positive evaluation of boundary crossing a stage further in the argument that the Garden of Eden is where human beings grow up.[82] They enter there as children, unaware of their differentiated being and leave as adults fully aware of the possibilities as well as the difficulties of life. The garden as the place of change is not connected with sin so much as a natural rebellion against divine parental authority.[83]

So far human beings have been treated as a species but one of the key issues for the message of moral order in Genesis chapters two and three is the role of man and woman. The traditional view regards woman as secondary to man, as a dependent being who then leads her superior astray. Feminist scholars attack this perspective as patriarchal oppression. Schungel-Straumann raises the issue of this exegetical tradition, in which blame is placed on Eve for the loss of paradise.[84] In counterpoint she

76  Carmichael, C., *The Paradise Myth*, p. 57.
77  Carmichael, C., *The Paradise Myth*, p. 57.
78  Donaldson, M., *Bordercrossing: Fall and Fantasy in Blade Runner and Thelma and Louise*, in Aichele, G. and Pippin, T. (eds), *The Monstrous and the Unspeakable*, Sheffield, Sheffield Academic Press, 1997.
79  Donaldson, M., *Bordercrossing*, pp. 19 f.
80  Donaldson, M., *Bordercrossing*, p. 25.
81  Donaldson, M., *Bordercrossing*, p. 25.
82  Bechtel, L., *Re-thinking the Interpretation of Genesis 2:4b – 3:24*, in Brenner, A. (ed.), *A Feminist Companion to Genesis*.
83  Bechtel, L., *Re-thinking the Interpretation of Genesis*, p. 85.
84  Schungel-Straumann, H., *On the Creation of Man and Woman in Genesis 3* in Brenner, A. (ed.), *A Feminist Companion to Genesis*, Sheffield, Sheffield Academic Press, 1997, p. 58.

argues that the origin of woman as 'helper' to man "does not imply anything subordinate, like the help of a maidservant".[85] Eve's openness to dialogue with the serpent indicates rather her developing curiosity in her environment and willingness to look for broader frontiers than wilful disobedience. Furthermore, she is justified in searching for truth since she does not immediately die as God had foretold. Rather than promoting whole hearted supremacy for one gender or the other, some commentators point to the complexity of the issues here. Adam (masculine) comes from *Adamah* (feminine) but *Ishah* (female) comes from *Ish* (male). This linguistic play indicates a subtle relationship between human beings and their place of existence.[86] Central to all the moral perspectives is the fact that gender is built in to created order and operates to express the role of mutuality in the cosmos.

## The City

Central to the debates over the garden narrative is the issue of the similarity and difference between God and human beings. John Sawyer indeed argues that the garden scene is placed in the text deliberately as an expansion on the theme of the image of God in Genesis chapter one.[87] The Tower City of Babel is another place where this theme is debated.[88] In the story the Tower 'ascends' to the heavens and establishes a name for the builders there while God 'descends' to see and to prevent this link to the heavens becoming permanent. This parallelism is emphasised by the fact that the two sections of the story, the account of the builders and the account of divine response, each begins: 'let us . . . make name/go and see'.

---

85  Schungel-Straumann, H., *On the Creation*, p. 66.
86  Simkins, R., *Gender Construction in the Yahwist Creation Myth*, in Brenner, A. (ed.), *Genesis: A Feminist Companion* (second series), Sheffield, Sheffield Academic Press, 1998, pp. 45-49.
87  Sawyer, J., *The Image of God, the Wisdom of Serpents and the Knowledge of Good and Evil* in Morris, P. and Sawyer, D. (eds), *A walk in the Garden*, Sheffield, Sheffield Academic Press, 1992.
88  In Genesis chapter eleven, the builders are sometimes described as making a tower, which rises up to the heavens, in the mode of a Ziggurat temple structure. And they are sometimes pictured as speaking to each other in a manner, which assumes that there is a large group of humans living together in this structure. This allows for two modes of relating to Babel, both as tower, and as city.

For Hubert Bost the tower and the city are one reality.[89]   The tower
represents the political power of a great city and provides a religious focus
for political activity.  Bost suggests that this represents that human beings
are on a par with God.  They do not attempt to replace God as in the Greek
Titan myth, but they do claim equality since the top of the tower is in
heaven.[90]  This approach to world order is countered in the story by God's
response, which offers the alternative attitude – that human beings are not
capable of achieving this equality.  Their attempts to do so, in creating a
monolithic community, will lead to absolutism and tyranny in human
society; it is this evil which God prevents by dispersing the tower's
inhabitants.[91]  This offers a morality in which a paternalistic deity acts to
prevent the consequences of faulty human wisdom, but it would be equally
possible to take the view that it is divine supremacy which is threatened by
the building skills of humans.  In this perspective God uses his superior
force to prevent human beings achieving their reasonable goals.


## The Deity and the Cosmos

This last point raises issues about the role of the deity in world order.
Brown assumes God can be trusted and relied on as a stable feature of the
world being beyond the story: "As lawgiver and creator, God is the
ultimate cause that brings about the moral coherence of nature."[92]  Steven
Brams takes a different approach in his book *Biblical Games*.[93]  Here he
argues that God does not always get his way, [so] he can properly be
viewed as a participant, or player, in a game:[94] "To make the world less
predictable and therefore more alive and engrossing, it was in God's
interest to give man free will.  The price he paid, of course, is having to
contend with a creature who continually frustrates him and occasionally
drives him to the brink of despair."[95]

This game-playing deity is overall a positive figure, though one who is a
participant alongside his own creation in a series of cosmic games.  But

---

89  Bost, H., *Babel. Du Texte au Symbole*, Geneva, Labor et Fides, 1985. Cf. for example, p.
    56.
90  Bost, H., *Du Texte au Symbole*, p. 65.
91  Bost, H., *Du Texte au Symbole*, p. 66.
92  Brown, W., *The Ethos of the Cosmos*, p. 13.
93  Brams, S., *Biblical Games: A Strategic Analysis of Stories in the Old Testament*,
    Massachusetts, MIT Press, 1980.
94  Brams, S., *Biblical Games*, p. 5.
95  Brams, S., *Biblical Games*, p. 14.

game-playing is not always judged to be a positive activity; it can be read as a form of manipulation. Norman Whybray, writing on the immorality of God, takes up two texts,[96] both instances where humans are coming close to divinity, with regard to immortality and omnipotence, respectively.[97] God acts to deal with this intrusion into his boundaries. In chapter three God tells human beings a lie, for they do *not* die on eating the fruit.[98] In Genesis chapter eleven God is vulnerable, according to Whybray: "although he rises effectively and apparently in the nick of time, to the challenge, he recognises human victory as a possibility".[99]

David Penchansky takes this negative approach to God further still.[100] Employing the genre of fantasy, he suggests that in the garden scene, God is monstrous. Using the problems of the text – such as why did God make available a tree from which he did not want humans to eat – he moves to the folktale genre in which a hero or heroine grows up. This usually occurs by breaking through the prohibitions set in place by a wicked adult, often a parent. In this reading "Yahweh/Elohim becomes an imprisoner, seeking to keep the humans in the Garden of Eden in ignorance and dependency".[101]

At the heart of this discussion is the view that God and human beings are forever linked in time and place. God is not alone in the cosmos just as Adam is not alone, for now they have each other. Although the relationship is uneasy and God wishes to have control of it he is drawn into the human experience, accompanying human beings on their journeys outside the garden and overseeing their fruitfulness in the earth. God and human beings inhabit the same spaces in the narrative and it is the interweaving of their responses to this indwelling which triggers the plot sequences of Torah.

96  Genesis 3 [22] and 11 [6-7].
97  Whybray, N., *The Immorality of God*, in *Journal for the Study of the Old Testament*, Volume No. 72/96, 1996, p. 90.
98  Whybray, N., *The Immorality of God*, p. 93.
99  Whybray, N., *The Immorality of God*, p. 96.
100 Penchansky, D., *God the Monster: Fantasy in the Garden of Eden* in Aichele, G. and Pippin, T. (eds), *The Monstrous and the Unspeakable*, Sheffield, Sheffield Academic Press, 1997.
101 Penchansky, D., *God the Monster*, p. 54.

## Summary: Cosmos, Community, and Person
## in Genesis Chapters One to Eleven

In the debates concerning these wider issues of morality in the world order, time and place run together, with stress on time as primal time, and on primal time as giving meaning to life as an ongoing reality in historical time. This primal time is examined via places – the world itself, earth, garden, city – to which can be added the Ark and the vineyard, in Noah's story. Issues of general moral vision emerge from this, for modern readers:

> the need to re-think human-centred attitudes to the rest of creation.
> the importance of gender, but equally the problems of gender distinction as a basis for oppressive human society.
> the possibilities of scaling the heights of wisdom, as human beings; and the possible destructive consequences of this pride in human achievement.

The question arises whether these issues can be discussed in the setting of development theory, a growth to fuller understanding, away from ignorance and error in human knowledge, or whether they can only be debated in the context of breaking basic law and order. There is a tension here, in the use of the word sin, between the evaluation of boundaries and limits as a positive cosmic reality and the belief that they endorse oppressive, socially-entrenched attitudes which colour power structures in a human group. In Genesis chapters one to eleven these issues are dealt with in such a manner that the cosmos is not an impersonal material environment but is, rather, personified into a being who can be named and whose works can be described. Community, on the other hand, remains somewhat abstract, representing any human group and the overall underlying roles of gendered beings in society. The human person is more visible as a topic since it is dealt with through a number of characters whose stories are narrated; yet each character also gathers up into her or himself the communal interests of a reading audience concerning the significance of world order.

# Chapter Nine

# Morality and World Powers
# in Daniel Chapters One to Seven

The previous chapter focused on the moral vision, which can be drawn from stories concerning the creation of world order and the ensuing threats to that order. One message, which can be arrived at, is the significance of human responsibility for maintaining or fragmenting that world order. This chapter adds a further dimension to the subject of human involvement with world affairs since it explores, through a separate narrative, the relationship between human systems of organisation, especially in the political structures of 'world powers', and the over-arching sovereignty of the God of Israel.

This investigation will be carried out by an examination of the literary structures of the first seven chapters of the Book of Daniel. Commentators usually split this book into two parts on the grounds of literary genre: chapters one to six, and chapters seven to twelve. The first six chapters are stories about dreams and visions and their interpretation, whereas the last chapters are in the style of vision-reports. This move entails a shift in narrator from a third person account to a first person narrator. However, there is room for manoeuvre here since the literary boundaries are blurred. Chapter seven is written in Aramaic rather than Hebrew and so fits, linguistically, with the previous material rather than the remaining sections of the book. There are parallels between chapter seven and the stories, especially with regard to the play on four kingdoms in chapters two and seven. In addition, the king becomes, temporarily, a beast in the story section while the kingdoms are portrayed as four beasts in chapter seven. It is possible, then, to link the first seven chapters of Daniel together.

The advantage of aligning chapter seven with the earlier units of material is that this provides a key to the theological meanings of those earlier sections. In the first chapters the stories are about matters on earth, but heaven continually influences events there. In chapter seven the order reverses, with heaven at the forefront of the scene and earth coming in later. Earth is symbolised by the court of a foreign king, and the events deal with how a Jew will fare at such a place. In chapter seven the nature of what earth is appears to have shifted to faithful Jews in Judah/Israel. But in both cases the stress is on the place which political systems have in human affairs. The argument is that human governments do not rule the earth without any reference to the deity who controls the heavens. The heavens and the earth are, as in Genesis chapters one to eleven, a single reality of cosmic dimensions.

It is the story of the young man, Daniel, and his colleagues, which holds the individual units together as the reader follows his career development at the courts of Babylon and Persia. The focus is on the training of Daniel to be a court official with special skills in advising the ruler through dream-interpretation.[1] In this way Daniel comes close to the presentation of Joseph in Genesis, where Joseph can interpret Pharaoh's dream because of divine assistance from the living God.[2] The successes of a Jew at a foreign court are balanced by scenes in which the Jewish person is in great danger: the three men in the furnace and Daniel in the lions' den. The reader is kept in suspense as the ups and downs of court life are revealed. Since the final scene leaves Daniel retrieved from the lions and his enemies destroyed it can be argued that this material forms a comedy, just as the story of Esther, another Jew at a foreign court, can be classed as comic, since Jewish fortunes end in the ascendant.[3]

In the first chapters of Daniel, the reader has been able to watch the hero in action; in chapter seven the reader is given an insight into the interior understanding which Daniel has of what is happening, and going to happen, around him. The reader has been prepared for this revelation at points in the earlier scenes. In the first chapter the context of the story of Daniel is that of the foreign invasion of Jerusalem and the seizure of the Temple and its destruction. The God of Israel allows these events to happen, but the corollary is that honour and worship are no longer available to this deity in his own place and from his own people. The looting of the Temple implies the weakness of the God to defend his own dwelling and the potential superiority of the gods of the Babylonians. This theme is reflected in chapter five, where Belshazzar calls for the Temple vessels to be used for profane purposes, and where the court drink from these vessels and toast the honour of their own deities. What is the reality of the cosmic balance of power? The immediate appearance at the banquet of the mysterious

---

1   The presentation of Daniel as a diviner, or dream interpreter, fits the book into a broader ancient near-Eastern pattern of mantic wisdom at the service of kings. The same format occurs for Joseph in the book of Genesis. In both cases the hero of the story is one figure among many other types of mantic sage at the royal court. See, for instance, Cryer, F., *Divination in Ancient Israel and it Near-Eastern Environment*, Sheffield, Sheffield Academic Press, 1994.

2   See here Chapter Six on the story of Joseph.

3   See her Chapter Four on the character of Esther.

hand, which writes on the palace wall, gives the answer. The God of the Jews is in charge of affairs, even those of foreign nations, and this God will redeem his own honour. That night the arrogant king will die and his kingdom will collapse as it falls to an invading power in its turn.

It is this invisible cosmic force which presides over history and whose nature is made plain in the heavenly vision material in the later chapters of Daniel. The text therefore presents world affairs as a struggle between nations carried through against the backdrop of the cosmos where the struggle is mirrored in the theme of cosmic warfare. The nations have their cosmic equivalents and the contest between them is active also among their supernatural counterparts. There is, in this book, a tension between history and timeless cosmic balances. On one level the book can be read as a historical novel which aims to use actual historical events as a means of exploring deeper issues of moral vision. Ancient commentators took up this view of the first part of Daniel, but there are problems of inaccuracy here.[4] The kings mentioned do not always fit in name and date with non-biblical historical data relating to the Babylonian and Persian Empires.[5] The narrative cannot be read as straight historiography. What can be salvaged from this approach is the idea of a novel. The text can be read as a series of 'court tales', which explore, through literary fiction, the nature of human society in an imperial setting.

## Court Tales in Daniel Chapters One to Six

As Pamela Milne notes: "Of the many sub-classifications which have been used for these stories . . . the one most often chosen is that of the 'court tale'."[6] In particular W. Lee Humphrey's analysis of Esther and Daniel as court tales has gained attention among scholars.[7] He suggests that the basic structure of such tales is that:

---

4    See, for instance, Collins, J., *Daniel*, Minneapolis, Augsburg/Fortress Press, 1993, pp. 24-
     28, on issues relating to composition. A key question is whether the text has serious
     historical links with the events of the Persian period or whether it belongs fully to the
     Hellenistic period.
5    See eg. Collins, J., *Daniel*, pp. 29-33.
6    Milne, P., *Vladimir Propp and the Study of Structure in Hebrew Biblical Narrative*,
     Sheffield, Sheffield Academic Press, 1988, p. 180.
7    See eg. Milne, P., *Vladimir Propp and the Study of Structure in Hebrew Biblical Narrative*,
     p. 181.

at the centre is a courtier whose qualities are outstanding and who is recognised as such.

he finds a place at court.

the life of the courtier is endangered through other courtiers or court events.

through various means the courtier manages to counter these dangers.

the courtier is exalted to higher rank and any enemies are destroyed.[8]

They may then subdivide into further genres – that of court conflict (where the focus is danger to the courtier) or court contest (where the courtier encounters challenges to his skills and career). An example of this latter form is the type of scene where the king is confronted with a dream or a sign which cannot be understood. Wise men fail to cope but the hero (in this case, Daniel) succeeds and then is exalted.[9] By contrast the account of the conspiracy by chief officials against Daniel in chapter six reflects more the genre of the conflict tale. Paul Redditt adds to the debate about court tale genres by referring to the work of Muller, who is unhappy about the split outlined above into two types and who looks for one deep underlying structuralist understanding of this kind of Folktale.[10] It is further suggested, by Collins, that the best single type for these tales is Aarne and Thompson's category of clever words and deeds.[11]

Edwin Good argues that the plots of court narratives follow the pattern of a comedy. That is, they end on a positive note.[12] This is in contrast with chapters seven to twelve where, although God's faithful servants are vindicated, this is in the face of vehement opposition from Gentile world powers.[13] Judahites win in the end because disasters come to the kings of the earth. In chapters one to six it could be argued that the text allows for the absorption of Jews into Gentile kingdoms and culture so that only religious practice remains to provide a distinction in social identity. Even though chapter two shows that world kingdoms will come to an end, and

---

8   Milne, P., *Vladimir Propp and the Study of Structure in Hebrew Biblical*, p. 181.

9   Milne, P., *Vladimir Propp and the Study of Structure in Hebrew Biblical*, p. 184.

10  Redditt, P., *Daniel*, New Century commentaries, Sheffield, Sheffield Academic Press, 1999.

11  Collins, J., *Daniel*, p. 173.

12  Redditt, P., *Daniel*, p. 13.

13  Daniel chapter twelve contains the scene where the end and a judgement take place as the books of record are opened and the wise shine like stars. In this chapter the reward of the faithful is resurrection from the dead to a happy and noble future.

that there is a difference between them and the kingdom which the God of Israel initiates and supports, the tone of the chapter can be argued to be gentle. The kingdoms are still part of God's historical time-plans and have their place in these schemes. But the kingdoms in chapter seven belong to the 'sea', a symbol for chaos and not to heaven.[14] They are specifically judged and condemned by God as arrogant rivals to him and are destroyed because they are not of God in any way.

This shift in perspective is generally acknowledged by scholars who attribute it to the different time setting of the author(s) of chapters eight to twelve. Whereas there can be some support for arguing that the 'court tales' material did emerge in the early stages of the Exilic period, it is clear that the later sections of Daniel together with its final editing belong in the Hellenistic period of the second century BCE.[15] In this context the relationships between Gentile kingdoms and Jewish culture moved more to an 'us versus them' approach. Redditt remarks that "gone is the more or less sympathetic portrayal of the foreign king encountered especially in Daniel chapters two and six, as well as the general hope that things would go well for Judæans in exile. Gone too is the portrayal of life in the Diaspora, and in its place is an overwhelming interest in Jerusalem and Judah."[16]

Thus, Daniel chapters one to seven provide the reader with competing patterns of evaluating morality. In the court tale version there is optimism about the unity of the cosmos. God, at the cosmic level, holds together the experiences of community and person. There may be difficulties encountered on both of these two levels, historically, which make it necessary for persons to use cunning and prudence in their conduct of affairs in order to gain the best advantage for life. But there remains the belief that the judicious use of divinely enhanced personal skills will improve the opportunities for the community to which such persons belong. In the more pessimistic version the individual person is still required to act in faith with God and community but this may not lead to the removal of social and political dangers to the life of the community as a whole. Only the direct intervention of God in human history can reverse the fortunes of Israel as community, and this can only be achieved at the cost of destruction for other communities. For there is an inherent dualism in community relations in which only one side can win the battle for survival. The

---

14 For more information see Chapter Eight on the story of Jonah.
15 Cf: Collins, J., *Daniel*, p. 35; Davies, P., *Daniel*, Sheffield, Sheffield Academic Press, 1985, pp. 13-18.
16 Redditt, P., *Daniel*, p. 4.

individual may be asked to sacrifice not only advancement, but also life itself, in this struggle and must look for reward outside the sphere of earthly existence.[17]

## Apocalyptic Writing

The literary genre of the book of Daniel moves from court tale to visions of war, victory and defeat for Judah and world powers joined in a cosmic contest for existence. This somewhat pessimistic view of world order is not a major focus for the present chapter, but it must be given some attention, since it forms the backdrop for chapter seven. Ultimately, since the book of Daniel contains both genres in one work, both styles contribute to the overall message of the work and are mutually interpretive. Scholars have generally labelled this pessimistic vision 'apocalyptic', not because this is an ancient title for the works which share this viewpoint, but in line with the name of the New Testament work, the Book of Revelation (in Greek, the Apocalypse). The question then arises what exactly is apocalyptic writing, what constitutes its literary genre? There have been intense debates on this matter in the twentieth century, but it is useful to consider the definition offered by J. J. Collins, a notable scholar in this field.[18] He describes the style as "a genre of revelatory literature with a narrative framework, in which a revelation is mediated by an otherworldly being to a human recipient, disclosing a transcendent reality, which is both temporal, insofar as it envisages eschatalogical salvation, and spatial, insofar as it involves another supernatural world".[19] It is apparent from reading the visions of Daniel chapter seven that the above definition offers a working description of what occurs there.

17  This is evidence of the beginnings of a martyr theology, which is developed in later texts such as the second book of Maccabees which contains the tale of a mother and her sons, and in the New Testament book of Revelation.

18  This is a subject of huge debate. Earlier scholars working on apocalyptic suggested a late date, in the Persian period, for the origins of the genre, because they detected signs of Zoroastrian dualism and the presence of angelic figures in the material. A greater knowledge of archæological evidence from Syro-Palestine has shown a continuity in the region from the second millenium of pantheons of deities which include messenger gods (see Edelmann, D. (ed.), *The Triumph of Elohim*, Kampen, Kok Pharos, 1995). Attention has thus turned to exploring the internal Israelite forms of apocalyptic thought. A key scholar in this area is John Collins. See *The Apocalyptic Imagination*, New York, Crossroad, 1984.

19  Collins, J. (ed.), *Apocalypse: Morphology of a Genre*, Missoula, Scholars Press, 1979, p. 9.

Thus both parts of Daniel have an interest in world order and particularly in the world powers which claim authority over that order. In the court tales the king is warned that he will become less than human, as in chapter four, or that his kingdom will be seized by others, as in chapter five. The reason for this is human arrogance, which makes the human ruler into the controller of the cosmos and of all human affairs. The same arrogance is attributed to the little horn mentioned in Daniel seven and, likewise, the same destruction awaits his human kingship.

## Time and Place in Daniel Chapters One to Seven

Consideration of literary genres leads on to the issues of time and place settings in Daniel with regard to the moral perspectives of the book. Clearly both time and place are important areas for consideration since both are essential to a work which examines the meaning of both historical time and historical places such as the courts of great kings.

Time comes to include the further topics of history, and of exile as a point in time, which is central to the moral vision of identity in the Old Testament. On a smaller scale, time operates internally in the work, giving meaning to events by placing them in one particular sequence of happening. Place can be broken up into places, spaces in which Jews and Gentiles interact. Thus the theme of the gentile court can be sub-divided into several topics: that of the great kingdom, represented by the person of the king himself; the court banquet, as a symbol of power and luxury; the furnace and the pit – the places of punishment for those within the court who defy its power.

## Time, Narrative and History

In the previous chapter some account was given of the role of time as a literary device used to structure narratives. Behind such a consideration lie deeper philosophical issues about the significance of time itself. Time is usually defined by its measurements – past, present, future. But there is a logical difficulty about this definition of time as a thing, which really exists, since the past is no more and the future is not yet. Only the present moment has any real existence, but this is not enough to give to time a function as providing meaning in life, whether daily existence or the life of the symbolic worlds of narratives. Only as moment is linked to moment, event to event, does the structuring of meaning by temporality make sense. Paul Ricoeur argues, in this context, from ancient philosophy to the narrative order of time.[20] He draws on Augustine's view that time becomes a useful concept for ordering and evaluating experience through the operation of the human mind. The mind forges a tool for time as a moral device through memory (of the past), attention (to the present) and expectation (of the future).[21] This gives an order to temporality, which allows past, present and future to be used to measure events and allows for the gathering of individual occurrences into a whole picture of life's events.

Ricoeur draws from this balance of the wholeness of a set of events against the discordance of individual moments of time, a particular approach to the narrative use of time. He aligns narrative time with Aristotle's theory of the literary style of the tragic poem, as a means of creating a whole which gives ultimate significance to events.[22] This approach allows for the discordance of episodes (the unexpected happening) but argues that these separate elements of the story flesh out the plurality of meaning to be taken from a narrative as a whole. The individual moments of time only reveal their true significance when placed in the over-arching narrative, which provides the framework for interpreting each of them in relation to the others. The link is emplotment, which creates a literary, narrative use of time, which is not the same as the passage of real time since it is governed by the ending of the story, which is already known and fixed by the story-teller. Ricoeur argues that it is the re-telling rather than the telling, of a story, which allows the closure of narrative meaning to be seen.[23]

These reflections on time are important because apocalyptic writing in general, and Daniel chapters one to seven in particular, is closely linked to the idea of time. John Collins points out that modern scholarship has become more aware of the manner in which material such as that in Daniel chapter seven builds on Creation time theories, bringing together *Ur*time and endtime in one temporal whole.[24] Moreover, although the beginnings of time set the context for this literary activity, it is the endtime which is the more significant, for it closes the meaning of world order by its ending of the temporal sequence. Ancient Near-Eastern myths contain the concept of creation as battle and this is picked up in Daniel chapters seven to twelve,

20  Ricoeur, P., *Time and Narrative*, Volume 1, Chicago, University of Chicago Press, 1984.
21  Ricoeur, P., *Time and Narrative*, pp. 20.
22  Ricoeur, P., *Time and Narrative*, pp. 38 f.
23  Ricoeur, P., *Time and Narrative*, pp. 66 f.
24  Cf. Collins, J., *Daniel*, p. 61, and the commentary on Daniel chapter seven.

where the theme of battle among nations opens out into cosmic warfare, the climax of which will lead to the trials of the Last Days and the cessation of history.[25]    Ricoeur suggests that apocalyptic use of time epitomises the reversal of temporality by which the end of a narrative, rather than the gradual development of events, establishes its meaning: "This reversal is magnified by the apocalyptic model to the extent that the end is the catastrophe that abolishes time and prefigures the horrors of the last days."[26]

Chapter seven of Daniel, as also chapter two, foresees a definitive end to time and this provides the moral vision from which to consider the value of human systems of government.    Great kings may see themselves as invincible and as holding supreme power within their empires but this is illusory.    Only the closure provided by gathering together beginning and ending of cosmic time can provide the proper tools for developing a moral perspective on kings and empires.    Time in Daniel is thus intimately connected with history – and again there are issues relating to the deeper significance of events, which need to be aired here.

Ricoeur's comments, on the *longue durée* approach to history, which has been adopted by some French historians of the twentieth century, are useful here.    He notes the emphasis put by this school not on events or individuals but on long term trends in social and economic affairs: "By means of slowness, weightiness, silence of long lasting time, history reaches an intelligibility that belongs only to the long time-span."[27]    This perspective is applicable to the literary world of Daniel where the workings of the cosmic forces, which are the foundations of human existence can only be understood through a long-term approach to political affairs.    The division maintained by chapter two, of political structures into four major kingdoms, none of which endures, explains to the reader that only the still centre of divine supremacy provides meaning to human history, not the succession of kingdoms and reigns.[28]    It is not human power which is eternal but that of the living God of Judahite belief.    In this manner Daniel offers a literary version of metahistory, in which the procession of events take on new shape.    The endless succession of rulers, the many battles between kingdoms for control of the earth, are seen not to determine the

---

25    See Chapter Eight on world order in Genesis.
26    Ricoeur, P., *Time and Narrative*, p. 73.
27    Ricoeur, P., *Time and Narrative*, p. 104.
28    Cf. Redditt, P., *Daniel*, pp. 6-10, where the historical kingdoms are outlined and pp. 62-63 and 118-124, where the theological use of these kingdoms in the book of Daniel is discussed.

proper view of history. Rather, it is the ultimate power of the divine cosmic force which determines the shape of human experience. The reader is encouraged to take on board this metahistorical explanation of human experience and to view community as conditioned by cosmos rather than cosmos as controlled by community. In this approach world order and world powers are not synonymous. World order is measured by the fixed points of a beginning and end of world affairs, not by the variety of world events in the temporal progression between start and finish.

## Time in Daniel Chapters One to Seven

As well as opening out into questions about the nature of time and history, the time settings of Daniel raise more local issues. The concept of exile becomes significant here, both as a cultural symbol, an aspect, which will be examined below, and as a bridge between text and the historical experience of its early readers. As a period of real time the Exile is important because it is in the post-Exilic setting that the Old Testament texts were edited.[29] It is in the light of the community experience of invasion, military defeat and deportation that these texts reflect on the significance of ancestral religious traditions. This historical context raises religious problems related to the strength/weakness of Judah's God. Was God too weak to prevent the exile of his people? Or did he not care about them? Should ancestral deities have any place in the new, post-Exilic community? Daniel chapters one to seven, as the book of Esther also, argues that the God of the ancestors is still operative and that this deity controls all nations while still electing Judah as his own people, provided that Judah worships him.

Time, then, is measured by politics and the way in which these mark the high and low points for Jewish characters in the stories. It is the development of royal politics, which also reveals the essential ambiguity of

---

29 This topic has been noted across the several chapters of the present work. There is little certainty as to when the text of the Old Testament came into existence. There is very little written material from Israel/Judah outside of the Old Testament with which to compare the text as it was finally transmitted. The best source is the Dead Sea material from the first century CE. The two most popular positions are either that the texts emerged from a long period of editing, between ninth century BCE and the fourth century BCE, or that all the material as it now stands developed between the fifth century BCE and the second century BCE. In each case the texts emerged within a post-exilic frame and are likely to have been shaped by the viewpoint of those who lived within a larger political unit of foreign empire.

Gentile rulers towards their Jewish subjects.   On the one hand they welcome skilled men into court positions but, on the other, are sensitive to how the advancement of these men may threaten their own power. Although one scene may show a ruler won over to the culture of the court official, the next starts all over again with a relational gap between king and courtier – a gap which can be exploited by other courtiers anxious for the role of king's friend.  The instability of the relations between Gentile and Jew prevents the ruler's acceptance of full exclusive monotheism, and, as a result, Gentile kingdoms are flawed political entities.

Inside the overall time-span of a number of reigns not all events are recorded.   This is not a chronicle of the ruler's achievements.   Rather, symbolic sequences of timing are used to illustrate an over-arching view on the nature of world powers.  Within this context there is a focus on the role of dreams and visions in court affairs.  This means that a further unit of time is significant, namely night-time.  Night is a time for the critique of world power, when, in the dreams of kings, the truth about their power emerges.   The statue of many metals, the mighty tree and the ox, the writing hand, are riddles – mysteries which carry an encoded message, summed up in the interpretation of the writing that these rulers are weighed and measured, by the judgement of the fullness of time.  As opposed to Genesis chapter forty-one where the dream of the ruler is important for the immediate policy-making in Egypt, the dream of Daniel chapter two has wider significance.  Both are royal dreams but the one in Daniel chapter two "extends far beyond the fate of the kingdom", according to Husser: "Essentially, what the reader retains is a revelation about the course of history in general and about God's intervention in the near future."[30]

Dreams merge, in Daniel chapters one to seven, with night visions. Chapter seven deals with what is called a dream, although its format is actually that of a vision, and leads into ascent to heaven combined with throne-vision mythology.[31]   Indeed Husser argues that dreams in Daniel chapters two and four show a different literary structure from other royal dreams in the Old Testament.  They seem "no longer to be concerned with recreating in any way the ordinary experience of dreams; the rich, highly

---

30  Husser, J.-M., *Dreams and Dream Narratives in the Biblical World*, Sheffield, Sheffield Academic Press, 1999, p. 119.
31  An essential motif of an apocalypse is a face to face encounter of the visionary with the heavenly powers. This entails an out-of- body experience described as an ascent to heaven (for example, see the first book of Enoch, chapters one to thirty-six and Daniel chapter seven). The throne is the literary symbol of the presence of God and of divine power. To see that throne is to have an authentic message about cosmic meaning.

elaborate symbolism, with mythological and quasi-universal overtones, makes the reader forget the dreams of his situation and instead highlights a message that one expects to be all the more true for the mysteriousness of its language".[32] Night time equates with the revelation of cosmic truths in a major way and it is appropriate that the recipient of messages from 'the beyond' is uneasy and troubled. Even when there are no dreams the king may lie uneasy at night, as in Daniel chapter six, where the ruler prays and laments over Daniel only to rise at dawn to a miraculous salvation of the courtier from the intended fate of being eaten by lions. Night forms the backdrop for the revelations of the miraculous, in a dawning of religious enlightenment in the darkness of Gentile ignorance.

## Place and Meaning in Daniel Chapters One to Seven

The use of place setting in Daniel chapters one to seven balances and mirrors the function of time sequence. If the Exile is the time setting of the court tales, it also provides the place-context of the foreign court. The young Jews are placed at the heart of the court; they are to be educated as Babylonian courtiers. Education here implies more than the skills of numeracy and literacy, it signifies the absorption of a young male citizen into the full duties and identity of the Babylonian state. Behind this setting is the issue of whether Judahite identity can survive at all in the new Diaspora framework. The issue is played out in the narrative through the topic of food. Daniel seeks to avoid defilement through eating gentile food. John Collins refers here to Mary Douglas's study on the connections between food and social identity.[33] Eating certain foods or abstaining from them reflects on a person's social status, while the macrocosm of community boundaries is expressed and preserved through the microcosm of food laws. In Daniel chapter one the contest over food is really a conflict of social identities. By avoidance of gentile food Daniel expresses his religious belief in a Judahite identity based on worship of YHWH alone.

His commitment is rewarded, for God ensures that he grows tall and strong, ready for a public career. This story sets the tone for the other scenes at the foreign court. It establishes both a potential harmony between foreign ways and Jewish identity, and a gap between Gentile and Jewish culture. Collins asserts this message to be the moral vision of this chapter

---

32  Husser, J.-M., *Dreams and Dream Narratives*, p. 120.
33  Collins, J., *Daniel*, p. 146.

and of succeeding ones. "Daniel and his companions prove themselves loyal and devoted subjects of the gentile king and embrace much of the gentile culture. Yet they also insist on a limit to assimilation."[34] Symbolic issues such as dietary rules are necessary for this moral perspective. "Although such observances are less engaging for modern western society ... their importance in maintaining religous communities should not be under-estimated."[35]

## The Great Kingdom

The theme of the foreign court then moves into the place of the great kingdom. In the court tales the great kingdom is the world of the text; all action occurs inside the foreign court, which is at the heart of the great kingdom or world empire. But is this equation of a single kingdom with total world power a reasonable and inevitable conclusion? In chapter two the dream of the statue reveals that this interpretation is flawed. The present ruler may be a figure of strength, as seen in the metaphor of the golden head, but his power, as it passes on, will be diminished to the point where it will be smashed completely. There is, then, a finitude to the great kingdom although this is a relative boundary since the kingdom will last for a long while before reaching its diminution. As Collins remarks, the reader is invited to view the message from the king's perception: "To be sure his kingdom will pass, but its destruction is not imminent."[36] On the other hand eschatology is still present in this scene. The crucial concept is that of the kingship of God as opposed to that of humans. Even the state chosen by God to take over from empire is only a reflection of divine authority to rule. To attribute cosmic power to human communities is a form of idolatry.[37]

It is not only the kingdom, which is an issue here, but the figure of the king himself. For the king represents in his person the honour of the whole community of the kingdom but yet stands above that community claiming personal links with the cosmos itself. In chapter four this role of the material presence of power in the person of the king is addressed. The symbol of a great tree (or mountain) is frequently applied to rulers in the ancient Near East and its size and height mirror a great king's claim to

---

34  Collins, J., *Daniel*, pp. 146 f.
35  Collins, J., *Daniel*, p. 147.
36  Collins, J., *Daniel*, p. 174.
37  Collins, J., *Daniel*, p. 147.

enter heaven and to be a force alongside cosmic powers.[38]   The irony is that, by claiming to be superhuman, the king turns out to be less than human.  His ignorance of the boundary between cosmos and kingship turns into the physical fact of a man lowered to the state of an irrational beast.

There is a further layer to moral vision here since the king is told he has a chance to retain sanity by acknowledging the proper bounds of his power. But instead the king is beguiled by the material evidence of his kingship.[39] Immediately the great city becomes the place of disaster, of cosmic judgement, as the sentence passed in the dream comes into force.  Collins indicates that this scene is traditionally read as a paradigm of hubris and humiliation,[40] and adds that this understanding of the city as the place of the fall of the arrogant is reinforced in the book of Daniel as a whole.[41]  Yet one thing is different in chapter four from the parallel scenes in chapters eight and eleven: the king is given a reprieve.  He repents of his arrogance, acknowledging his place as less than heaven and his power as defined by cosmic authority.

### The Great Feast

There is then some leeway in Daniel chapters one to six for the place of the great kingdom and the mighty ruler.  The great kingdom offers a place for Jews and their faith to survive and to provide a basis for the conversion of foreigners.  On the other hand this is not enough to ensure the eternity of either kingdom or ruler.  In Daniel chapter five the great foreign power is summed up in the symbol of the great feast.  Eating and drinking stand for community existence, which is here the community of the kingly court. King and high officials, the elite classes, revel in their power and luxury. Great wealth leads to great consumption and this can imply to the consumers that their resources are unlimited, as is their own control of destiny.

Luxury as a force for misleading persons and communities is summed up in the use of the Jerusalem Temple vessels for the royal table.  In the great hall, lit by flickering torches, the great and the good eat and drink

---

38  LaCocque, A., *Daniel in His Time*, South Carolina, University of South Carolina Press, 1988, p. 103.
39  Archæologists have revealed that Babylon was indeed a very large city for antiquity.  Cf. Redditt, P., *Daniel*, p. 84.
40  Collins, J., *Daniel*, p. 234.
41  Collins, J., *Daniel*, p. 234.

their fill, complacent in their honouring of their gods of gold and silver, wood and stone. A hand suddenly appears and starts to write the judgement, which God passes on great kings. As Collins states, "the story is a legend, since it is not only concerned with the wonderful but also aimed at edification . . . the God of heaven has power over human kingdoms and can humble those who fail to respect him and who practise idolatry".[42]

This scene at the place of the feast shows a similarity with the scene in chapter four, but it goes further in its attack on royal power. This time there is no space for retrieval, no hope for redemption. That very night the king dies and his kingdom passes to another. Thus a variety of messages is to be found with regard to court, kingdom and king in these court tales. There are some signs that human governments are part of the plan for the cosmos and that they can image divine authority over person and community, but equally they frequently go astray and become the means of human oppression. Collins notes: "The most enduring effect [of chapter five] . . . is bound up with the image of the writing on the wall, which has passed into common speech as a potent metaphor for impending doom and the transience of all human power."[43]

### The Furnace and the Pit

If the king is one kind of human person which is examined in Daniel chapters one to six the Jewish courtier is another. Here the stress is on the one who is powerless, who is at the mercy of the great king and his authority. Such a person may be exalted, as in several scenes, but equally may be thrown down, exposed to death. The place of the one who is different from the court, who separates himself from the king's will, is to be found in the furnace and the pit. The court retains places, then, spaces where punishment is administered to those who threaten its identity. The fire stands for the wrath of the great king, described in earlier verses. It will eat up those who threaten human power. But, instead, the men are untouched by fire or anger. The place of fire becomes a sacred space of peace and quiet where a fourth figure walks and talks with the outcasts as they make their prayers to their God. Collins notes that "the accusation is refusal to commit idolatry, and the deliverance is by a dramatic miracle. The appeal to the supernatural here is consonant with the appeal to divine

42 Collins, J., *Daniel*, p. 254.
43 Collins, J., *Daniel*, p. 255.

revelation in chapter two."[44] Thus the courtly place of punishment turns into the cosmic place of salvation. The space outside the court becomes the heart of the cosmos.

In a similar vein the lions' den becomes, in chapter six, a place of danger transmuted into a place of refuge. This time the cosmic protection results in the shutting of the lions' mouths. As a result Daniel is a quasi-martyr, a symbol of hope for the Jewish community, according to Collins.[45] This reading of Daniel in the pit connects with chapter seven. In Daniel chapter six, Darius converts, apparently, on seeing the place of death becoming the space for life. But Daniel could have died, would have died. It is that death, which is required in Daniel, chapters seven to twelve, of all pious Jews whose faith is threatened by great kings. Here the world powers are not generous and no immediate deliverance prevents the death of God's faithful. What is required is perseverance in faith to the end – the end of a person's life and of the last days of time.

## Evil in Daniel Chapters One to Seven

Telling these stories leads to the production of a dualistic viewpoint in which the struggle is between king and court on the one side and Jewish heroes on the other. One part of this contest involves the evil inherent in a foreign court, as in chapter one. However, the theme of foreign evil is nuanced with relation to the kings themselves. Chapter three sets out an evil profile of a king who demands worship of alien deities; but this decree is revoked later in the scene. Only in chapter five is the alliance of king and sacrilege so intimate that the ruler stands under an irrevocable punishment. Even in chapter six it is the courtly conspirators rather than the king who are the source of evil for Daniel. Evil, in these chapters, is the by-product of human activity. It is evil but an evil brought about largely through human ignorance and unthinking arrogance.

When the court tales are put in the context of Daniel as a whole, however, the context for this human wrongdoing is the evil to be found in chapter seven. The evil here is a more thoroughgoing type whereby the kingdoms of the world partake in chaos. Collins states: "The tales had envisaged the possibility of a successful life for Jews in the service of gentile kings. Chapter seven considers no such possibility but looks for the divine judgement, where the most offensive and immediately present

44  Collins, J., *Daniel*, p. 192.
45  Collins, J., *Daniel*, p. 273.

gentile kingdom will be destroyed."[46] In this perspective the great king, the great kingdom, and the foreign court, are all alike, all destined for destruction. The court space is now defined as a community of evil from a cosmic perspective, with an evil person at its head. The moral vision of chapter seven, for Collins, makes an "appeal to ancient myth to show that the disturbing events of the period conform to a pattern that has reverberated throughout history. Creation is threatened by the eruption of beasts from the sea, but the threat will be overcome by the rider on the clouds."[47]

## Daniel Chapters One to Seven in Socio-Cultural Perspective

The material discussed above produces several individual cultural symbols, both temporal and spatial, such as exile, end, empire, which can be treated from a wider perspective than the immediate literary context of Daniel. These symbols take their original meaning from the historical setting of the work, in the periods of the Babylonian and Persian supremacy.   Jon Berquist argues that Daniel, like the rest of the present Old Testament, originated against the background of a Jewishness existing in a foreign, imperial culture.[48] Indeed Daniel is written to effect a social integration of Yahwism and imperial society in which "there is no inconsistency between faithful Yahwism and the service of a foreign empire".[49] Berquist notes that the political situation behind such a message is one which falls under the rubric of imperial-colonial relations.[50] In this model, Persian officials are the controllers and the planners but the leaders of Judah are allowed to insert their own local culture into the over-arching imperial plan: "Yehud [Judah] constructed the physical and social apparatus by which Yahwism would be the official religion of the colony."[51] This reality can be viewed both positively (as shown above) and negatively: "Persian domination of Yehud created the conditions of colonialism, with all its negative ramifications for the independence of the people."[52]

Thus the combination of Persian power and the rule of Yahweh provides a local cultural identity but only within the confines of the imperial system

46  Collins, J., *Daniel*, p. 323.
47  Collins, J., *Daniel*, p. 324.
48  Berquist, J., *Judaism in Persia's Shadow*, Minneapolis, Augsburg/Fortress Press, 1995.
49  Berquist, J., *Judaism in Persia's Shadow*, p. 227.
50  Berquist, J., *Judaism in Persia's Shadow*, p. 234.
51  Berquist, J., *Judaism in Persia's Shadow*, p. 235.
52  Berquist, J., *Judaism in Persia's Shadow*, p. 237.

and by the 'great king's' permission. This social context provides its own interpretation of world order in which the human beings concerned fall into one of two community categories, being either exiles, persons who have lost their social autonomy, or empire, those who carry out the orders of the sovereign state. The exiles must co-exist with empire in order to survive but they may also long for the end to this unequal political relationship.

## Exile

The experience of separation from one's roots and the lack of social cohesion leaves persons and community unsupported. Thus the exile of the Babylonian period includes both despair and hope: despair for the loss of the past certainty about the world and human order, and hope that, notwithstanding loss and defeat, a new order will arise which will mirror the old structures but in a changed guise. As such, exile comes to be a free floating religious symbol standing for this experience of rootlessness and insecurity which can be addressed to any readership experiencing parallel conditions.

Walter Brueggemann argues, in *Cadences of Hope*, that the symbol of exile can be re-used for late twentieth century North American Christians.[53] As the Jews of the past had come to doubt themselves because of the undermining of their beliefs so also there has been a collapse of the old value system in western society, with the failed text of white, male, western hegemony.[54] As the book of Daniel deals with the possibility of living in a foreign culture without total assimilation so also this text can be used for the same purpose in the United States of the twenty-first century. Brueggemann supposes that, then and now, the company of exiles are not weak personalities or intellectually inferior.[55] However, they are in an insecure state, since they are seeking to maintain an alternative identity and an alternative vocation in a societal context where the main forces of

---

53  Brueggemann, W., *Cadences of Home*, Louisville, Westminster John Knox, 1997.
54  Brueggemann, W., *Cadences of Home*, p. 36.
55  It has generally been suggested that the social context of apocalyptic is among marginalised groups who are politically weak and uneducated people. Stephen Cook has recently countered this view by arguing that central groups who are educated and potentially powerful may have recourse to this genre if their political hopes are frustrated by a dominant overlord power. See Cook, S. L., *Prophecy and Apocalypticism*, Minneapolis, Fortress/Augsburg Press, 1995.

culture seek to deny, discredit or discard that old identity.[56] Such a new perspective or moral identity will work not just for the exiles but will have a knock on effect on the imperial culture itself. As in Daniel chapter four, the king is reprieved from madness and offers praise to Daniel's God, so "the public life of the empire may be transformed, not away from Babylon's true character, but away from Babylon's inappropriate, unacceptable and now to be abandoned brutality".[57]

This reading makes of exile a vision of hope, both for the deportees and for the deporters. The exiles, those who are socially estranged from the host culture and forcibly integrated to it, who are outsiders, experience a renewed cultural coherence round a moral vision of hope and so, among themselves, become once again insiders. Thus enabled they can continue to survive as an independent social entity. The social boundary here is ambiguous; exiles are part of the empire and yet not fully so. This is typified in the symbol of the eating of food, according to Brueggemann: "The invitation is to cease taking life and food and nourishment and hope from the Empire."[58] The experience of exile in one place, at one time, widens out into a moral symbol for community identity in any time and place where there has been a shattering and re-establishing of society.

## A Sense of Ending

This use of the exile as a spatial symbol moves the reader on to a temporal level since it contains within it the concept of a decisive end, and a new beginning. This does not preclude the continuity of some links with the past in which older cultural patterns are adapted to new times, but it does give a special significance to the idea of the end. In Daniel the old Israel continues into the future in the life of faithful Jews, but this life is shaped by new social conditions. This symbol of an end also can be re-used in different cultural circumstances. It comes into western culture through the function of the Christian Bible as literature, which provides western society with a language for discussing social reality. Frank Kermode argues that Apocalypse themes, represented by the symbol of the end, have had a major part to play in western literature.[59] The end has become a tool for interpreting and expressing social malaise. A final end-time has been

---

56 Brueggemann, W., *Cadences of Home*, p. 41.
57 Brueggemann, W., *Cadences of Home*, p. 94.
58 Brueggemann, W., *Cadences of Home*, p. 131.
59 Kermode, F., *The Sense of an Ending*, Oxford, Oxford University Press, 2000.

transmuted into crisis language. Apocalypse is "immanent rather than imminent. Thus . . . we think in terms of crisis rather than temporal ends; and make much of subtle disconfirmation or elaborate peripeteia."[60]

In literary terms apocalypse merges with Tragedy; a set of characters struggle with the apocalyptic crisis of their own time, as in the play King Lear, for instance. As the social framework of the world of the play collapses, producing chaotic and destructive relations between characters and an era ends in the midst of this crisis, the characters left alive in the final scene acknowledge their sense of ending and a lesser time beginning. Thus also in Daniel chapter five the Jews in the Babylonian court will survive the death of Belshazzar and the crisis surrounding the end of his kingdom. So, for Kermode, "the humble elect survive . . . the one king whose typical story is enacted before them".[61] As the kingdom collapses so does the certainty among human beings in community that they understand the cosmos in which they exist. The cosmos itself appears to shake and chaos threatens.

Although this approach limits the end to relative significance within a cosmos which, in fact, does not cease to operate at world level, the concept of the end of all time is important for giving meaning to life as a whole. Kermode argues that human beings live 'in the middest', that is without sight of the first act of creation or of the final eschaton and so seek for a symbol to give some coherence to this plateau experience of time. It is the end, which produces an ultimate moral vision of meaning for time, establishing both ordinary time (*chronos*) and special times connected to the eschaton (*kairoi*), together with the fullness of time (*pleroma*). Kermode argues that "the end is a fact of life and a fact of the imagination, working out from the middle, the human crisis . . . we re-create the horizons we have abolished, the structures that have collapsed . . . old patterns . . . adapting them to our new worlds".[62]

## Empire

The stress on a sense of end is linked, for Kermode, with other apocalyptic types – empire, decadence and revolution, progress and catastrophe.[63] The moral spotlight here is not on exile but on empire. 'Empire' as a symbol is

60 Kermode, F., *The Sense of an Ending*, p. 30.
61 Kermode, F., *The Sense of an Ending*, p. 30.
62 Kermode, F., *The Sense of an Ending*, p. 58.
63 Kermode, F., *The Sense of an Ending*, p. 29.

drawn from the existence of historical empires. Power, wealth and status are gathered into the centre where the elite classes are supported by the resources taken from the margins. This reality creates an image of empire as strong but oppressive, of wealthy but also as lethargic, complacent and so decadent. In the end empire collapses back into itself, through the vortex of revolution and change. This is the theme of the book of Daniel where the seeming invincibility of the Babylonian and Persian Empires is presented as an illusion, the only lasting sovereignty being that exercised by YHWH.

As Berquist argued, empire and colonialism are two faces of a single political reality – in the ancient world but in the modern world also.[64] Politics, culture and religion are interwoven; in Daniel, the kings want to assert their control by legislating for the worship patterns of their subjects. In the modern global empires, political power and religious symbols have worked together as Christian missionaries helped to replace native religions with the imperial religion of Christianity. Thus, Segovia argues, "the political, economic and cultural centre also functions as a religious centre . . . so the margins related to the centre must be brought to religious submission".[65] As the earlier stages of western imperialism give way to the re-establishment of local autonomy so the study of the Old Testament shifts around. Now the margins of old empires, the colonies, can engage on their own terms with religious material, which has become part of their cultural heritage. Not surprisingly the first movement in this re-owning is coloured by a reaction to colonialism itself. For Segovia "post colonial studies is a model that takes the reality of Empire . . . as an omnipresent, inescapable and overwhelming reality in the world".[66] Empire thus turns into another free-floating cultural symbol – an anti-symbol for the colonised. But this symbol is rooted in pragmatics, the "structural reality, political, economic, and cultural . . . more often than not symbolised in a city".[67] In Daniel, Babylon operates as such a city-symbol.

---

64  Cf. Berquist, J., *Judaism in Persia's Shadow*, pp. 26-32, 222.
65  Segovia, F., *Biblical Criticism and Postcolonial Studies: Towards a Postcolonial Optic*, in Sugirtharajah, R. (ed.), *The Postcolonial Bible*, Sheffield, Sheffield Academic Press, 1998, pp. 59 f.
66  Segovia, F., *Biblical Criticism*, p. 56.
67  Segovia, F., *Biblical Criticism*, pp. 56 f.

## Politics and Irony

Thus political issues are important to these religious texts as world powers and world power are investigated through the court tales in Daniel chapters one to six. D. S. Russell suggests that the parallel with the apocalyptic setting of these tales is the political cartoon.[68] In Daniel chapters one to six "we have a series of political cartoons in the form of dreams and visions telling of the fall of king and empire".[69] Each tale has its cartoon format – a great statue, a mighty tree, a disembodied hand. Whereas Collins and Davies tend to argue that politics are subordinated to religion and that the texts show Gentile kings in a positive light, this approach is not adopted by all readers.[70] David Valeta has recently proposed that Daniel chapters one to six and seven to twelve form a better literary coherence if the literary structures of chapters one to six are viewed as satire or parody with a 'resistance' background.[71] Into this category fits the presentation of the great king as a figure of weakness, needing interpreters, failing to perceive the conspiracies that surround him.

The king as an ox is a subtle caricature suitable for 'little' people with which to resist the lure of symbols such as the great statue, the idols, which represent the cultural values of imperial control. Into the same mould fit the presentations of the excessive nature of the foreign court. In chapter three emphasis is laid on the extreme height of the statue and the inclusion of every kind of musical instrument.[72] There is caricature also in the furnace scene where the executioners are themselves killed.[73] The satire reaches a climax in chapter five, where the decadence and complacency of the court is underlined as the contrast to the moving hand. There is a dramatic irony in the moment where the king sits proudly at ease, savouring his past conquests, worshipping his material gods since, a minute later he cringes fearfully before the manifestation of a truly cosmic power. The Septuagint version of Daniel makes the satirising more obvious in the case of the conspirators in Daniel chapter six. Meadowcroft details the scene with its patent absurdity that a large group of officials crashing on

68  Russell, D., *Apocalyptic Imagery as Political Cartoon?* in Barton, J. and Reimer, D. (eds), *After the Exile*, Georgia, Mercer University, 1996.

69  Russell, D., *Apocalyptic Imagery*, p. 193.

70  See Collins, J., *Daniel*, p. 51; Davies, P., *Daniel*, p. 93.

71  Valeta, D., *Satire and the Book of Daniel*. Paper read to the Millennium Conference in the University of Oxford, April 2000.

72  Collins, J., *Daniel, with an Introduction to Apocalyptic Literature*, Volume XX in the series *Forms of Old Testament Literature*, Grand Rapids, Eerdmans, 1984.

73  Collins, J., *Daniel*, p. 60.

and off stage could expect that nobody would notice their plans:[74] "Absurdity lies in the knowledge of the reader, the ignorance of a king blinded by his pride, and the lack of awareness on the part of the plotters that Daniel and . . . his God still hold the upper hand."[75]

Through irony and satire the narrator's viewpoint peeps through the telling of the story and reveals itself as more malicious in its assessment of the king and his world power than the surface level of the text. The ambiguity reflects the place of 'little' people in an empire needing to keep up the appearance of consent, while privately separating themselves from the self-identity of the empire. As D. Smith-Christopher has shown texts have two faces.[76] They can appear, on the surface, to uphold the status quo while at the same time quietly undermining it.

The African-American use of the book of Daniel is an instance of this community use of texts to undermine oppressive reality.[77] It has been argued, Kampen states, that texts, which look for freedom were used by slaves only with an otherworldly meaning. Freedom was only for the hereafter. But he argues that this is a misleading idea. Songs such as *Didn't my Lord deliver Daniel from the lions*, express the real hope for liberation now.[78] In 1829 David Walker used such biblical ideas in a strong anti-slavery work.[79] Those deriving economic benefit from slave labour are the great kings of the modern world and the God of Armies can, and will, attack them. Walker insisted on the inevitability of revolution, of a total destruction, only to be averted by a highly unlikely repentance on the part of the white population.[80] This approach to the reading of apocalyptic texts by slaves provided the visionary basis for a number of attempted slave rebellions on the grounds that the cosmic deity supported the community of slaves against the slave-owning society.

There is a tension, then, between two moral perspectives, representing ruler and ruled respectively. This tension is visible in the modern world and can find its origins in the ambivalence of texts like Daniel towards the role of Jews in foreign courts. There is a coherent link between the

---

74 Meadowcroft, T., *Aramaic Daniel and Greek Daniel*, Sheffield, Sheffield Academic Press, 1995.
75 Meadowcroft, T., *Aramaic Daniel and Greek Daniel*, p. 97.
76 Smith-Christopher, D., *The Book of Daniel*, Massachusetts, Hendrickson, 1996.
77 Kampen, J., *The Genre and Function of Apocalyptic Literature in the African American Experience* in Smith-Christopher, D. (ed.), *Text and Experience*, Sheffield, Sheffield Academic Press, 1995.
78 Kampen, J., *Genre and Function*, p. 48.
79 Kampen, J., *Genre and Function*, pp. 52 f.
80 Kampen, J., *Genre and Function*, p. 53.

ambiguity and the historical setting in which it emerged. To understand the role of irony in the text the reader needs to know these historical realities. As Wayne Booth notes,[81] the reader finds the parody by examining "the historical context – personal and social – in which the piece was written".[82] A further understanding of the coherence of irony in a text is through its literary context. In Daniel the clue to the satire which gives the book its darker side is found in chapters seven to twelve. There is less incoherence in the work if the reader decides that the first part exactly balances the second, while employing different literary genres to achieve the same end.

The use of irony in Daniel chapters one to six is to stress the nature of the judgement, which is passed upon the oppressive world powers. The judgement that is passed is a political one, leading to an actual decline of the world powers. But the force behind that condemnation is a religious one. It is a religious moral vision, which argues for a cosmos broader and higher that the political imperial framework just as it is the cosmic authority of a personal deity which will actualise the moral vision.

### Daniel and the Cosmic Perspective

Thus Daniel takes one person, a young Jew, as a representative of a whole community and sets him up against another person, a great king, who represents a second community. There is productive social intercourse between the two, but there is always tension for the one is subordinate, as person and as community, to the other. The narrator describes the stories of the encounters of these two from the perspective of the minority group, which accepts practical reality and wishes to make the exile a place, a space, for positive living and not total social fragmentation. But there is also the continuing hope that this situation will unpick itself and that independence will be re-asserted. The latent hostility between the two communities is picked up in chapter seven. Whereas the cosmos as context for community struggle is present but in the background in the earlier chapters, the cosmos is now fore-grounded. This move reflects the urgent need for a final solution for the burning issue. What is the absolute moral value of the respective communities? The text of this chapter makes it clear that the narrator endorses the Jew rather than the king.

Yet it is possible to read the court tales on their own, more peacefully. Maybe foreign culture can be acceptable. That is a message, which has

81  Booth, W., *A Rhetoric of Irony*, Chicago, University of Chicago Press, 1974.
82  Booth, W., *A Rhetoric of Irony*, pp. 96 f.

been perceived in this material by modern commentators.[83]   However, it could be argued, in this regard, that most commentators have been white, male and belonging to the empire of their own time, hence likely to find any signs in the text of an openness to the rule of the majority.  The final verdict could be one of ambivalence not clarity, that Daniel chapters one to six, in their textual setting, are capable of being interpreted in varying perspectives without any absolute weighting on good or evil.  As Booth states, "poets often create deliberate ambiguities . . . many literary works . . . not only can, but should be read in several different and even contradictory ways".[84]

---

83  This argument can be drawn from a reading of the text of the stories, which stresses the author's mild approach to gentile monarchs. They are capable of repentance and even of conversion.  Such a viewpoint admits the gentile world of the empire to be a possibly fruitful setting for Jews, one which is capable of giving them freedom of worship and allowing them a place in the political elite.

84  Booth, W., *A Rhetoric of Irony*, p. 127.

# Chapter Ten

# Morality, Suffering, and Evil
# in the Book of Job

The last two chapters have been primarily concerned with issues of world order; both divine responsibility for that order, and the nature of human contributions to it. In the previous chapter the focus was on human claims to control world affairs, through vast empires ruled over by great kings. This involved an evaluation of world order from the human perspective. In the present chapter a further treatment of foundational matters of moral vision in relation to world order will be made. The book of Job is concerned with order both in cosmic and in human affairs, and with disorder as the cause of human suffering. The text raises once again queries with regard to the nature of the cosmos as a moral environment and its creator as a moral agent.

Strictly speaking, in the book of Job only chapters one, two and forty-two are basic narrative, but the narrative establishes a recognisable situation within which issues of world order can be investigated, by setting up a plot line in which a good man finds himself the subject of bad fortune. The Job of chapters one and two is the same Job who cries out against his fate in chapter three, even if his companions find him much altered by his experiences. Moreover, aspects of events in the first two chapters are brought into the debates of the middle section of the book. What appears to be polite academic debate is a vehicle for the expression of strongly held beliefs and strongly felt emotions. When the friends speak of the justified suffering of the wicked (as in chapter four) they implicitly attack their erstwhile colleague, Job himself, since he is now included in those who suffer through wrongdoing.[1] In turn, Job accuses his comforters of being

---

1  The book of course assumes as its base line the idea of Retributive Justice: that human beings get back in life the mirror of how the behaviour that they put in. This involves the division of human beings into two opposing pairs of categories – wise/fool: righteous/wicked. This theory underlies all three Old Testament wisdom books though Proverbs is more optimistic about its value for giving meaning to life experience that the other two. If someone does well it must be the result of good actions while sickness is a sign of punishment. Since there is no life beyond this one, in most Old Testament books, rewards and punishments must come in this world. See for instance, Whybray, N., *Job*, Sheffield, Sheffield Academic Press, 1998, Introduction.

traitors and oppressors (as in chapter six), who have no common human feeling with himself.

The hinge of this animosity is the moral vision concerning the deity. It is because of strongly divided perspectives on cosmic order and disorder that the human persons involved break their communal ties and each claims to have the true perspective on God. The friends view the deity as an agent of retributive justice; Job defines God as absent, silent, and, ultimately, as oppressor. God reveals himself as mystery, ambiguity and yet as creator-controller of the universe. The reader may choose between these opposing opinions, at the heart of which are two moral matters: theodicy, and human suffering.

The high tone of the discourses can appear at odds with the simplicity, even banality, of the initial narrative. Job is so pious; God is so much king in his own realm. But is Job really pious – or does he go through the motions of public worship just in case? Then, too, is God so all-powerful? If so, how does he so quickly come to doubt Job, and, if he is a friend to Job, how can he allow the man to undergo such losses simply to carry through a heavenly wager? Read carefully, the opening story already hints at the ambiguities of personal moral intention, human and divine, which will be explored in the dialogue scenes.

## Literary Genres and Job

The book of Job clearly deals with serious issues of cosmic proportions – matters of justice, world order and divine faithfulness to his creatures. Yet the work is not a tightly structured systematic treatise nor is it a single narrative, nor a series of inter-connected short stories. The complexity of the book's meanings issues partly from the variety of genres, which are used therein. The narrative of the first two chapters appears to fit a fairly simple folktale mode in which stock characters play out a conflict. But this opens into the deep lament of chapter three, a literary style close to the form of psalms of lament and to the Book of Lamentations. This genre leads the reader to encounter a despair, which is not found in chapters one and two. The long middle section of the book takes the form of discourses – partly legal debate, partly philosophical reflection. These debates are structured formally in three cycles with the friends and Job each having a turn to speak in each cycle.[2]  Again, the style might appear fairly simple with each speaker setting out his position in a fairly rigid and formal manner.  But the debates as a whole raise deep questions concerning the nature of God and whether a God of justice (as understood by humans) rules over the cosmos.  At the same time, despite the impersonal tone of the speeches, the debate is fundamentally acrimonious with the friends engaging in personal attacks on Job who reciprocates in kind.  In justifying their world view the friends are not afraid to draw on the death of Job's children as evidence for divine punishment of human evil, for example.[3]

These speeches are interrupted by chapter twenty-eight, which contains a poem on the meaning of wisdom.  They are followed by the appearance of Elihu whose style is that of the monologue as he also discourses on theodicy.  Finally, a climax comes with the entrance of God in chapter thirty-eight.  In the following section God's rhetorical questioning of Job outlines his own nature as this is evidenced in creation and in nature, that is, at the level of cosmic events.  Job accepts this view,[4] and the book closes with God's approval of Job and condemnation of the friends, followed by a return to the folk-tale narrative style of the first part of the work, wherein Job comes to live happily ever after.

Each of these styles has its own content to contribute to the over-arching message of the book and each can be read as a separate piece of text in its own right.  But it is reasonable to view the work also as a whole, since it now exists as such; in which case it is fair to ask what genre dominates overall.  William Whedbee has argued for the view that Job is overall a Comedy, a view which is conditioned by putting emphasis on the narrative

---

2   There are generally assumed to be three cycles of speeches, although the third in the series is not as coherent as the other two.  It is not always clear who is speaking nor how Job Twenty-Eight fits into the pattern of debates; is it a speech of Job as placing would imply? Or is it to be read as a totally separate insertion, breaking up the text order?  See for example, Habel, N., *The Book of Job*, London, SCM Press, 1985, for a detailed treatment on these issues.  With regard to the problems about which speaker is operating in Job chapters twenty-four to twenty-seven see for instance, Whybray, N., *Job*, pp. 106 f.

3   Cf. Job 8[4].

4   The Hebrew text at this point is ambiguous in terms of how Job chapter forty-two, verses one to six fits together, especially, verses three and four are hard to fit together with the other verses to make a coherent, linear statement.  See for example, Whybray, N., *Job*, p. 170.  The text here allows for the abasement of Job before the deity or for a more aggressive Job who nonetheless accepts God's superiority.  In both approaches Job accepts God as mystery but the difference in tone gives a variety of interpretations of Job's own personality here.

framework of Job.[5] In this frame there is a movement of events from happiness to decline to happiness again. This fits the u-shaped curve of the comic plot as outlined by Northrop Frye.[6] Pauline Shelton suggests that "Whedbee argues that the book of Job is a comedy – not in the sense that laughter is the appropriate response – but rather that Job embodies 'that vision of comedy which has two central ingredients: first, its perception of incongruity that moves in the realm of the comic, the ludicrous, and the ridiculous; and second, a basic plot-line that leads ultimately to the happiness of the new'".[7]

By contrast, Shelton herself argues that Job should be read as a form of Tragedy.[8] Admittedly the work does not fully fit a normative literary definition of Tragedy: there is no obvious error of judgement on Job's part at the beginning and there is a happy ending, both with regard to the assertion that God is benevolent and to Job's personal safety.[9] However, Shelton suggests that the work is more tragic than comic. She finds a way forward here by comparing Job with Pirandello's work, *Six Characters in search of an Author*.[10] In both works, she argues, there is a major crisis of existence for human beings in search of answers: "It is the tragedy of Pirandellian drama that behind all the illusions – of theatre, characters, actors, masks – there is no ultimate reality."[11] This is comparable to the existential crisis experienced by Job. However, in the book of Job, God does arrive to give a foundation for answers, though those answers reject the human frames of reference previously utilised both by Job and his friends. Yair Hoffman also discusses Job as Tragedy, in connection with the issue of theodicy and its variety of solutions to the theological uncertainty about cosmic justice.[12] If God is above and beyond matters of human justice, for example, then the tragedy lies in the meaninglessness of human experience and of human attempts to provide a rational explanation for what happens in the world of creation.

5   Whedbee, W., *The Bible and Comic Vision*, Cambridge, Cambridge University Press, 1998.
6   Whedbee, W., *The Bible and Comic Vision*, p. 227.
7   Shelton, P., *Making a Drama out of a Crisis? A Consideration of the Book of Job as Drama* in *Journal for the Study of the Old Testament*, Volume No. 83/99, p. 72.
8   Shelton, P., *Making a Drama out of a Crisis?*, pp. 69-82.
9   Shelton, P., *Making a Drama out of a Crisis?*, pp. 71 f.
10  Shelton uses the Pirandello play as a schema for an exploration of the book of Job.
11  Shelton, P., *Making a Drama out of a Crisis?*, p. 77.
12  Hoffman, Y., *A Blemished Perfection*, Sheffield, Sheffield Academic Press, 1996.

## The Moral Imagination of the Poet

Moving from the question of genre to that of author it is possible to describe the author(s) of Job as poets – telling stories, weaving pictures of heaven and earth, balancing natural creation against human existence. Robert Alter, for instance, reflects on the balance between sections of the text, across genre boundaries.[13] He points out that the first thirty-seven lines of God's answer to Job brilliantly reverse, in structure, theme and image, the initial poem of Job in chapter three.[14] There, Job called on cloud and deep darkness to obliterate his birth-day. God relates to the same cloudy cover, not as a means of terror, but as "a matutinal blanket over the primordial seas".[15] Alter says "the finest illustration of this nice match of meaning and imagery between the two poems is the beautiful counterbalance between the most haunting of Job's lines wishing for darkness, and the most exquisite of God's lines affirming light".[16]

William Brown argues that it is through such poetic structuring that the book produces its moral vision:[17] that the poet engages here in a form of moral imagination.[18] In this world of the moral imagination the issues of creation and justice, of morality and cosmology, cannot be separated.[19] There is a direct link between the chaos caused by suffering in Job's own life and global chaos, world evil.[20] The mode for exploring these intertwined themes is fantasy. The issues of suffering, evil and justice are investigated, according to Brown, in "an imaginative world . . . full of unspeakable predicaments and exotic beasts, a fantasy in the richest sense".[21] Forced by events to seek for meaning at the furthest extremes of his understanding Job "flirts with mythic powers beyond his control by exhorting the predacious darkness to seize and destroy . . . the cosmos":[22] while, in the balancing chapters (thirty-eight to forty-one), "the cosmic journey from land to sea is part of Job's journey of displacement, a fantasy into the frontiers of the cosmos inaccessible to human experience".[23]

---

13 Alter, R., *The Art of Biblical Poetry*, Edinburgh, T. and T. Clark, 1990.
14 Alter, R., *The Art of Biblical Poetry*, p. 96.
15 Alter, R., *The Art of Biblical Poetry*, p. 97.
16 Alter, R., *The Art of Biblical Poetry*, p. 98.
17 Brown, W., *The Ethos of the Cosmos*, Grand Rapids, Eerdmans, 1999.
18 Brown, W., *The Ethos of the Cosmos*, Grand Rapids, Eerdmans, 1999, p. 320.
19 Brown, W., *The Ethos of the Cosmos*, pp. 318 f.
20 Brown, W., *The Ethos of the Cosmos*, pp. 318 f.
21 Brown, W., *The Ethos of the Cosmos*, p. 319.
22 Brown, W., *The Ethos of the Cosmos*, p. 322.
23 Brown, W., *The Ethos of the Cosmos*, p. 342.

## Cosmos, Community and Person

The reflections on literary style set out above lead the reader back to the
question of overall meaning. What form of morality does this work offer
its readers? The text does indeed have something to say on the three levels
of cosmos, community and person. Person and cosmos open the text, while
community comes in strongly once the debates begin among the human
characters. It is not just that Job and his three friends constitute a
community in self-dialogue. Both sides in the argument also refer
constantly to the wider community to which they belong. They draw upon
the traditional religious views of their social group, on the nature of elite
society, on an elite's view of poorer and weaker social group members, in
order to put forward an argument, which will be convincing to their fellow
citizens. Job's dilemmas are not simply personal but challenge community
bonds and cosmic beliefs. God's testing of Job is not just an idea in
heaven, it is the same reality as the succession of messengers bearing their
news of disasters which strike him as blow after blow. Thus Job is
constantly set in a community context, from his introduction as a keen
family man to his problems with his social peers, and his experience is the
basis for community reflection on the meaning of the cosmos.

Answers to matters of cosmic meaning are not straightforward.
Ambiguity and even absurdity are present, as Ellen van Wolde and Dermot
Cox have argued. Van Wolde points out that, from the first chapter,
ambiguity in the created order is a matter of significance:[24] "How can God
look himself in the eye as creator if all his creatures, even the most pious,
love him only for what they can get out of him?"[25] God views Job's piety
as ambiguous here, and God's own self becomes ambiguous for the reader,
as he allows such great pain to one who strives for loyalty. At the same
time Job himself is ambiguous. Why was he so anxious about the letter of
the law regarding public worship of God? Was it because he knows that
his children have no real concern with the cosmic ruler, being sewn into
their luxurious life of feasting? Is Job papering over the cracks in his own
household's religious attitudes?

The situation which emerges in chapter two produces a further
ambiguity about world order. But this ambiguity only emerges if the reader
has a theistic approach to the cosmos, otherwise there is no need to search
for an answer beyond the obvious. Van Wolde comments: "If God did not
exist for Job, as God no longer exists for many people now, the problems of

24  van Wolde, E., *Mr and Mrs Job*, London, SCM Press, 1997.
25  van Wolde, E., *Mr and Mrs Job*, p. 3.

the book would not arise . . . life would be absurd. But Job believes in God so has to confront the questions which this raises."[26] The focus of the ambiguity becomes, then, the nature of God. Job moves through a series of putative images of the deity in his search for the reality beyond the ambiguity. God is, for example, a gangster figure, always after him.[27] Then God is the great gaoler who is also completely arbitrary.[28] As van Wolde notes, "Yahweh as creator and the creation are to be evaluated separately and the human moral order is not to be regarded as a guiding principle of the order of creation".[29] Once Job ceases to impose a theory of retributive justice on God, ambiguity lessens. It is not for God to sort out justice among righteous and wicked. If human beings want this system it is up to them to run such a human community.[30]

Dermot Cox also engages in reviewing the book of Job along lines of ambiguity, more specifically as an example of the absurd.[31] He argues that the text shows that the justice of man is balanced by the injustice of God. Yet the human person and the community continue to feel that it is essential to be in accord with an absolute cosmic design which should be sought through the layers of ambiguity. Cox argues that Job's "enquiry into God is an analysis of the absurd, since existentialism's basic concern is a concern with ethics and God is unethical".[32] Job discovers a God who is Lord of absurdity, a deity who cannot be explicated by reason, who cannot be tied into neat intellectual boxes, but who constantly breaks free. Intellectually, then, Job must opt for a religion of absurdity where the order is constantly blurred by random, disordered occurrences.[33] Paradoxically it is this vision of disorder, which leads directly to an appreciation of the mystery of God.[34] Ambiguity and absurdity thus mark out the poetic imagination in Job. In the comic view, ambiguity is resolved in the direction of God as a fixed reality, holding chaos at bay, though himself rejoicing in chaotic world power and raw aggression. In the tragic view, person, cosmos and community are all undermined as positive concepts.

26  van Wolde, E., *Mr and Mrs Job*, p. 36.
27  van Wolde, E., *Mr and Mrs Job*, p. 48.
28  van Wolde, E., *Mr and Mrs Job*, p. 61.
29  van Wolde, E., *Mr and Mrs Job*, p. 69.
30  van Wolde, E., *Mr and Mrs Job*, pp. 129, 127.
31  Cox, D., *Man's Anger and God's Silence*, Slough, St Paul's Press, 1990.
32  Cox, D., *Man's Anger and God's Silence*, p. 83.
33  Cox, D., *Man's Anger and God's Silence*, p. 84.
34  Cox, D., *Man's Anger and God's Silence*, p. 85.

### Suffering and Evil in Job

The ambiguity consequent on the possibility of reading the text in either of these ways raises further questions concerning suffering and evil. Behind suffering is the cause of suffering, namely the regulating forces of cosmic power. Are these cosmic forces acting appropriately in causing human pain? If not, the search for meaning raises the matter of cosmic powers as evil beings. God is the creator of, and one who rewards, human beings, in Job, but the Satan is his other self, a figure who queries apparent human goodness and is the direct cause of human suffering. Satan, in the New Testament, is clearly an evil being who seeks to distort truth and destroy God's creation, as can be seen in the Gospel stories of the temptations of Jesus and in the book of Revelation. But it is not clear, in Job, that the Satan is such a figure; he is, indeed, an officer at the divine court rather than an outcast from heaven (as in Revelation chapter twelve).[35]

The equivalent of the Satan on earth is Job's friends who cause him great pain and anxiety by querying his past actions and accusing him of sin. Just as the Satan provokes God's doubts about Job's worth so the friends accuse Job of blasphemy and sacrilegious views. The appearance of God in mighty wind and storm appear to support their vision of deserved punishment, and God does question Job with some force. But, in the end, the friends are definitely put in the wrong by the text. The Satan himself is not dealt with accordingly. He simply disappears from the narrative.

The themes of suffering and evil thus move around and share in the ambiguity of the text. They are linked issues, but what moral perspective actually holds them together in a meaningful explanation of human life experience? What exactly is the place of human suffering in the cosmos? Is it deliberately caused by cosmic controllers or is it the inevitable result of the play of random forces? Can the word evil be properly used in assessing the place of suffering? Suffering itself may be labelled an evil, but is there an evil cause of pain or is it merely a spin-off from life experience generally? It is useful to return here to the comments of van Wolde; the

---

35 That is the major difference of context. The Satan is part of the divine council, relied on here by God. In the New Testament Satan becomes a fallen angel in the account in the book of Revelation, chapter twelve. There is no clear line of development between these images between Old and New Testament texts, but the Satan as a court official may have been acting as a court spy, or *agent provocateur* on God's behalf. It is possible that the idea of testing then moved into that of tempting, that is, a deliberate entrapment of human beings in disloyalty to God. Indeed the koine Greek *peirasmon* means both test and temptation.

intellectual problem of evil and suffering may be the result of trying to link together realities which cannot be so tied together, namely God and human justice. Yet the Satan lingers on in a reader's mind as a symbol of the ambiguity of the cosmos. Does he (and God) not know what he is doing, in terms of its human consequences? In chapter two God has viewed the results of the test, but he still allows more disasters to occur. So, does he not care about human persons at all? Is that the content of evil from a human viewpoint, that there exists an indifferent cosmic figure, concerned only with his own agendas, rather than a comforting parent figure?

## Time and Place in Job

Having thus explored some of the broad issues of morality in regard of the book of Job, it is time to turn more specifically to the narrative structures of time and place settings and their contribution to the work's moral approaches to cosmos, community and person. Time as the external setting of the work is both historical and timeless. Job is a rich ruler in Uz which seems to be a fictional place, though set in the world of the ancient near-east, in a society which engages in agriculture but has a central habitation area.[36]

Internal time belongs to the movement of events within the symbolic world of the story. Internally, time rushes past in chapters one and two. The swift passage from scenes in heaven to those on earth and the arrival of new messengers as the last was still speaking stress the speed of blows and losses, and set out the narrative frame for the middle of the book. Time then stands still for much of the book as Job stays at the dungheap. The effect of slowing the pace is to emphasise the depth of Job's solitariness and pain. When his friends see him they are dumbstruck and silent for seven days – an indication of the need for perfect silence in awe before such a calamity. As silence moves to discourse, the writer draws in the past time of the characters to their present state by *analepses* which refer the reader to the past of Job in his community. Chapter twenty-nine especially

---

36 There is much discussion among commentators as to whether Uz is meant to be an historical site; a number of commentators take the view that this is a fictional place setting. For a discussion of the options see for instance Habel, N., *Job*. In chapters one and two Job has a household dispersed in homes as well as flocks and herds which implies an agricultural existence. Later, especially in Job chapter twenty-nine, the picture is of village/city society where many households live close together and with a centralised leadership of Elders, possibly with a king or chieftain as ultimate authority.

works by this use of time structuring. This device serves also to look to the future. Job cannot go back to 'the past' but needs to move to a yet unknown future. The coming of God moves the action forward to that future time, and the last part of chapter forty-two returns to a swift time frame as in the first scenes. Here the losses endured by Job are made good in swift succession.

Since chapters one, two and forty-two provide a narrative framework for the text, the book can be described as defined by that strong delineation of events in time. That is, its message deals with what happens between what can be seen as a series of losses and gains from a human perspective, while, from a divine perspective the same period is defined as what happens between the first outcome of a heavenly wager and its long term goal of waiting to see if Job will curse God. He never does but circles round this possibility via his doubts and questions concerning God's nature and intentions. God's direct intervention cuts short this waiting period.

But, since the discourses of the middle section of the book, take place in one spot, and are presented as continuous dialogue, it would be possible to view this part of the text as 'timeless'. And to describe it as a time out of life, set apart from ordinary time to make a space for intellectual activity. This is the time of the rubbish heap. The one who sits there no longer has to worry about 'business time' but has the chance to engage in a moral vision of reality opened up to the *longue durée* of a whole life-time's experience which progresses to the world order within which such a life is lived. It is this long view which gives the opportunity for an indepth search of morality, where moral attitudes emerge from holding together the movement from creation to chaos, from chaos to creation.

### Place Setting and Moral Vision

Although some of the moral perspective in Job is focused on time, the spatial setting is equally important since the moral issues dealt with in the book are worked out within the spatial framework of the cosmos. The world of the text parallels the world of the real cosmos. As in one so in the other, the world is divided into two parts – heaven and earth – and it is the interaction of these two levels which provides a foundation for moral world order. Heaven is the place of God and is thus the key to events. It is God's council meeting, which sparks off the plot. Yet earth, as the place of humans, is not a passive partner to heaven; Job's response from the earth is as important as God's action in the heaven. Indeed it is that response which is being elicited by the difference of opinion between God and the Satan and by the Satan's tests of Job's loyalty. As these story elements unfold, heaven is further delineated as the council chamber of God, and a great storm; while earth is featured as the household of Job, and as the dungheap, where Job lives as a social outcast on account of physical disease.[37]

## Heaven and Earth

It is the context of the executive committee in heaven, which sets in motion a major moral issue in the book. Whybray remarks that "the first scene with the Satan introduces a crucial issue that will continue to be debated throughout the book: that of theodicy".[38] God does not come out of this scene as perfect justice. Whybray comments that "this caricature. . . is reminiscent of the informal and sometimes comic scenes in polytheistic myths".[39] The caricature opens the way for the reader to view God as a doubtful source of authority and so creates the dramatic irony that the reader knows what Job does not, that his sufferings are part of the internal debate in heaven. As Carl Jung remarks: "The inner instability of Yahweh is the prime cause not only of the creation of the world, but also of the pleromatic drama for which mankind serves as a tragic chorus."[40] The interaction of heaven and earth, then, is not morally stable, but produces the context for an open-ended exploration of the content of cosmic morality.

One of the key terms here is bless (*Barak*).[41] Does Job really bless God when he utters vows of praise, from his heart? Will Job go on uttering words of blessing if circumstances change or will he curse? When Job speaks of his losses he re-iterates a blessing on the one who is beyond human control. Faced with a second round of troubles Job is challenged by his wife to 'bless' God and die. This is surely a euphemism, creating a linguistic ambiguity, for it assumes an act of cursing, which will be met by immediate divine force. But Job refuses that way out of his sickness and loss. Yet he does not actually utter words of blessing in this situation. He did not sin with his lips but what is moving in his depths? In the past God

---

37 According to the purity laws in Leviticus, skin disease is a blemish, which ritually defiles the person who so suffers. Since impurity is contagious the law stipulates that the person is to be sent out from the community.

38 Whybray, N., *Job*, p. 29.

39 Whybray, N., *Job*, p. 29.

40 Jung, C., *Answer to Job*, London, Hodder and Stoughton, 1965, p. 108.

41 Consider here the complexities of usage of the term 'bless' as discussed in van Wolde's commentary on chapters one to three of the book of Job.

has blessed Job by hedging him round by good things, but now that divine protection has gone and Job is hedged in by sorrow and distress as he himself states in chapter three.


## The Dungheap

Bruce Zuckerman suggests that, in the scenes from the dungheap, "the author has transformed the tradition into a devastating satirical tool, utilised to surprise the reader, to shock him into seeing the Joban conventions in an unconventional manner".[42]   The silent Job of chapter two who accepts suffering is transformed into an angry, challenging voice, raising the question as to whether God can be validly seen as a moral deity.  At the heart of this material which acts as a parody, undermining the model of passive acceptance of life's fortunes, is the topic of cosmic justice.  In an ordered state in the Ancient Near East the king would be the source of order, in a manner similar to the self-presentation of Job in chapter twenty-nine.  In this setting the key to justice is the royal court of appeal.  God is the ruler of the heavens and so his court is the final source of cosmic arbitration, but Job queries the legality of God's judgement and so calls on God to become a co-litigant.[43]   Thus the poet endeavours to divorce God from his ultimate legal authority.[44]   In this context the death wish of chapter two and the legal claims that follow unite to offer a truly nihilistic and disjunctive moral perspective.  The author of Job, according to Zuckerman "will not be content simply to discredit an ancient and beloved folktale; this serves merely as his point of departure for an all-encompassing onslaught against the most basic, conventional assumptions about the nature of God and his relation to mankind".[45]   The place of the dungheap, then, is one of sorrow and challenge where the concerns of the human person face directly out to the cosmos itself.  Even while conducting debates with his friends, Job never loses this belief that it is only the cosmos which can provide a suitable answer to his pains.


42  Zuckerman, B., *Job the Silent*, Oxford University Press, 1991, p. 48.
43  Zuckerman, B., *Job the Silent*, p. 109.
44  Zuckerman, B., *Job the Silent*, p. 111.
45  Zuckerman, B., *Job the Silent*, p. 137.

## The Storm

The fulfilment of such a moral view of the cosmos comes in God's own words in chapters thirty-eight to forty-one. God speaks to Job from the heart of the storm. Just as the dungheap symbolises the rock-bottom state of Job's personal fortunes, so the storm aptly encapsulates the fierce cosmic power which Job has invoked in chapter three, and which comes now in answer to his growing human anger and distress. But the Lord of the storm does not deal in legal terms, nor is he the weak figure of chapter one, engaged in self doubt. Instead this God demands of Job answers to divine questioning on wisdom and knowledge. The theme of a great storm is appropriate also because it embodies an ancient Palestinian religious metaphor for the deity, who is viewed as a form of weather-god.[46] The storm-god metaphor moves into the field of mythology as it finds expression in the title of Divine Warrior. Leo Perdue stresses the role of mythological motifs in shaping the moral meaning of Job.[47] He argues that Job's lament in chapter three points towards a God who is a warrior figure, one who is on close terms with chaos.[48] In the Discourses, Job envisages the wrath of such a 'divine warrior' as turned against himself.[49]

In the whirlwind, according to Perdue, God takes on the mythological profile touched on by Job and comes "to engage in combat mortal revolutionary and immortal chaos monsters" and to assert a "re-description of the reality in which the creator fights chaos to continue creation".[50] Faced with this alignment of God's person with the traits Job has identified as truly cosmic Job abandons the lament, which threatens the cosmic order on account of his cursing.[51] God remains a mythological figure full of wrath and power. But only such a deity can, indeed, control cosmic energies and produce, sometimes at least, positive benefits for human persons. The ultimate moral vision here requires mystery as the medium of God's freedom as against a dogma of strict retribution.[52]

---

46  The image of God of Israel as a weather god, attached to rain and storm, which is a feature of Old Testament poetry, appears to be linked to Syrio-Palestinian religion and Mesopotamian deities. See notes on this issue in the chapter on Genesis.
47  Perdue, L., *Wisdom and Creation*, Nashville, Abingdon, 1994.
48  Perdue, L., *Wisdom and Creation*, p. 134.
49  Perdue, L., *Wisdom and Creation*, pp. 141, 145.
50  Perdue, L., *Wisdom and Creation*, p. 168.
51  Perdue, L., *Wisdom and Creation*, p. 181.
52  Perdue, L., *Wisdom and Creation*, p. 192.

## The Relevance of Place and Space in the Morality of Job

Thus the morality of relations between heaven and earth are examined through the places of 'dungheap and storm'. The reader learns to view human affairs from such a cosmic perspective in chapters one and two, where the narrative shifts regularly between heaven and earth.[53] Ironically Job, in chapter one, understands the intimacy of such a connection and knows that his peace on earth can only be prolonged by a focus on peace with heaven. In chapters one and two it is the same inter-connectedness which is the cause of his suffering. Seen from a divine plane, Job is a servant, valued, but not 'one of us'. Heaven's wagers come first, together with heavenly uncertainty about humanity's true self. Heaven and earth thus become opposed places and it is this contrast which structures the rest of the book: "When several places, ordered in groups, can be related to psychological, ideological and moral oppositions, location may function as an important principle of structure . . . far-near, open-closed, finite-infinite, together with familiar-strange, safe-unsafe, and accessible-inaccessible are oppositions often encountered."[54]

Mieke Bal here stresses the importance of locating paired, opposing places – an importance indicated above with regard to heaven and earth as key places in the book of Job. Bal goes on to state that "a special role may be played by the *boundary* between two opposed locations . . . the shop, as a transitory place, between outside and inside, the sea between society and solitude . . . all function as mediators. It is possible to be trapped in such places".[55] In Job the dungheap functions as such a boundary – a liminal site. It sits between heaven and earth as a transitory mode, though one in which Job has become trapped. In chapter one Job accepted misfortune; his loss of family and possessions did not result in a loss of sense of place. Job was still in earth and knew where heaven was located. In chapter three, however, Job cries out against a spatial disorientation. He is no longer an earth dweller, but has moved outside social community meaning. Even the day of his birth is lacking in value for it did not bring him safe to community membership but left him stranded in a liminal place, though not, like death, one of peace.

Only as the storm breaks over the rubbish dump can Job move from a liminal to a social status. Yet he does not move directly to earth – rather,

---

53　Heaven and earth are typically the pair of terms by which the world is delineated in the Old
　　Testament. Their place in the cosmos is established in Genesis chapter one.

54　Bal, M., *Narratology*, Toronto, University of Toronto Press, 1988, p. 44.

55　Bal, M., *Narratology*, p. 45.

he is invited to become a citizen of heaven, to be caught up in the moral vision of the God of the storm. His failure to become an equal citizen with God is emphasised by the pouring out of rhetorical questions on Job, questions unanswerable by human reasoning and experience. Yet, paradoxically, it is this visit to heaven which allows Job to return to earth and renew his family and household identity.

These several places in the text of Job provide a spatial ordering of the narrative in which places are linked to certain points of perception.[56] Bal says: "These places seen *in relations to their perception* are called space."[57] Using Bal's language it can be argued that the dungheap and the storm are spaces, insofar as Job's experience of them as locations for human activity produces a shift in moral vision with regard to the heaven/earth basis on which the text is built.

The storm is expanded in significance with whirlwind and thunder claps. As a great upheaval of nature it mirrors Job's inner state and the intensely-felt cut and thrust of the dungheap debates. Its further development is through nature in the wild and by the creatures Behemoth and Leviathan. In both spaces, dungheap and storm, using the language of Bal, "space is 'thematised': it becomes an object of presentation itself, for its own sake. Space thus becomes an 'acting place' rather than the place of action. It influences the *fabula*, and the *fabula* becomes subordinate to the presentation of space."[58] The return to the heaven/earth space and place setting of the initial story is achieved through the journey into dump and storm; but this journey is itself influential in defining the contents of the places, heaven and earth. God and Job come to a form of relationship in the end but the terms are new ones, at least from the viewpoint of a human reader.

## Parallel Worlds and Moral Vision in Job

It can be argued that there are a number of parallel places/spaces in the text of Job which operate as parallel worlds. By moving into and out of such worlds the reader grows in moral understanding. One method of investigating the role of these worlds in the reading process is that offered by Roland Boer.[59] In his chapter on science fiction Boer suggests that the

56 Bal, M., *Narratology*, p. 93.
57 Bal, M., *Narratology*, p. 93.
58 Bal, M., *Narratology*, p. 96.
59 Boer, R., *Novel Histories*, Sheffield, Sheffield Academic Press, 1997.

basic mode of science fiction is a representation which allows us to recognise the familiar but, at the same time, makes it unfamiliar:[60] "It is . . . a fundamentally dialectical activity, moving the line of sight or of analysis into an opposite of the original so as to view the original at work in the opposite and from the perspective of the opposite."[61]

In Job this can be related to ideological issues – seeing the world of creation through new eyes, via a tale of human suffering. The initial world here is the normal religious one in which God in heaven balances the human person on earth. It can be known and understood. But the dungheap is a place outside this normative world, a place of parallel existence from which the normative world can be seen differently and evaluated accordingly. Although science fiction presents a new perspective through the use of future worlds, while Job moves to a timeless world, both Job and science fiction deal with problems of contemporary human experience, as Susan Sontag suggests concerning science fiction, that therein lurks the deepest anxieties about human experience.[62]

In 'Mutant on the Bounty' Boer moves on to consider the role of utopian literature within the science fiction network. He argues that "a utopia requires a radical disjunction with this dismal world as a condition of its possibility, yet in order to be possible in the first place it must find another way to re-open the connection".[63] It is from this utopian perspective that Job reflects on his 'rubbish dump world'. In chapter twenty-nine he looks back to his past world as an ideal place from which he is now barred, but which he desires to re-enter. For Job the past ceases to be a real event, and becomes the core of a symbolic existence in which pain and suffering would be excluded. For the reader, chapter twenty-nine mirrors chapter one in terms of its place setting within the human community. By comparing the presentation of material in these two chapters, the reader can come to a new evaluation of the historical world of chapter one. In the initial chapter the community world of earth is taken for granted; it is the place of existence and there is no other. In chapter twenty-nine a step has been taken away from this identifying of the self with the community world, since Job views it as a spectator who has once been a participant. What Job derives from that world and its frame is control over life. In his utopian dream Job is always in command – of self, of other human beings, even of the cosmos itself. But the reader may now

60  Boer, R., *Novel Histories*, p. 109.
61  Boer, R., *Novel Histories*, p. 110.
62  Boer, R., *Novel Histories*, p. 110.
63  Boer, R., *Novel Histories*, p. 121.

be led to a questioning not found in his or her response to chapter one. Is this Utopia not tied too much to one man's needs and does it not provide a moral vision in which a human person is prioritised over community and cosmos?

From Job's viewpoint, however, this world is home, and he is now banished from it – seemingly forever. As he sits on his dungheap he can be described as feeling place-bereaved.[64] As he senses the gap between past and present to be that between two parallel worlds, only one of which is currently available, Job laments his social and cosmic exclusion. Using Boer's terminology it is possible to argue that to leave elite society behind, for him, "is perhaps the ultimate farewell and the ultimate expression of the feeling that home is always elsewhere".[65] Job's farewell to the past, combined with his statement of life intent (chapter thirty-one) prepares the way for a new world to emerge, this time that of the whirlwind and storm. As characters in science fiction move from terra to cosmos so also Job moves to the cosmic, to an environment of outer-space mælstrom and to a voice which rages from the cosmic storm. In this world Job encounters nature, to which he has often made reference in his speeches, in a new manner. The ostrich, the horse and the eagle are viewed afresh, as ambiguous characters – beautiful, strong, stupid, bloodthirsty. Yet beauty and strength cannot be separated from stupidity and violence. Behemoth and Leviathan move the language from the natural to the abnormal, appearing as mutant creatures, half animal and half mythical.

Job is invited to live in this world and to own it as his historical home. As a parallel world, the land of the storm contrasts with the place of the human household. As Boer states: "Both science fiction and utopia have as a central feature the construction of [alternative] worlds . . . science fiction is also an exercise in the collision of worlds in which the comparisons and the disparities between the worlds of the reader and the narrative come to the fore."[66] Job is a human person who goes through a process of re-imaging his world – especially his moral vision of the cosmos. This is achieved through the alternative worlds of 'the dungheap and the storm' which collide with his original world.

---

64  Boer, R., *Novel Histories*, p. 128.
65  Boer, R., *Novel Histories*, p. 128.
66  Boer, R., *Novel Histories*, pp. 123 f.

### Power, Class, and Status in the Morality of Job

It is certainly possible for a reader to address the book of Job at the level of timeless matters of world order, of the relationship between divine justice and human pain. However, to stay at this stage of reading would be to forget that the text originally emerged within a particular period and with a particular audience in mind. What sort of persons, what sort of community, find their concerns mirrored in Job? David Clines suggests that the text "implies a highly literate public, with a rich vocabulary, a taste for imagery and a stomach for elaborate and extended rhetoric. It implies a readership that is not literal-minded, one that delights in irony, exaggeration, misdirection and whimsy."[67]

In other words, Clines believes that the book is written for an elite group within a wider society. Job is not a poor man, but a rich one who becomes poor, thus acting out the nightmare of every rich person. Job's main concern is loss of status not how to obtain bread to live on. At the end of the book his reward is the return of all his possessions. Moreover, wealth as such is not a problem in the book.[68] Although chapter twenty-four offers a sympathetic picture of the actual poor in Job's community it is a rhetorician's portrait, dealing with stock situations such as loss of income by widows and orphans.[69] Job begins as, and remains, the prototypical patriarch who commands society from his lofty social and economic status. The answers and the questions themselves are in many ways based on reasoning and argument of an intellectual kind rather than on the pragmatic logic of a peasant in a subsistence economy.[70]

Whereas Clines stresses the need to read Job as the literary expression of upper class culture, Gustavo Gutierrez uses the book for the benefit of the lower classes of Latin America.[71] He notes the potential universality of a figure like Job.[72] As a human person he represents the weakness of utilitarian religion which lacks depth and authenticity.[73] Job has to make progress in deepening his faith through a dramatic crisis:[74] "The problem of speaking correctly about God and unjust suffering is not limited to the case

67  Clines, D., *Interested Parties*, Sheffield, Sheffield Academic Press, 1995, chapter six, p. 124.
68  Clines, D., *Interested Parties*, p. 128.
69  Clines, D., *Interested Parties*, p. 127.
70  Clines, D., *Interested Parties*, p. 141.
71  Gutierrez, G., *On Job*, Maryknoll, Orbis, 1987.
72  Gutierrez, G., *On Job*, p. 4.
73  Gutierrez, G., *On Job*, p. 5.
74  Gutierrez, G., *On Job*, p. 6.

of Job, but is a challenge to every believer."[75] Gutierrez can then apply the universal crisis of a human being specifically to the poor in Central America: "How is a human being to speak to God in such bad times – we ask the same question today in the lands of want and hope that are Latin America. Here the masses of the poor suffer in an inhuman situation that is evidently undeserved."[76]

He casts Job anew in the guise of a Latin American peasant. Job takes on poverty and suffering and rebels against them in a hunger and thirst for justice.[77] The garbage heap of the city is a good place to start in the search for language about God since it is the abode of the underdogs of society.[78] Retribution is a theory for the wealthy and Job's rejection of it makes him a champion of the poor with whom he now identifies.[79] The end of Job's searching is the discovery of God as a principle of loving gift: "Job left his own world and entered that of the poor. [This] meant that he came to see God as gratuitous love rather than justice."[80] Such a moral vision is the foundation of a preferential option for the poor and suffering.

## A Material Reading of the Book of Job

These two contrasting readings emerge from moving from text to audience. They are arguing for a connection between literature and the material culture – whether that of the original readers or that of another set of readers. This approach to literature has connections with Marxist literary criticism. Terry Eagleton suggests that Marxist criticism "means grasping . . . forms, styles and meanings as the product of a particular history"[81], and that to understand literature means understanding the total social process of which it is a part.[82] All literary works are therefore forms of perception, particular ways of seeing the world,[83] and no work of art is entirely devoid of ideological content.[84] The book of Job is viewed by Clines as a part of a patriarchal elite community in the Ancient Near East. Gutierrez views the

75  Gutierrez, G., *On Job*, p. 11.
76  Gutierrez, G., *On Job*, p. 12.
77  Gutierrez, G., *On Job*, p. 14.
78  Gutierrez, G., *On Job*, p. 16.
79  Gutierrez, G., *On Job*, p. 31.
80  Gutierrez, G., *On Job*, p. 94.
81  Eagleton, T., *Marxism and Literary Criticism*, London, Routledge, 1989, p. 3.
82  Eagleton, T., *Marxism and Literary Criticism*, pp. 5 f.
83  Eagleton, T., *Marxism and Literary Criticism*, p. 6.
84  Eagleton, T., *Marxism and Literary Criticism*, p. 17.

book as having a home in a revolutionary peasant community in twentieth century Latin America. In each case the place setting of the work provides a different moral vision for the reader of the text.

From a materialist viewpoint the book of Job acts as a channel of communication for moral vision within a given cultural setting. It takes up issues from that environment and transposes them in such a way that material cultures, human beings as a means of production, can use that vision in re-shaping the community. Here the spotlight falls on the human character, who is engaged in the re-thinking of given values rather than on the areas of community and cosmos directly. The person needs to look out from community to cosmos (world order) in order to shift community values but the onus is on the human community to make the moves. It is not a matter of faith – belief in a personal world being – as a solution. Rather it is an engagement with a fragmented and hostile material environment on the part of human beings which counts. This is a moral vision in opposition to that of putting the cosmos first and relying on the divine to sort out life's problems. Although this is endorsed in the last speeches in Job, a great part of the text has set out the task among human beings in community of trying to make sense of life and find a way forward. Job himself comes to the conclusion, before the storm, that there is no certainty that God will give an answer, which explains the nature of experience.

## Job and Biblical Criticism

The material interpretation of Job may be extended to the task of reading the biblical books more widely. This involves acknowledging the cultural condition of a modern Bible readership, in what has been generally labelled a postmodern world. As Boer states: "The growing feeling that we have been living for some time in the millennium after 'the end of history' has been dubbed the postmodern. This sense or feeling manifests itself on the personal level as an overwhelming impression . . . of uncontrollable and bewildering change."[85]

In this context the reader experiences the loss of over-arching explanations of the cosmos and the fragmentation of community living. This is the state of those whose culture has come to stress the subjective before the communal and to dispose of the supernatural as an explanation

85  Boer, R., *Novel Histories*, p. 170.

for the origins of life and the universe. Boer outlines postmodern features: anti-essentialism, irrationality and nominalism – each of them in their own ways refusals of depth, understood as a rejection of the ideal or essential being of a text and its meaning.[86] This literary open-endedness combines with an experience of a disintegration in life, as social customs cease to prevail and as globalisation moves ahead with the world-wide nature of economic activity.[87]

When all this is applied to biblical criticism, Boer states, it leads to a market-entreprise reading method in which a variety of meanings vie for status: "An understanding of biblical interpretation in terms of the stock market is entirely appropriate: my interpretation of a particular text must take its chances in competition with others, its value falling in the face of a new challenge or rising over against its competitors, taking in the losses and dividends where appropriate."[88] Following this line modern readings of Job emerge within the moral boundaries created by a capitalist market economy society. This is to tie in the reading of biblical works with the contemporary culture of Western Europe. Boer argues that biblical commentators need to own this reality and consciously use it in their reading. "The future, utopian promise of postmodern biblical criticism lies in the border crossing it undertakes, in the interpretative risks it is willing to attempt, in the conjunction of the odd and the incongruous . . . a certain playfulness in interpretation, and a healthy disrespect for the sanctity of the item being interpreted."[89]

Such a plan for literary endeavour with regard to biblical works will not suit all readers, nor is it the only methodology currently available. But it does resonate with the construction of the book of Job itself and thus with the moral vision which the authors of that text were constructing. For it is, in many ways, a book about border crossing where the characters and the readers have to take risks to move forward from stagnation and decline. It is a work where the moral vision of a liveable-in universe comes from looking anew at the odd and incongruous elements of the material world and where a healthy disrespect for the sanctity of traditional moral perspectives is endorsed from the cosmos to the person, for the community. The moral world of the text of Job involves a material context where person, driven beyond current community, offers a fresh perspective to that same community, through a re-alignment of person with cosmos.

86  Boer, R., *Novel Histories*, p. 177.
87  Boer, R., *Novel Histories*, p. 179.
88  Boer, R., *Novel Histories*, p. 197.
89  Boer, R., *Novel Histories*, p. 198.

## Morality, Time and Place: A Summary

In this last section of the work the narrative-critical approach has been maintained, but in this case in relation to time and place settings, rather than characterisation and plot. As has been argued the organisation of a story around a timeframe and places where persons operate is an important facet of narrative structure.

### Time and Place

Time and place are themselves revealed to be complex concepts through the reading of texts given in this third section of the present book. Time is, in some ways, a fluid and content-less term, until given depth through the human mind and its imaginative powers. Time then becomes a tool for putting value on events by sequencing them; here the *longue durée* approach is significant for these biblical narratives. Only afterwards can events be examined for their fuller significance. Even the start of time only gives moral content when the reader reviews it from a period long after the imagined events. The end of time has not yet come in the fullest sense, but, by conjuring up images of endings, a story gives a moral vision concerning what occurs now, in the light of that posited end-time.

Place also gains depth as its many particular contents are developed. Thus these stories refer to many individual places which each gives a context for events. Place opens out, by this means, into space – the space within which an act takes place. Place and act are united in the concept of narrative space. Places become part of the story itself and are not merely cardboard cut-outs, providing a convenient but insignificant backdrop.

### Cosmos, Community and Person

Time is very much tied to cosmos. Time begins and ends with the created world and is coæval with it. But there is also internal time within stories, providing their beginnings, middles and ends, which sometimes rushes along and at other times drags its feet. The cosmic structuring of the world, by time periodisation, is balanced by this fast/slow time motion, within particular narratives. The beginning of time in Genesis chapter one offers the picture of a good world, a positive creator, but this is conditioned by human acts in time which connect with chaotic disorder as much as creative order. In Daniel the end-time is the chance for a caring national deity to rescue his own people and to punish their oppressors. In Job the time of the heavenly wager ties the hero into a prolonged period of extreme suffering and raises the question of divine morality. There is, indeed, considerable ambiguity about the nature of the cosmic deity, both in Genesis chapters one to eleven, and in Job. Places such as the garden and the dungheap balance the ark and the storm, and raise (in terms of practical details) queries concerning what God is doing, exactly, and how just that activity is in its effects on human persons.

The three narratives are written about characters, persons, but as a vehicle for the presentation of community values. Adam and Eve, Cain and Abel, Noah, Daniel, and Job, reflect to the community of readers the importance of individual human acts in connection with the fortunes of the community. These human persons are not always positive models. Adam and Eve are ambivalent paradigms for behaviour, Cain certainly loses his roots in human society through his murderous act, Daniel is faithful and so preserves Jewish identity – a model for diaspora Jews perhaps. Job's move from patience to anger and accusation endorses the place of the questioning of tradition in religious dialogue. Through such personal histories the community seeks to understand the cosmos as the place of human habitation and reflects on the moral vision necessary to harmonise with the forces of the cosmos to best advantage.

# CONCLUSION

CONCLUSION

# Chapter Eleven

# The Variety of Moral Perspectives

It is now appropriate to come to a summary and conclusion of the present investigation into Old Testament narratives and their moral perspectives. In the first chapter it was stated that, while the Old Testament does provide moral frameworks for the attention of the reader, this is not done, in the main, by narrowly legal or forensic material. It is necessary rather to view specifically ethical passages in their overall literary context – and that is often as part of a narrative, since so much Old Testament literature is of a narrative genre.

Since that beginning, the study has been wide-ranging in terms of the separate stories interpreted, with each narrative taken up in its own right, together with the complexities of interpretation that are attached to reading that particular story. In each case a plurality of different readings of the text with their accompanying diversity of moral vision, has emerged. Responding to this plurality of ideas involves listening to positive and negative aspects of evaluation. These evaluations stem from two sources, first, the narrative voice, and secondly, readers themselves. Both sources are culture-bound, to the culture of the writer(s) of the narrative, or to the particular readership carrying out the evaluation of meaning. The breadth of this interpretive process leads to an understanding that morality, in any given text, is not a single message but consists of a plethora of interpretations, some contradictory to others.

## Character

A character acts as an individual human being. He or she can be a stock figure, but major Old Testament characters tend to be developed in some depth, resulting in a rounded view of the human person. In such a profile there are often contradictory elements, unresolved attitudes and views and a mismatch of beliefs and acts. Ironically, the more fully that a character is treated, the more ambiguous she or he tends to become to the reader. Characters remain ambivalent in terms of their merits and flaws. This was particularly clear in the treatment made of Abraham and David. Abraham was described as both saint and savage, and David as both golden boy and abusive father in a dysfunctional family. Here two opposing poles of moral evaluation are brought together. In the case of Abraham the title of saint is appropriate on a cosmic level, that of the relationship between Abraham and God, and of divine endorsement of Abraham's trust in divine promises. If, however, that level is taken away and Abraham is read from the perspective of a human being in a community of other human beings, it is less clear that Abraham demonstrates outstanding virtue. In relation to his wives, and to the sacrifice of his son in Genesis chapter twenty-two, Abraham comes off less well.

As well as negatives produced by reading Abraham at the level of society dynamics, there are some advantages to reading him in this manner. The main advantage of reading Abraham from the angle of ordinary social relations is precisely that he becomes ordinary, a man alongside ordinary male and female readers. In this interpretation Abraham's trickster games in Egypt and Gerar, and his pragmatism vis-à-vis a God who promises but fails to deliver, provide a foil for human actions which occur on a daily basis as human beings engage with their circumstances and attempt to produce benefit from sometimes problematic situations. Which approach to Abraham is more desirable – the cosmic or the social – depends on who is doing the reading and which details in the narrative are prioritised.

The same comments may be made in relation to David. David is the chosen of God, a man viewed as the originator of a temple-state, which renewed itself in Judah in the Persian Empire, and a figure idealised in the Books of Chronicles.[1] If, however, the reader turns to the career of David as a human being, who grows up in a family, comes to the notice of Saul and Jonathan and takes the kingdom for himself, she or he has to pay attention to the ambiguities present in the narrative. These are relative to David as a real person rather than an ideal figure. The text of the first and second books of Samuel continue to support David as one approved by God, while acknowledging on his part adultery, murder, apparent indifference to rape, and a lack of control of his sons. Again, this can be viewed neutrally: here is a man making the best of life's opportunities for self-aggrandisement and then floundering in a maze of bad decisions, just as any ordinary person may do. This mixed personality offers readers a tool for reflecting on their own life-patterns, for evaluating the positive and negative effects of their own actions. The term dysfunctional, used above for example, stands for a reading from within the culture of twenty-first century Western Europe where family relationships are frequently adduced

1    In the account of David found in the books of Chronicles he is idealised as a model for a
     renewed leadership in a temple state. See chapter three for more information on this topic.

as the key to problems of socialisation among adult citizens. Once again, it matters who is doing the reading.

Esther comes in for less negative portrayal than Abraham or David, though she is also perhaps less fully developed as a character than either of these two men. On the other hand, God is not a direct actor in the story so something of the cosmic level of the other two narratives is missing. God never appears to approve or condemn the heroine. Esther, then, is profiled from a community rather than a cosmic perspective, although community here includes the two spheres of family and state government as her function in the story turns on her ability to handle the inter-action of these two social contexts with prudence and discretion. Even so, some commentators have objected that Esther is a manipulator who tricks a weak king and his bombastic official, while the end of the story makes of her a person who supports ethnic attacks.[2] Yet the interior tone of the book leaves Esther as a figure to be admired: "The role of Esther is central, her character clearly drawn for the audience as a person who moves through a series of reversals from passive . . . to active, now one whose influence with the king can save the Jews."[3]

## Plot

Female submission to male authority structures is seen also in the book of Ruth. Ruth is approved by the story line, because she becomes wife to Boaz, and is the ancestress of David. She is a foreigner, unlike Esther, but fulfils a true kinswoman's function for the Judahite Naomi. This raises wider questions of male and female social roles, and whether these roles remain a valid source of moral vision for all periods and cultural backgrounds of readership. The subject of social location of a character is relevant, too, and not unconnected, on one level, with male and female social roles. Another aspect of living on the fringe is connected to Ruth's status as a foreigner. Here the topic of insider/outsider becomes a significant aspect of moral vision, as in the Joseph and Jonah stories.

The Joseph story begins precisely because Joseph is cast out from his own family and, as a slave, has no personal identity in society. He becomes

---

2  Luther has been a key figure in the development of the idea that Esther is a work which presents an anti-Gentile polemic, which makes the book unacceptable for Christian readers. This issue is discussed in more detail in chapter four.

3  Wills, L., *The Jewish Novel in the Ancient World*, Ithaca, Cornell University Press, 1995, p. 102.

an outsider in Egypt where he nevertheless makes good, and becomes an insider at Pharaoh's court. Yet the second half of the story reverts to the issue of Joseph's own culture. Will he be an outcast forever from that culture? The plot allows for Joseph to be an insider again, albeit in changed family circumstances, not the least of which involves the passing of many years. At the same time the story makes it possible for Joseph to bring his own family the best benefits of belonging to an outside culture, with the migration to Egypt and the staving off of famine and death for his extended family.

The story of Jonah, meanwhile, turns totally on insider/outsider issues in its linking of the Judahite prophet with the foreign oppressor. The prophet views the Ninevites as rank outsiders. Like the sailors, they are shown, in the story, to be as important as insiders, and to have the ability to be insiders in terms of a commitment to fear God. Jonah, by contrast, does not fear God, since he attempts to evade divine plans in his regard. In this approach the story of Jonah is dominated by the cosmic, unlike the plots of Esther, Ruth or Joseph. Despite the underlying message that God is right, however mysterious or unpalatable his commands on human beings, which strongly emerges from the book, one commentator, at least, believes that it is right for Jonah to try to evade God's call to go on mission to the foreign oppressor.[4] In Ruth, too, the narrative can be read against the grain, so that Orpah, who clings to her own marginalised culture, becomes a heroine of the text, rather than Ruth who allows herself to be colonised by Naomi's culture.[5]

## Time and Place

The book of Esther is not unlike that of Daniel chapters one to seven, in its concern with how the God of Israel controls the time and place of foreign rulers and kingdoms, in the interest of Jewish subjects. The story of Joseph, too, shares a long view of the movement of events across time and of the control which the deity exerts over foreign places. Ultimately all these stories share the same cosmic frame as Genesis chapters one to eleven and the book of Job. But different stories occupy different sections of this time frame. Genesis chapters one to eleven focus on its origins, Daniel on

---

4  Frolov, S., *Returning the ticket. God and his prophet in the Book of Jonah, Journal for the Study of the Old Testament*, Volume 99/86, 1999.

5  These issues of joining another culture and leaving one's own society were discussed in chapter five with regard to the book of Ruth.

its yet-to-appear end.    Joseph, Jonah and Ruth operate in the middle spectrum of ongoing history, as do Abraham and David.    Job floats somewhat in a timeless relationship to the chronological movement of time, belonging to a moment when such a crisis could occur, whenever that might be.    Cosmic time is paralleled by cosmic space.    That is, by the heavens and earth, as the ongoing parameters of human activity.    Earth is a general term, in the usages of narrative structure, which is developed in many individual places where narrative action occurs, such as the garden, the ark, and the dungheap, as well as foreign lands and cities – the lands of Judah and of all-Israel.

Historical time and place are thus linked to the timeless.    Though Esther, Daniel, and Joseph are fictions, if viewed as novels, they are set against real historical contexts, as are Abraham and David, Ruth, and Jonah.    But all the narratives, including Genesis chapters one to eleven and Job, share an internal historical structure, since they only function in relation to particular times and places as set forth in the story.    These time and place elements of the narratives make the story a genre relevant to human beings as a source of moral vision.    For their readers are beings who define themselves, directly or otherwise, via the time and place in which they live, and from the context of which they address the story itself.

It is within these treatments of characters, of stories and of their worlds, that Old Testament moral perspectives are produced.    As was argued in the first chapter, the bringing together of these three literary modes in a narrative creates a textual world from which the real world of the reader can be evaluated.[6]    There is here an important interaction between readers and texts, an issue reflected upon by Wolfgang Iser.[7]    He states that a literary text "presents reactions to and attitudes towards the world we live in, and it is these reactions and attitudes that constitute the reality of a literary text".[8]    In this view, meaning is not established by the text and it is not for the reader to absorb the one, intended message of the book being read.    Rather, meaning is something, which emerges when a text comes alive in the act of reading.    Thus a literary object can never be given a final definition.[9]    Instead the text belongs to no one message but is a no-man's

---

6    'Real' here indicates the actual historical world of a reader but is not meant to suggest that textual worlds are not significant and so not real in terms of their value for the creation of moral perspectives.

7    Iser, W., *Prospecting: From Reader Response to Literary Anthropology*, Baltimore, John Hopkins University, 1993.

8    Iser, W., *Prospecting*, p. 7.

9    Iser, W., *Prospecting*, p. 9.

land of indeterminacy. Iser argues that "gaps open up and they offer free play in the interpretation of specific ways in which various views can be connected . . . [they] give the reader the chance to build its own bridges, relating different aspects of the object which thus far has been revealed".[10]

Such an opening up of the text was remarked upon in chapter three, with regard to the scene where David does not go out to campaign as kings do, the critical hinge in the text being the meaning of the connecting conjunction. It is only when the text is read by a human audience that its moral boundaries emerge; indeed, the production of these moral boundaries is itself part of the text-reader interaction. It is probable, then, that different readers of the same texts will arrive at differing moral meanings. Returning to the case of David and Bathsheba, for instance, some readers will blame David for his being available to view the woman, while others will blame the woman for being on view.

## Narrative and Narrator

Text and reader are the two central aspects of the reading process. In the case of the Old Testament, the texts are literally the source and endpoint of the production of meaning, of moral vision, so it is significant that the literary genre that is under scrutiny here is that of narrative. A key issue for narrative is the role of the narrator, since it is through the narratorial voice that a story comes into being and can be heard by the reader. As Mieke Bal asserts that: "The identity of the narrator, the degree to which and the manner in which that identity is indicated in the text, and the choices that are implied lend the text its specific character."[11]

Bal goes on to debate the various styles of narration, including first and third person accounts. For most biblical narratives it is the significance of the third person narrative style, which is to be stressed. Most biblical narrators do not name themselves and thus the narrative voice may be taken for granted by a reader. It is important to remember that "in principle, it does not make a difference to the status of narration whether a narrator refers to itself or not. As soon as there is language, there is a speaker who utters it, as soon as those linguistic utterances constitute a narrative text, there is a narrator, a narrating subject."[12]

10  Iser, W., *Prospecting*, p. 9.
11  Bal, M., *Narratology: An introduction to the Theory of Narrative*, Toronto University of Toronto Press, 1988, p. 19.
12  Bal, M., *Narratology*, p. 22.

With regard to Old Testament material Meir Sternberg has made a major contribution to the study of the narrator's role in creating meaning.[13] For Sternberg the narrator controls the development of meaning because the narrative voice is both reliable (consistent and with the intention of straightforwardly informing the reader of events and persons) and omniscient. Despite gaps and ambiguities in the telling of stories the overall picture points to the transcendent power of a single deity. Indeed the tendency is to align the narratorial voice with that deity's thoughts and utterances. David Gunn has commented on this approach, with regard to its tendency towards confusing of theological meaning with appreciation of literary art:[14] "For Sternberg . . . right reading is essentially a matter of poetics . . . this is because, in his view, biblical ideology and biblical poetics mirror each other."[15]

Gunn counters Sternberg's view of narratorial stability by arguing for the unreliability and lack of overall knowledge of biblical narrators. In his view the gaps and ambiguities in what is narrated point towards limits on the narrative voice, as, for instance, in the final ambiguity of the text as to who actually killed Goliath in the story of David and Goliath.[16] Whereas Sternberg argues that a major input source for moral vision in Old Testament narratives comes from clear direction on the part of the narrator, then, Gunn is happier to read the narrative voice as a means of expression for moral boundaries which are incomplete and ambiguous.

Behind the issue of the narrator's reliability lurks a further point – Sternberg's viewpoint concerning the omniscient narrator links narrative to the divine. God is, in this sense, the author of the story and the narrator speaks with the weight of divine authority. Once again this points to the argument that the text has a right reading, one which the narrator simply reveals. Gunn argues, rather, that the narrator is very much a human figure. The narrator's human status is also discernible through the cumulative effect of the narratorial point of view, which is to say a human point of view.[17] Only Genesis and Job start from a divine perspective and both move quickly to a human stance on affairs.

---

13  Sternberg, M., *The Poetics of Biblical Narrative*, Bloomington, Indiana, 1985.
14  Gunn, D., *Reading Right: Reliable and Omniscient Narrator, Omniscient God and Foolproof Composition in the Hebrew Bible* in Clines, D., Fowl, S. and Porter, S. (eds), *The Bible in Three Dimensions*, Sheffield, Sheffield Academic Press, 1990.
15  Gunn, D., *Reading Right*, p. 54.
16  Gunn, D., *Reading Right*, p. 57.
17  Gunn, D., *Reading Right*, p. 58.

The linking of God and narrator provokes reflection on the position of God's self in the narratives. God, in Old Testament stories, is a character like others; this is the deity of the symbolic world of the text. Gunn argues that "to claim that God-as-character in the Bible is not the creation of the author/narrator is, in my view, perverse".[18]   The effect of Sternberg's approach is to make a circular interpretation in which the narrator points to God who points back to the narrator; that is, the cosmic level defines human person and community values through the literary structure of the story. Gunn's viewpoint is that the human originators of the text shape the character of God in their shaping of the narrator.

Once 'God' has taken on certain lineaments within a particular story he is defined by those personal and social boundaries and cannot be other than a character developed via plot and time and place contexts. This would mean that in Ruth, for instance, where God is barely present, the deity is established through Boaz's speech to Ruth and the belief that God sees Ruth's loyalty to Naomi as a trust in God himself. Such a God will bless that loyalty with nurturing in practical terms in a new social setting. On the other hand, in Genesis chapter one, God is coæval with time and space and as such is the ground of all human life. Here God is a commanding voice who speaks his plan that human beings should be made (by us) in the divine image. God is a partaker in moral meaning, then, but does not stand above the textual frame to give moral vision; rather, God is shaped, within a given book, according to the literary perceptions at work there.

## The Reader

This focus on the creation of meaning as an aspect of individual texts leads to the treatment of each text, individually, and also brings attention back to the role of the reader as the author of meaning. Clearly the term author properly applies to the ancient compiler of the narrative and a search for the author and authorial meaning in this context would situate the moral content of the text in the past of that writer's time. The historical approach to text construction belongs with this style of exploration and has its points to make. But the literary-critical method of reading stories focuses on the continuing creation of meaning via the open-ended nature of the texts. Amos Wilder remarks that, in the literary mode, "we begin to realise that these fictions cannot be shut off in the past tense. These characters and

---

18  Gunn, D., *Reading Right*, p. 61.

plots have backgrounds which outlast them, orientations which continue to operate on us also."[19] Although narratives have their own worlds to present and the reader is called upon to enter willingly into these environments, the end result is not a loss of contact with the current life experience of the reader. According to Wilder "fictions do not take us out of time and the world. Their sequences and vicissitudes are woven of the same contingencies, surprises and reversals which attend on our own uncertainties."[20]

## Morality and Biblical Fiction

The use of the word fiction here may startle readers of the Bible for whom these works offer a means of finding the absolute boundaries of human existence. Surely fiction implies a relative and not an absolute meaning? This would stand in opposition to the viewpoint of M. Sternberg that God as the creator and keeper of moral order is to be discovered in biblical poetics. It is true that the position concerning the role of the reader in finding meaning in text, outlined above, has as its corollary that there is no one unchangeable message to be discovered. New meanings emerge through the intimacy of text and reader in a given act of reading. But that does not mean that no over-arching values are to be found in the narrative nor that the text produces deceitful or frivolous ideas of little long-term significance.

In the chapter on Job mention was made of William Brown's references to poetic imagination.[21] Imagination is a useful term, here, relative to the exploration of moral perspectives in the context of text-reader relations. Lawrence Wills, dealing with the Jewish novel in antiquity, stated that "fiction, the art of creating narratives that do not have a referent in past events, is not really a lie, it is a mutually agreed upon flight of the imagination, a playful reflection on what reality is and what it is not".[22] Iser goes further when he says that "fictions are inventions enabling humankind to extend itself",[23] and it is through imagination that this enabling takes place: "Perception cannot take place without a proportion of

---

19  Wilder, A., *The Bible and the Literary Critic*, Minneapolis, Augsburg/Fortress, 1991, p. 133.
20  Wilder, A., *The Bible and the Literary Critic*, p. 143.
21  Brown, W., *The Ethos of the Cosmos*, Grand Rapids, Eerdmans, 1999.
22  Wills, L., *Jewish Novel*, p. 223.
23  Iser, W., *Prospecting*, p. 265.

imagination."[24] The perception referred to here involves a transcendence of the understanding achieved so far on the part of the reader and brings a new entity into being, an entity which challenges the reader to further explorations of the world and meaning. Iser argues that "the fictional . . . is an 'as if' construction, which goes beyond itself in order to act as the bearer for something else. In so doing, it imposes a perspective upon what it is not but which it bears."[25]

## Moral Cultural Perspectives

Imagination is an aspect of the human mind which draws its symbols from the cultural experiences of the reader. Cultural diversity thus becomes the foundation of the making of moral vision through the act of reading Old Testament narratives. In previous chapters attention was constantly drawn to the variety of cultural readings, reflecting frequently on the issue of boundary crossing. Two areas emerging from that process, referred to above, are male/female gender boundaries and outsider/insider group boundaries.

Cheryl Exum has recently offered an overview of male/female boundaries in relation to the current development of feminist critique of texts and how these developments are producing other forms of moral imagination.[26] Exum focuses on Mieke Bal as a great forerunner who paved the way for new styles of feminist biblical criticism. Alice Bach, in particular, has developed an inter-disciplinary style of reading, following Bal's lead, as in her study of Madame Potiphar where she moves between biblical text and the novel of Thomas Mann.[27] Bringing biblical text into contact with other texts, or the bringing together of biblical texts not usually treated simultaneously, in a method called juxtaposition is, for Exum, a fruitful approach. Here the commentator jerks the reader into making new literary connections and thus crossing intellectual boundaries, which have previously regulated reading of biblical material – often those

---

24  Iser, W., *Prospecting*, p. 273.
25  Iser, W., *Prospecting*, p. 277.
26  Exum, J. C., *Developing Strategies of Feminist Criticism* in Clines, D. and Moore, S. (eds), *Auguries*, Sheffield, Sheffield Academic Press, 1998.
27  See Chapter Six with regard to the Joseph story, where Alice Bach's work is commented on and attention is drawn to her critique of the Joseph/Mrs Potiphar scenes. Bach, A., *Women, Seduction and Betrayal in Biblical Narrative*, Cambridge, Cambridge University Press, 1997.

of a male dominant culture. Bach, working on Numbers chapter five, for instance, "finding that traditional interpretations of the ritual of the Sotah disturbingly re-inscribe the biblical author's sense of suspicion about women . . . reads the bizarre text with the intention of 'stir[ring] up a new brew', where men's attempts to control women's bodies are read as male vulnerability".[28]

Insider/outsider issues are linked to the boundaries between and within social groups – any group – but an important aspect of social boundaries is currently that which relates to biblical interpretation and regionalism, and the promoting of readings of Old Testament stories from one geographical region above those from other regions. In *Voices from the Margin* biblical commentators from the third world offer their readings of biblical texts.[29] This is not a matter of adding-on readings to the master narrative, as colonies were added to empires. Rather, non-European readings stand on equal terms with European readings; no one region's readings have greater weight. All readings offer moral perspectives worth attending to. Thus there are no pejorative insider/outsider roles to reading of Old Testament narratives in an ideally balanced moral vision of texts and their meanings.

Two examples from the volume will help to reveal the issues at stake here. Stanley Samartha moves from globalisation, which has made the Old Testament a part of world heritage to what this means for biblical culture:[30] "When the Scriptures cannot be regarded as the monopolistic possession of any one particular people, but should be accepted as belonging to the heritage of the whole world, the hermeneutic question may be stated: How can the Bible, a Semitic book . . . appropriated and interpreted . . . by the West . . . now be interpreted in Asia by Asian Christians for their own people?"[31] In the interface of Christianity and (other) Asian religions Samartha argues that the biblical texts can have no predominance simply because they talk about God; they sit alongside the sacred texts of other religious faiths in a wide cultural multiplicity of religious traditions. What is important is to go behind the question of biblical authority to "bring out the insights, guideposts and directions to which the Bible points",[32] a task in which images and stories have a particular part to play.[33] Once more imagination comes to the fore, in this case in the service of communication

---

28 Exum, J. C., *Developing Strategies*, pp. 216 f.
29 Sugirtharajah, R. (ed.), *Voices from the Margin*, London, SPCK, 1995.
30 Samartha, S., *Scripture and Scriptures*, in Sugirtharajah, R. (ed.), 1997.
31 Samartha, S., *Scripture and Scriptures*, p. 21.
32 Samartha, S., *Scripture and Scriptures*, p. 22.
33 Samartha, S., *Scripture and Scriptures*, p. 22.

of religious meaning in a largely non-Christian environment. It is by appeal to images and stories that moral vision can be most easily fleshed out.

Canaan Banana, speaking from an African viewpoint, argues that "holiness is a product of human imagination. Legitimation of meaning is not immutable."[34] Here he indicates his belief in a plurality of modes by which to give voice to religious views. He goes on to say that "logic requires us to recognise that, religiously speaking, there is no difference between Abraham and Mbuya Nehada".[35] Banana thinks that there is a commonality of moral vision concerning religious heroes, persons whose strengths may be emulated. In this setting the characters of Old Testament narratives are on a par with other such figures in the folk memories of the readers concerned. Moral vision is thus composed of biblical and non-biblical symbols, all of which carry weight equally as part of a local culture.

## Biblical Interpretation in the Western World

Although the idea of the crossing of social boundaries within biblical interpretation has been outlined here in a non-European context, it is equally important within Europe. The need to transcend boundaries and to find new frameworks of moral perspective by which to order life applies equally to European commentators. On both academic and popular fronts the dominance of Christian culture is waning, as Philip Davies has argued.[36]

In this situation there is a need to find new meeting points between contemporary culture and actual or potential readers. An obvious point of contact is story, since narratives are easily accessible and a frequently used method of handing on ideas. It can be argued, therefore, that Old Testament stories and the moral vision(s) they express can be an ongoing community resource, which can be interpreted through the use of moral imagination. Roland Boer addresses some of the cultural issues in biblical exegesis in the context of popular culture, in *Knockin' on Heaven's Door*.[37] His stated aim is to put the Bible into the area of popular culture where

---

34  Banana, C.S., *The case for a New Bible*, in Sugirtharajah, R. (ed.), 1997, p. 71.
35  Banana, C., *The Case for a New Bible*, p. 81.
36  Davies, P., *The Future of 'Biblical History'*, in Clines, D. and Moore, S. (eds), *Auguries*, Sheffield, Sheffield Academic Press, 1998.
37  Boer, R., *Knockin' on Heaven's Door: The Bible and Postmodern Culture*, London, Routledge, 1999.

there are still some echoes of a past influence of the Bible on culture.[38] Taking as aspects of popular interests, sex, violence, and food, Boer makes an inter-disciplinary connection between biblical material, contemporary literature and popular concerns. The base for Boer's choice of topics derives, he argues, from his appreciation that capitalist consumer culture is the dominant social worldview and that is to be combined with the cultural outlook of the working classes. The combination of these two cultural areas effects the collapse of high/low cultural boundaries and so brings into being another kind of boundary crossing.

In the chapter on *Queer Heroes*, for instance, Boer taps in to contemporary interest in gender and orientation boundaries: "Are all our heroes queer? It seems so, at least with regard to the action hero, found mainly in contemporary film, and with regard to the biblical hero."[39] Boer continues by discussing queer theory: "The specific contribution of [which] is to focus on the operation of the heterosexual/homosexual binary and on the politics of knowledge and difference" and moves on to consider some of the manifestations of this approach in film and story.[40] This forms a bridge to the exploration of the biblical David, in the first book of Samuel chapters eighteen to twenty especially, where the text deals with the relationship between David and Jonathan. Boer asserts that the gender issues and social boundaries involved here are complex matters, in which it is important to understand the social context of sexual acts in different societies: "The crucial point . . . is that in the ancient Mediterranean . . . penetration signifies male, dominant, citizen and active, whereas being penetrated signifies female, subordinate, non-citizen and passive."[41]

Boer takes this as a measure for the account of David's social life. In fact David is extremely active in the world of war but passive in social affairs.[42] He receives love/hate from Saul, love from Jonathan, love/hate from Michal in a complex interaction between his adopted family and himself: "It is as though the impotent and unfruitful marriage between David and Michal . . . comes to fruition with David and Jonathan."[43] Despite the intimacy in the text between the two men, Boer notes that "I have not located any explicit reference to sex, although my search has been

---

38 As companion to this approach see Clines, D., *The Bible and the Modern World*, Sheffield, Sheffield Academic Press, 1997, which discusses how much British culture still shows traces of biblical concepts, characters and language.
39 Boer, R., *Knockin' on Heaven's Door*, p. 13.
40 Boer, R., *Knockin' on Heaven's Door*, p. 14.
41 Boer, R., *Knockin' on Heaven's Door*, p. 24.
42 Boer, R., *Knockin' on Heaven's Door*, p. 26.
43 Boer, R., *Knockin' on Heaven's Door*, p. 27.

for the active/passive dynamic".[44] Yet David absorbs all that is thrown at him in terms of fame, status and regard: "Perhaps this should be read as not only an accumulation of power, but also of sexual power?".[45] Is David active or passive? Does he gain virility or become subordinate? Boer's conclusion is that David "may better be seen as a sort of biblical Herakles . . . whose gender identification and sexuality are highly ambiguous, both as a virile man and lover and as a 'feminine' passive figure".[46]

In this account Boer deals in detail with a Hebrew text while, at the same time, widening the interest of the story to make a point of contact with a contemporary cultural concern. In the volume *Biblical Studies: Cultural Studies* there is another example of the use of cultural perspectives to aid the reading of biblical texts.[47] The essay *David the Musician and Poet: Plotted and Painted* by Erich Zenger provides a suitable foil to Boer's work.[48] While Boer concentrates on new meanings Zenger examines a whole history of cultural re-use of the David story in Europe. Zenger is interested in the after life of this biblical figure. He explores "the peculiar phenomenon that, in early Judaism, David was progressively promoted to the figure of royal musician and poet and that he, as such a cultural model, was subject to a diverse reception in the post-biblical period".[49]

From this Zenger moves to pictures of David in the Dura-Europos Synagogue, a third century CE site in modern Turkey. One wall painting in particular shows a lyrist, linked to trees and animals. Zenger thinks that this figure is David-Orpheus, an image which combines biblical material with that of Hellenistic religious thought.[50] David's cure of Saul's evil spirit here equates with the power of Orpheus' lyre. Thus David is interpreted for a new social setting and becomes a key to understanding the Old Testament. As Zenger points out, David, now revered as the author of the five books of Psalms, comes to have a religious authority in a new age.[51]

---

44 Boer, R., *Knockin' on Heaven's Door*, p. 30.
45 Boer, R., *Knockin' on Heaven's Door*, p. 31.
46 Boer, R., *Knockin' on Heaven's Door*, p. 31.
47 Exum, J. C. and Moore, S. (eds), *Biblical Studies: Cultural Studies*, Sheffield, Sheffield Academic Press, 1998.
48 Zenger, E., *David the Musician and Poet: plotted and Painted*, in Exum, J. C. and Moore, S. (eds), *Biblical Studies: Cultural Studies*.
49 Zenger, E., *David the Musician*, p. 264.
50 Zenger, E., *David the Musician*, pp. 268-274.
51 Zenger, E., *David the Musician*, p. 274.

Zenger traces the continuation of these traditions in Christian Europe, with reference to the door panels of San Ambrosio in Milan. He asserts that the representations of David on this door pick up the biblical traditions of a soldier figure and combine them with that of a lyrist and musician. By the time of Ambrose, then, in the fourth century CE, "the psalms of David were interpreted as songs of battle against the powers of evil, especially if they were seen in a christological *and* ecclesiological perspective".[52] From there Zenger traces the re-shaping of the David traditions through the tenth, the twelfth and the seventeenth centuries.

He shows how, in the seventeenth century, the biblical David was the source of artistic imagination for Rembrandt and his school. In Lucas van Leyden's painting of David playing for Saul the meaning is interpreted in a new way: "In contrast to the (rare) mediæval representations of the scene . . . it is an innovation here that the evil spirit no longer appears as a demon . . . instead, the evil is portrayed as a mood, a disease."[53] In Rembrandt's own painting of this scene "two worlds confront each other in Saul and David. Saul appears in the glaring light as the embodiment of the evil power . . . David is placed in shadows."[54] Zenger suggests that, in the context of seventeenth century Europe the two figures represent the political and cultural struggle between the overlord, Catholic Spain, and the protestant rebel heroes who sought for independence.[55] From these disparate elements, all linked to the David stories, Zenger argues that past and present are fused in the pictures. This "demands from viewers a creative examination of the *sujet* . . . *and* of the associations . . . that do not come from the Bible but from different historical periods . . . a biblical model . . . can thus become a cultural and political model that influences individual and collective action".[56] In their similarity and, yet, their differences, these treatments of the story of David exemplify the importance of multiple readings of texts and the production of multiple moral frames. Each interpretation is itself a world with its own boundaries within which David performs particular moral roles.

---

52  Zenger, E., *David the Musician*, p. 281.
53  Zenger, E., *David the Musician*, p. 296.
54  Zenger, E., *David the Musician*, p. 296.
55  Zenger, E., *David the Musician*, p. 297.
56  Zenger, E., *David the Musician*, p. 298.

## Cosmos and Boundary Crossing

It can be seen from these several examples of reading biblical books in different regions of the world that very different questions exercise the minds of the various commentators. Whereas Samartha and Banana are concerned with the moral vision, which can be brought into communication with that of other religious traditions, Boer and Zenger are taken up with the task of exploring the wider social and political impact, which biblical characters have on European culture, both now and in the past. Not that any of these views are the only ones to be found either in the third world or in Europe, but they do indicate the wide diversity of imagination needed to evaluate the importance of biblical texts across a range of cultures. Boundary crossing is linked to boundary blurring as part of re-forming fictive worlds, which impact on the historical world of the reader or writer. Such boundary crossing may be examined from the viewpoint of a whole region or from the narrower focus of gender grouping within a single society.

It can be argued that each Old Testament story is its own world in which there is a particular slant on God and the transcendent nature of life; in the canonical collection these stories stand side by side. They can, therefore, be viewed as parallel worlds, time and space zones into which a reader travels to experience a diversity of cosmic understanding. What holds this together as a common entreprise is the perception of the reader that these several reading experiences are coherent. Cosmic order is consequent on this reading process. For the reader there may be a sense that there is a oneness about the deity involved (with regard to a person's perception of coherence of meaning) but not a 'sameness'. This view seems to prioritise a subjective and individual reading of the text, but reader could mean a group of readers with a common interest or cultural background; though here too the oneness may include variant shades of meaning on the part of group members.

## Community and Language

Turning from cosmos to community, moral imagination deals with inter-communication between human beings. In this setting it is relevant to consider Mikhail Bakhtin's essay *Discourse in the Novel*.[57] As part of his

---

57  Bakhtin, M., *The Dialogic Imagination*, Austen, University of Texas, 1998, chapter four.

analysis of the poetics of the modern novel Bakhtin explores the nature of verbal discourse in its widest sense: "Verbal discourse is a social phenomenon – social throughout its entire range and in each and every one of its factors."[58] From this starting point Bakhtin comes to the view that "the novel orchestrates all its themes, the totality of the world of objects and ideas depicted and expressed in it, by means of the social diversity of speech types . . . authorial speech, the speech of narrators, inserted genres, the speech of characters, are merely those fundamental compositions . . . with whose help heteroglossia can enter the novel".[59]

Prose narrative, as a result, is not a single, unitive passage of writing but contains within itself diversity and even oppositions. It is as a result of the intercommunication of the diverse elements of the discourse that meaning emerges, in prose. Dialogue, between aspects of the language of texts-narrator, speeches by characters, embedded narratives – brings a fuller meaning.[60]

This approach to the nature of prose narrative reminds the reader of the essentially social nature of human existence, a social environment from which literature comes and within which it has its life. At the simplest level, a writer offers a reader speech concerning a social situation. The reader engages in reading the story with the assumption that the text will engage with that reader's own social experience and will add a depth of meaning or an extra layer of meaning to that experience. At a more complex level the reader encounters different responses to the plot of the story on the part of the characters or of the narrator and it is by entering into dialogue with these varieties of response that the reader develops his or her own appreciation of events.

## Diversity and Opposition

In producing summative comments on biblical moral perspectives it cannot be denied that a proper mode would be to leave each text to speak for itself, recognising that moral vision is not a single viewpoint held by all Old Testament narratives. This recognition of pluralism in Old Testament works formed the basis for method in *Images of God in the Old Testament*,[61] and, indeed, the diversity of the biblical character 'God' has

---

58  Bakhtin, M., *The Dialogic Imagination*, p. 259.
59  Bakhtin, M., *The Dialogic Imagination*, p. 272.
60  Bakhtin, M., *The Dialogic Imagination*, p. 282.
61  Mills, M., *Images of God in the Old Testament*, London, Cassell, 1998.

been touched on already above. Yet there is some value in estimating whether any common features of moral vision can be discerned in Old Testament stories.

What has emerged, across the chapters, is the linking of two opposing poles of thought. Thus, in characterisation, harmonious and disjunctive elements were noted. Abraham the pious worshipper is in harmony with the cosmos but the Abraham who washes his hands of Hagar in her dispute with Sarah is disjunctive in terms of social, community order. Other forms of polarised assessment have been addressed above – insider/outsider, male/female, tragic/comic. Within the three sections it has often been significant to define a text as comic or tragic. As, for instance, with Genesis chapters one to three, where it can be stated that a tragic fall occurs with an ongoing lack of cosmic harmony and human fulfilment as consequence, or that here is a comedy in which mistaken decisions lead to the opening up of new and beneficial vision. With regard to all these paired symbols border-crossing has been a significant part of finding moral meanings.[62] There is no either/or, but rather both/and; more especially, the stress is on the point, the border, at which A crosses over into B. When does a saint become savage, where does an outsider turn in to an insider or vice versa, how can tragic events move over into constructive goals? It can be argued that moral vision resides at this point of liminality where two identifiable and separate aspects meet and dialogue.

## Cosmos, Community and Person: Final Remarks

On another level the members of the dialogic process are not paired opposites but the three levels cosmos, community and person, insofar as the human context of seeking understanding involves all three of these perspectives. When boundaries are crossed it is within the linguistic and social framework of the cosmic, the communal and the personal. In Genesis chapter three, for example, it is the persons Adam and Eve who do the crossing, they do so in a dialogic community of themselves and the serpent and the effect of their crossing is found immediately at personal and cosmic levels. At all three levels of existence gaps open up with disharmony among humans, between humans and nature and between humans and God.

---

62  For further uses of this concept as a means of explaining Old Testament narrative style see chapter eight on Genesis chapters one to eleven, discussing genre of the garden and fantasy.

Thus, despite the lack of a single unitary message, which every reader of an Old Testament narrative will discover and own as moral vision, there are objective means of reflecting on biblical morality. The starting point and its final closure is the biblical text itself. It is in the act of reading that the text produces moral vision, while a willingness to sample the findings of other, parallel readers, offers a deepening of vision consequent on, and not in spite of, the diversity of moral imagination. It is, perhaps, appropriate to conclude with a quotation from Boer's experience of reading biblical texts in a new cultural environment. In this passage he holds together pleasure and pain as companions in the act of reading – a reading sometimes carried through 'against the grain' of the world of biblical scholarship. Yet, it needs to be remembered that texts are kept alive within cultures and that each culture reads the texts in search of meanings relevant for it. Biblical morality will continue to be a topic of interest while there remain readers who wish to explore it. The content of their researches, however, remains to be revealed, or even to have an existence, until those future acts of reading actually occur.

Boer concludes: "Yet I want to evoke *jouissance* once again, the transgressive and painful enjoyment beyond pleasure, in the exercise of biblical studies at the end of the second millenium of the common era . . . the disparagement of a postmodern practice in biblical studies . . . is comparable to the common disparagement . . . of McDonalds . . . Instead of decrying the degeneration of standards . . . it might be better to sit down and partake of the painful pleasure, to enjoy in pain the sheer cleverness and consummate skill with which all the variegated parts of the postmodern moment operate."[63]

---

63 Boer, R., *Novel Histories*, pp. 199 f.

# Bibliography

Aichele, G. and Pippin, T., *The Monstrous and the Unspeakable The Bible as fantastic literature*, Sheffield, Sheffield Academic Press, 1997.

Alschich, M. translated, Shakar, R., *Ruth, A Harvest of Majesty*, Jerusalem, Feldheim, 1991.

Alter, R., *The Art of Biblical Poetry*, Edinburgh, T. and T. Clark, 1990.

Alter, R., *Genesis*, New York, Norton, 1996.

Alter, R. and Kermode, F. (eds), *The Literary Guide to the Bible*, London, Harper Collins, 1997.

Auerbach, E., *Mimesis. The Representation of Reality in Western Literature*, Princeton, Princeton University Press, 1953.

Bach, A., *Women, Seduction and Betrayal in Biblical Narrative*, Cambridge, Cambridge University Press, 1997.

Bach, A. (ed.), *Women in the Hebrew Bible*, London, Routledge, 1998.

Bakhtin, M., translated, Holquist, M., *The Dialogic Imagination*, Austen, University of Texas Press, 1998.

Bal, M., *Narratology: Introduction to the Theory of Narrative*, Toronto, University of Toronto Press, 1988 First edition, 1997 Second edition.

Bar-Efrat, S., *Narrative Art in the Bible*, Sheffield, Sheffield Academic Press, 1997.

Barton, J., *Ethics in the Old Testament*, London, SCM Press, 1998.

Barton, J. and Reimer, D. (eds), *After the Exile*, Macon, Mercer University Press, 1996.

Beal, T., *The Book of Hiding*, London, Routledge, 1997.

Beal, T. and Gunn, D. (eds), *Reading Bibles, Writing Bodies*, London, Routledge, 1997.

Berg, S., *The Book of Esther*, Atlanta, Scholars Press, 1979.

Berquist, J., *Judaism in Persia's Shadow: A Social and Historical Approach*, Minneapolis, Fortress, 1995.

Bible Collective, *The Postmodern Bible*, New Haven, Yale University Press, 1995.

Boer, R., *Novel Histories The Fiction of Biblical Criticism*, Sheffield, Sheffield Academic Press, 1997.

Boer, R., *Knockin' on Heaven's Door. The Bible and Postmodern Culture*, London, Routledge, 1998.

Booth, W., *A Rhetoric of Irony*, Chicago, University of Chicago Press, 1974.

Bost, H., *Babel: Du texte au symbol*, Geneva, Labor et Fides, 1985.

Brams, S., *Biblical Games: A Strategic Analysis of Stories in the Old Testament*, Cambridge, Massachusetts, MIT, 1980.

Brenner, A., *The Isrælite Woman*, Sheffield, Sheffield Academic Press, 1994.

Brenner, A. (ed.), *A Feminist Companion to Ruth*, Sheffield, Sheffield Academic Press, 1993.

Brenner, A. (ed.), *A Feminist Companion to Esther, Judith and Susannah*, Sheffield, Sheffield Academic Press, 1995.

Brenner, A. (ed.), *Ruth and Esther*, Sheffield, Sheffield Academic Press, 1997.

Brenner, A. (ed.), *Genesis: A Feminist Companion*, Second series Sheffield, Sheffield Academic Press, 1998.

Brettler, M., *The Creation of History in Ancient Isræl*, London, Routledge, 1995.

Brown, W., *The Ethos of the Cosmos: the Genesis of Moral Imagination in the Bible*, Grand Rapids, Eerdmans, 1999.

Brueggemann, W., *David's Truth in Isræl's Imagination and Memory*, Philadelphia, Fortress, 1985.

Brueggemann, W., *Texts Under Negotiation: the Bible and Postmodern Imagination*, Minneapolis, Fortess/Augsburg, 1993.

Brueggemann,W., *Cadences of Home. Preaching among the Exiles*, Louisville, Westminster John Knox, 1997.

Charlesworth, J. (ed.), *The Pseudepigrapha of the Old Testament, 2 Volumes*, New York, Doubleday, 1985-88.

Clines, D., *The Esther Scroll*, Sheffield, Sheffield Academic Press, 1984.

Clines, D., *What Does Eve Do To Help? And other readerly questions*, Sheffield, Sheffield Academic Press, 1994.

Clines, D., *Interested Parties: the Ideology of Writers and Readers*, Sheffield, Sheffield Academic Press, 1995.

Clines, D., *The Theme of the Pentateuch*, Sheffield, Sheffield Academic Press, 1997.

Clines, D., *The Bible and the Modern World*, Sheffield, Sheffield Academic Press, 1997.

Clines, D. and Moore, S. (eds), *Auguries*, Sheffield, Sheffield Academic Press, 1998.

Clines, D., Fowl, S. and Porter, S. (eds), *The Bible in Three Dimensions*, Sheffield, Sheffield Academic Press, 1990.

Cohn, N., *Cosmos, Chaos and the World to Come*, New Haven, Yale University Press, 1993.

Collins, J., *The Apocalyptic Imagination*, New York, Crossroad, 1984.

Collins, J., *Daniel, with an Introduction to Apocalyptic Literature, Volume XX of the Forms of the Old Testament Literature Series*, Grand Rapids, Eerdmans, 1984.

Collins, J., *Daniel*, Minneapolis, Fortress/Augsburg, 1993.

Collins, J. (ed.), *Apocalypse: Morphology of a Genre*, Atlanta, Scholars MIT, 1979.

Cook, S., *Prophecy and Apocalypticism The Post Exilic Setting*, Minneapolis, Fortress, 1995.

Coppleston, F., *A History of Philosophy*, Tunbridge Wells, Burns and Oates, 1966.

Cox, D., *Man's Anger and God's Silence*, Slough, St Paul's Press, 1990.

Craig, K., *A Poetics of Jonah*, South Carolina, University of South Carolina Press, 1993.

Cryer, F., *Divination in Ancient Israel and its Near-Eastern Environment*, Sheffield, Sheffield Academic Press, 1994.

Culpepper, A., *Anatomy of the Fourth Gospel A Study in Literary Design*, Philadelphia, Fortress, 1983.

Davies, P., *Daniel*, Sheffield, Sheffield Academic Press, 1985.

Davies, P., *In Search of Ancient Israel*, Sheffield, Sheffield Academic Press, 1992.

Davies, P., *Whose Bible is it Anyway?*, Sheffield, Sheffield Academic Press, 1995.

Davies, P. (ed.), *Second Temple Studies I*, Sheffield, Sheffield Academic Press, 1991.

Davies, P. and Clines, D. (eds), *Among the Prophets. Language, Image and Structure in the Prophetic Writings*, Sheffield, Sheffield Academic Press, 1993.

Davies, P. and Clines, D. (eds), *The World of Genesis. Persons, Places and Perspectives*, Sheffield, Sheffield Academic Press, 1998.

Day, J., *God's Conflict with the Dragon and the Sea*, Cambridge, Cambridge University Press, 1985.

Day, J., Gordon, R. and Williamson, H. (eds), *Wisdom in Ancient Israel*, Cambridge, Cambridge University Press, 1995.

Day, L., *Three Faces of a Queen*, Sheffield, Sheffield Academic Press, 1995.

Delaney, C., *Abraham on Trial*, Princeton, Princeton University Press, 1998.

Eagleton, T., *Marxism and Literary Criticism*, London, Routledge, 1989.

Edelmann, D. (ed.), *The Triumph of Elohim. From Yahwisms to Judaisms*, Kampen, Kok Pharos, 1995.

Esler, P., *The First Christians in their Social Worlds*, London, Routledge, 1994.

Eslinger, L., *House of God or House of David: The Rhetoric of 2 Samuel 7*, Sheffield, Sheffield Academic Press, 1994.

Exum, J. C., *Tragedy and Biblical Narrative*, Cambridge, Cambridge University Press, 1992.

Exum, J. C., *Plotted, Shot and Painted*, Sheffield, Sheffield Academic Press, 1996.

Exum, J. C. (ed.), *The Historical Books*, Sheffield, Sheffield Academic Press, 1997.

Exum, J. C. and Moore, S. (eds), *Biblical Studies: Cultural Studies*, Sheffield, Sheffield Academic Press, 1998.

Fewell, D. and Gunn, D., *Gender, Power and Promise, the subject of the Bible's First Story*, Nashville, Abingdon, 1993.

Fishbane, M., *Biblical Text and Texture*, Oxford, One World, 1998.

Fowl, S., *Engaging Scripture*, Oxford, Blackwell, 1998.

Fox, M., *Character and Ideology in the Book of Esther*, Columbia, University of South Carolina Press, 1991.

Frolov, S., *Returning the Ticket: God and his Prophet in the book of Jonah*, in *Journal for the Study of the Old Testament 99/86*, 1999.

Geertz, C., *The Interpretation of Cultures*, London, Fontana, 1993.

Gordis, R., *The Book of Job*, New York, Jewish Theological Seminary of America, 1978.

Goulder, M., *The Prayers of David*, Sheffield, Sheffield Academic Press, 1990.

Gow, M., *The Book of Ruth*, Leicester, Apollos Press, 1994.

Graham, S. and Thimmes, P. (eds), *Escaping Eden. New Feminist Perspectives in the Bible*, Sheffield, Sheffield Academic Press, 1998.

Gray, M., *Amnon: A Chip off the Old Block? Rhetorical Strategy in 2 Samuel 13:7-15 the rape of Tamar and the Humiliation of the Poor*, in *Journal for the Study of the Old Testament 98/77*, 1998.

Gunn, D., *The Story of King David: Genre and Interpretation*, Sheffield, Sheffield Academic Press, 1978.

Gunn, D. and Fewell, D., *Narrative Art in the Hebrew Bible*, Oxford, Oxford University Press, 1993.

Gutierrez, G., *On Job: God-talk and the Suffering of the Innocent*, Maryknoll, Orbis, 1987.

Habel, N., *The Book of Job*, London, SCM Press, 1985.

Hiebert, T., *The Yahwist's Landscape*, Oxford, Oxford University Press, 1996.

Hoffman, Y., *A Blemished Perfection: the Book of Job in Context*, Sheffield, Sheffield Academic Press, 1996.

Hollander, H., *Joseph as an Ethical Model in the Testament of the Twelve Patriarchs*, Leiden, Brill, 1981.

Horrell, D., *Converging Ideologies: Berger and Luckman and the Pastoral Epistles*, in *Journal for the Study of the New Testament 93/50*, 1993.

Hubbard Jr, R., *The Book of Ruth*, Grand Rapids, Eerdmans, 1991.

Husser, J.-M., *Dreams and Dream Narratives in the Biblical World*, Sheffield, Sheffield Academic Press, 1999.

Iser, W., *Prospecting: From Reader Response to Literary Anthropology*, Baltimore, John Hopkins University, 1993.

Janzen, W., *Old Testament Ethics: A Paradigmatic Approach*, Louisville, Westminster John Knox, 1994.

Jones, L. and Buckley, J. (eds), *Spirituality and Social Embodiment*, Oxford, Blackwell, 1997.

Josopovici, G., *The Book of God*, New Haven, Yale University Press, 1988.

Jung, C., *Answer to Job*, London, Hodder and Stoughton, 1964.

Kermode, F., *The Sense of an Ending*, Oxford, Oxford University Press, 2000.

Kugel, J., *In Potiphar's House: The Interpretive Life of Biblical Texts*, Massachusetts, Harvard University Press, 1990.

Kuschel, K.-J., *Abraham. A Symbol of Hope for Jews, Christians and Muslims*, London, SCM Press, 1995.

LaCocque, A., *Daniel in his Time*, South Carolina, University of South Carolina Press, 1988.

LaCocque, A. and Lacocque, P.-E., *Jonah: A Psycho-Religious Approach to the Prophet*, South Carolina, University of South Carolina Press, 1990.

Laffey, A., *Wives, Harlots and Concubines*, London, SPCK, 1988.

Lemche, N., *Israel in History and Tradition*, London, SPCK, 1988.

Levenson, J., *Esther*, London, SCM Press, 1997.

Limberg, J., *Jonah*, London, SCM Press, 1993.

Linafeldt, T. and Beal, T. (eds), *God in the Fray*, Minneapolis, Fortress, 1998.

Lowenthal, E., *The Joseph Narrative in Genesis*, New York, KTAV, 1973.

Lundin, R., Walhout, C. and Thistleton, A. (eds), *The Promise of Hermeneutics*, Grand Rapids, Eerdmans, 1999.

Magonet, J., *Form and Meaning: Studies in Literary Techniques in the Book of Jonah*, Sheffield, Sheffield Academic Press, 1983.

Magonet, J., *The Subversive Bible*, London, SCM Press, 1997.

Malina, B. and Neyrey, J., *Portraits of Paul*, Louisville, Westminster John Knox, 1996.

Mason, R., *Propaganda and Subversion in the Old Testament*, London, SPCK, 1997.

McConville, J., *Law and Theology in Deuteronomy*, Sheffield, Sheffield Academic Press, 1984.

McConville, J., *Grace in the End: A Study in Deuteronomic Theology*, Carlisle, Paternoster, 1993.

McDonald, J., *The Crucible of Christian Morality*, London, Routledge, 1998.

McKay, H. and Clines, D. (eds), *Of Prophets' Visions and the Wisdom of Sages*, Sheffield, Sheffield Academic Press, 1996.

Meadowcroft, T., *Aramaic Daniel and Greek Daniel*, Sheffield, Sheffield Academic Press, 1995.

Meeks, W., *The Origins of Christian Morality*, New Haven, Yale University Press, 1993.

Miles, J., *God – A Biography*, New York, Simon and Schuster, 1995.

Mills, M., *Images of God in the Old Testament*, London, Cassell, 1998.

Milne, P., *Vladimir Propp and the Study of Structure in Hebrew Biblical Narrative*, Sheffield, Sheffield Academic Press, 1988.

Moberley, R., *Genesis 12-50*, Sheffield, Sheffield Academic Press, 1995.

Morris, P. and Sawyer, D. (eds), *A Walk in the Garden: Biblical, Iconographical and Literary Images of Eden*, Sheffield, Sheffield Academic Press, 1992.

Noll, K., *The Faces of David*, Sheffield, Sheffield Academic Press, 1997.

Perdue, L., *Wisdom and Creation: the theology of wisdom literature*, Nashville Abingdon, 1994.

Perdue, L., Blenkinsopp, J., Collins, J., Meyers, C., *Families in Ancient Israel*, Louisville, Westminster John Knox, 1997.

Perry, M. and Sternberg, M., *The King through Ironic Eyes. The Narrator's Devices in the Biblical Story of David and Bathsheba and two excursuses on the Theory of the Narrative Text, Hasifrut*, 1968.

Person, R., *In Conversation with Jonah: Conversation Analysis, Literary Criticism and the Book of Jonah*, Sheffield, Sheffield Academic Press, 1996.

Pippin, T., *Apocalyptic Bodies*, London, Routledge, 1999.

Redditt, P., *Daniel*, Sheffield, Sheffield Academic Press, 1999.

Ricoeur, P., *Time and Narrative*, Volume 1 Chicago, University of Chicago Press, 1984.

Rhoads, D. and Syreeni, K. (eds), *Characterisation in the Gospels*, Sheffield, Sheffield Academic Press, 1999.

Rogerson, J., *Genesis*, Sheffield, Sheffield Academic Press, 1991.

Rogerson, J. (ed.), *The Pentateuch*, Sheffield, Sheffield Academic Press, 1996.

Rogerson, J., Davies, M., and Carroll, M. Daniel (eds), *The Bible in Ethics*, Sheffield, Sheffield Academic Press, 1995.

Salters, R., *Jonah and Lamentations*, Sheffield, Sheffield Academic Press, 1994.

Sasson, J., *Jonah,* New York, Doubleday, 1990.

Sasson, J., *Ruth*, Sheffield, Sheffield Academic Press, 1995.

Satterthwaite, P., Hess, R. and Wenham, G., *The Lord's Anointed*, Carlisle, Paternoster, 1995.

Schussler-Fiorenza, E., *In Memory of Her*, London, SCM Press, 1983.

Schussler-Fiorenza, E., *Bread not Stone*, Edinburgh, T. and T. Clark, 1984.

Shelton, P., *Making a drama out of a crisis? A Consideration of the Book of Job as Drama*, in *Journal for the Study of the Old Testament 99/83*, 1999.

Smith-Christopher, D., *The Book of Daniel*, NIB series Carlisle, Paternoster, 1996.

Smith-Christopher, D. (ed.), *Text and Experience*, Sheffield, Sheffield Academic Press, 1995.

Stahl, N., *Law and Liminality in the Bible*, Sheffield, Sheffield Academic Press, 1995.

Sternberg, M., *The Poetics of Biblical Narrative*, Bloomington, Indiana, 1985.

Stone, M. and Bergren, T. (eds), *Biblical Figures outside the Bible*, Harrisburg, Trinity Press International, 1998.

Sugirtharajah, R. (ed.), *Voices from the Margin*, London, SPCK, 1995.

Sugirtharajah, R. (ed.), *The Postcolonial Bible*, Sheffield, Sheffield Academic Press, 1998.

Trible, P., *God and the Rhetoric of Sexuality*, London, SCM Press, 1978.

Trible, P., *Rhetorical Criticism – Context, Method and the Book of Jonah*, Minneapolis, Fortress, 1994.

Valeta, D., *Satire in the Book of Daniel* Paper read to the 'Millennium' Conference, University of Oxford, April 2000.

van Wolde, E., *Stories of the Beginning Genesis 1-11 and Other Creation Stories*, London, SCM Press, 1996.

van Wolde, E., *Ruth and Naomi*, London, SCM Press, 1997.

van Wolde, E., *Mr and Mrs Job*, London, SCM Press, 1997.

Weeks, S., *Early Israelite Wisdom*, Oxford, Oxford University Press, 1999.

West, G., *The Academy of the Poor*, Sheffield, Sheffield Academic Press, 1999.

Westerman, C., *The Promises to the Fathers*, Philadelphia, Fortress, 1980.

Westermann, C., *Genesis: A Practical Commentary*, Grand Rapids, Eerdmans, 1987.

Whedbee, W., *The Bible and the Comic Vision*, Cambridge, Cambridge University Press, 1998.

White, H., *Narration and Discourse in the Book of Genesis*, Cambridge, Cambridge University Press, 1991.

Whitelam, K., *The Invention of Ancient Israel*, London, Routledge, 1996.

Whybray, N., *The Immorality of God: a reflection on some passages in Genesis, Job, Exodus and Numbers*, in *Journal for the Study of the Old Testament 96/72*, 1996.

Whybray, N., *Job*, Sheffield, Sheffield Academic Press, 1998.

Wilder, A., *The Bible and the Literary Critic*, Minneapolis, Fortress, 1991.

Wills, L., *The Jewish Novel in the Ancient World*, Ithaca, Cornell, 1995.

Woolff, H., *Obadiah and Jonah*, Edinburgh, T and T Clark, 1976.

Wright, A., *Living as the People of God*, Leicester, InterVarsity Press, 1983.

Zuckerman, B., *Job the Silent: A Study in Historical Counterpoint*, Oxford, Oxford University Press, 1991.